WORLD ATLAS OF
FLAGS

WORLD ATLAS OF
FLAGS

BRIAN JOHNSON BARKER

NEW
HOLLAND

NEW HOLLAND

First published in 2004 by
New Holland Publishers
London • Cape Town • Sydney • Auckland
www.newhollandpublishers.com

86 Edgware Rd
London W2 2EA
United Kingdom

80 McKenzie Street
Cape Town 8001
South Africa

14 Aquatic Drive
Frenchs Forest, NSW 2086
Australia

218 Lake Road
Northcote, Auckland
New Zealand

Publisher: Mariëlle Renssen
Publishing managers: Claudia Dos Santos, Simon Pooley
Commissioning editor: Alfred LeMaitre
Studio manager: Richard MacArthur
Editor: Gill Gordon
Designer: Christelle Marais
Design assistant: Jeannette Streicher
Cartographer: Genene Hart
Picture researcher: Karla Kik
Production: Myrna Collins
Consultant: Whitney Smith

ISBN 1 84330 721 9 (HB); 1 84330 722 7 (PB)

Reproduction by Hirt and Carter
Printed and bound in Singapore by Tien Wah Press

2 4 6 8 10 9 7 5 3 1

Contents

INTRODUCING FLAGS 10

Flying the flag 12

The history of flags 16

Military flags 22

Flags at sea 26

Common symbols and colours 30

International organizations 36

Flags in sport 38

FLAGS OF THE WORLD 42

World map 44

Europe 46

Western and Southern Asia 68

Eastern and Southeast Asia 82

Australia, New Zealand and Oceania 92

North America, Central America and the Caribbean 104

South America 124

Africa and adjacent islands 132

Glossary 154

Index 156

Vexillological Associations 159

Credits & acknowledgements 160

Foreword

Flags appear everywhere in modern society – on television, in sports arenas, for official ceremonies, election campaigns, in advertising, revolutionary actions, churches, and on homes and businesses. So common are they, we tend to take them for granted – in many cases forgetting that people have literally given their lives to advance the causes represented by those flags.

Their historical roots are often forgotten as well. Flags have played important roles in some of the great moments in history – the labarum associated with the conversion of the Emperor Constantine to Christianity, the standard flaunted by Genghis Khan as he created the largest territorial empire ever, the banners planted by the Crusaders on fortress walls in the Holy Land, the flag raised on the Moon when humans first landed there.

Today the creation and usage of flags is not limited to heralds, military leaders, and potentates. Anyone can devise a personal flag, a banner for neighbourhood or family, a pennant for yachting or for waving at a sports event. Each such flag in its own way expresses the sentiment "I am here; I am important; this is what I stand for!"

In their colours, varied designs, and in the stories of how they were created and used, flags have an appeal across generations, cultures, and lifestyles. This book will help the novice – as well as the vexillologist (flag historian) – better to understand the importance, usages, and symbolism of flags. Whether read cover to cover or sampled at random, it provides important knowledge about our world, present and past. Those who immerse themselves will discover not only a subject of significance but one which can bring great personal pleasure.

Whitney Smith
Director: Flag Research Institute

Introducing Flags

Flags have always had the power to stir the imagination, and poets and writers have been quick to capture this. In 'Childe Harold's Pilgrimage', the 19th-century English Romantic poet, Lord Byron, celebrates liberty, that most precious quality: 'Yet, Freedom! yet thy banner, torn, but flying / Streams like the thunderstorm against the wind'. Byron invests the flag of freedom with the power to fly against the wind, creating an almost mystic image. Another English poet, Alfred, Lord Tennyson, wrote of the flag as the image of dauntless resistance in 'The Defence of Lucknow', which recalls an incident in the Indian uprising of 1857–58: 'Shot thro' the mast or the halyard, but ever we raised thee anew / And ever from the topmost roof our banner of England blew'.

The 'Star-Spangled Banner' became the official anthem of the United States only in 1931, although it was written by Francis Scott Key as early as 1814. Stirring lyrics like 'O say, does that star-spangled banner yet wave / O'er the land of the free and the home of the brave?' resound through the consciousness of all Americans and ensure that they hold their flag in extremely high regard.

Flying the flag

Throughout the world, flags are associated with love of one's country. As symbols of nationhood, flags should always be handled with great respect. They are honoured by being saluted, protected and defended, but equally, may be shown disrespect by being torn or burned. Flags are associated with many emotions and qualities, such as pride, homesickness or contempt. They have attained their status through centuries of change and development, and have a fascinating story to tell us.

The flags of independent nations are regarded as being of equal status, no matter that one country may be among the largest and wealthiest in the world and another described as 'third world'. Where many national flags are displayed, as at the United Nations (UN) headquarters for instance, care is taken to ensure that no flag receives precedence. One way to accomplish this is to arrange the flagstaffs in a circle that has no beginning or end. Another is to place the flags in alphabetical order of the countries' names, either in English or in the language of the host country. This also applies when the flags of one or more nations are flown alongside a host country's flag.

The national flag always takes precedence over other flags, such as state or corporate flags. When two flags are flown on a podium, the national flag must be on the speaker's right side (the audience's left). In Europe, when three flags are displayed, the national flag is placed at the centre. A line of more than five flags should have a national flag at each end. In many countries, the national flag takes precedence over military colours, the latter being positioned according to the seniority of the regiments represented.

Left The best way to fly a flag is by using a proper flagpole and halyard.
Top Flags of participating nations on display during the 2002 Winter Olympic Games in Salt Lake City (USA).

Proper usage of national flags

International rules on the use of flags are necessarily a generalization, but following them should help to avoid giving offence. Many countries issue guidelines on how their national flag should be displayed, even if they have no laws concerning this. Military forces, in particular, follow strict protocol where their national and regimental flags are concerned, as do embassies and consulates.

Flags should not be put to undignified or inappropriate use. A flag should never drag on the floor or fall to the ground. A flag used to cover a commemorative plaque prior to its unveiling should not touch the ground when it falls away and, while it may be acceptable to trim a speaker's table with the national flag it should not be used as a tablecloth or seat cover. Rules may be broken for formal state funerals, but this ceremonial denoting respect for the dead is usually carried out by those well versed in flag protocol, such as a special military squad.

The USA has detailed regulations for the display and handling of the Stars and Stripes, even specifying how it should be folded, and how old flags should be disposed of.

Other countries that have legislated the use of their flags include Egypt, Bahrain, Romania, Monaco and Finland. Curiously, the UK has not written into law any regulations concerning its own Union Flag (often called the Union Jack) that, even after the demise of the great British Empire, still flies in various forms around the world.

The central European custom of draping flags or hanging them vertically as an alternative to flying them from a staff contains some potential for embarrassment. Hanging involves displaying a flag so the hoist (see p14) becomes the upper edge, with the field and all its designs turned through 90 degrees from the masthead position.

Simple bicolours and tri-colours can change their identity when draped. The flag of Poland, for instance, may be mistaken for that of Indonesia or Monaco, while the Dutch horizontal tricolour becomes the vertical tricolour of Yugoslavia. Because of the potential for confusion, some countries forbid the draping of their national flag, while others produce special versions of their flag that are designed to be draped or hung vertically.

When to fly a flag

Flags are generally flown from sunrise to sunset, although the hours may be specified according to the clock in those countries that lie in far northern and southern latitudes. For instance in Finland, the land of the midnight sun, the official hours for flying the national flag are between 08:00 and sunset, or not later than 21:00.

In most countries, government departments fly the flag during office or business hours, and civilians follow suit. No flag should be flown in the dark, so any flag flying after sunset must be well illuminated.

The size of flag to be flown in various weather conditions is usually left up to the person in charge of the flag station. In very windy weather it is best to fly a small 'storm flag' which will suffer less damage than a larger flag, and impose less stress on the flagstaff and halyard.

A national flag flying in a foreign country may be flown according to the customs of the guest country.

Right When the flags of many nations are hoisted simultaneously, care must be taken to ensure they rise at the same speed.

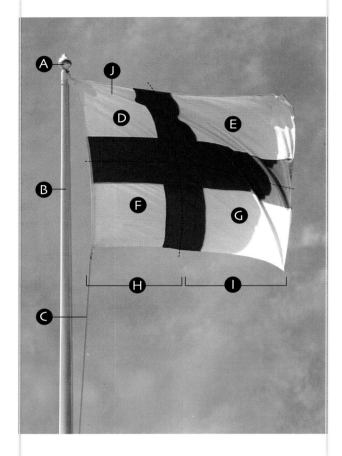

PARTS OF A FLAG

A	finial or ornament	F	lower hoist
B	flagpole	G	lower fly
C	halyard	H	hoist
D	upper hoist	I	fly
E	upper fly	J	canton

Practicalities of flying a flag

When a flag is flown, it is considered to be free to be unfurled by the wind. This suggests outdoor use, but flags are also used indoors, where they may be displayed either draped (falling naturally) or secured to show the full extent of the field.

The principal item for flying a flag is the flagpole, also referred to as a flagstaff (there are several towns in the world called Flagstaff) or a mast. (Strictly, masts belong aboard ship, and the expression 'half-mast' dates from early shipboard use of flags.)

A flagstaff may be made of any rigid material resistant to the adverse conditions in which it might be placed, such as rust or rot. The staff may be embedded in the ground or attached to a base so that the staff can be pivoted and lowered for repairs and maintenance, such as replacing the halyard or the truck. Portable flagstaffs are usually attached to a base, such as a heavy timber X-frame with a socket in the centre for receiving the staff, which is able to resist both wind and clumsy treatment.

Some countries decorate their flagstaffs. In Norway, for instance, the staff is usually white, while the finial (the ornament at the top of the staff) is often a simple knob or a spear point. Staffs from which Israel's national flag is flown are often painted blue for one third of the height, and white for the remainder. Flagstaffs in Belarus are usually painted with a form of golden ochre.

The size of flag to be flown in any circumstances may be specified by official instructions, but the most important consideration is that it should be impressive in its surroundings. For example, one would not fly a small flag in front of a very large building (unless it is a storm flag in windy conditions).

In a multi-national display, flags are usually reduced to the same size, or at least to the same depth (vertical height at the hoist). This means that some flags will not be of the prescribed proportions, but at least ensures that they are all of approximately the same size.

Flags flown in public should always be in good condition, not torn or faded. They should be easy to hoist and maintain. Some installations include double pulleys and halyards, but a single halyard should be sufficient if it is examined regularly for signs of wear. Most halyards are fitted with a toggle at one end and an eye splice or becket at the other. Some countries have clips on the halyards which attach to grommets in the heading of the flag. A length of rope sewn into the tube, or heading, on the flag's hoist is similarly fitted so that it can be attached to the halyard only when the flag is the right way up. (A flag flown upside down, or in any way but the right way up, is presumed to be a signal of distress.)

Flags used in mourning

Flags are flown at half-mast (half-staff) in mourning for the death of a prominent person, or to indicate a national tragedy. National flags are half-masted only on instructions from the highest authority. When a flag is to be flown at half-mast it is first raised to its full height and then slowly lowered to the prescribed position. Similarly, before being lowered and removed at the end of the day, a half-masted flag is slowly raised to full height.

At a state or military funeral, the coffin or casket is customarily covered with the deceased person's national flag. The hoist is placed at the head and the top edge draped over the left side of the deceased. The flag is removed before the coffin is placed over the grave and, in the case of US citizens, is ceremonially folded and presented to the next of kin. In an official funeral parade, officers and soldiers generally salute the deceased by dipping their colours as they pass by the casket. The courtesy of carrying a soldier to his grave under his country's flag is sometimes extended to enemy soldiers who die in captivity, or whose bodies are repatriated for burial at home.

There are some variations to half-masting. On days of national mourning in El Salvador, for instance, the flag is flown at half-mast and a length of black crepe is fixed to the top of the staff. In Morocco, to mark mourning on the death of King Hassan II in 1999, the national flag was raised, but was tied so that it could not unfurl. In Spain, mourning is indicated by attaching a piece of black material to the centre of flags that are draped or displayed with the hoist horizontal at the top. A length of black material may be attached to the flagstaff, and the national flag hoisted to half-mast.

Saluting a flag

A flag may be saluted at any time. Uniformed personnel salute according to their unit instructions, while civilians salute according to national custom, by raising a hat, for instance, or standing to attention and facing the flag until it has been raised and broken. Organizations and corporations that fly private or 'house' flags acknowledge them in accordance with their own customs.

Persons in the vicinity of a national flag that is being hoisted should halt and face the flag until it has been raised and broken. 'Breaking' a flag involves hoisting it in a rolled-up state to full height. A tug on the halyard then causes the flag to unfurl or break.

By far the majority of flags are identical on both sides, but it is possible to have a different design on the obverse (the more important side) than the reverse (the secondary side).

As generally depicted in publications, a flag is almost always assumed to have the hoist to the reader's left, although some Muslim and other flags have the hoist to the right when the obverse is visible.

Left When a member of the US armed forces dies in service, the flag used to drape the coffin is ceremonially folded before being presented to the next of kin.

The history of flags

The origin of flags lies in the human need to communicate. When early man roamed the plains and steppes, the waving of a leafy branch could convey essential information if he was beyond voice range, or out of sight of ordinary arm signals. The branch would later have been replaced by a banner of woven reeds, and later still by plain, coarse cloth. Thus a relatively sophisticated system of signalling may have evolved over time.

Humans seek comfort in the company of others who share the same beliefs, and whose numbers offer protection. Ancient examples of rock art show complex associations not only between groups of humans, but with animals, suggesting that clans were known and identified by their totemic figures. Over time, these figures were represented on banners or shields – the forerunners of today's flags.

Banners, emblems and coats of arms

Early flags or banners were primarily concerned with identification, so they needed to be readily visible and easily recognized. We imagine that warriors would choose powerful and predatory animals with which to identify themselves, but this was not necessarily so. For instance, the emblem of the Vikings, which aroused terror in those who saw it, was a raven. The 'fatal raven' was consecrated to Odin, the Danish god of war. Legend had it that if defeat lay ahead the raven would droop its wings, but if victory was certain, it adopted a soaring posture, urging its followers on.

Above This herald's tunic depicts the royal lions of England (gold on crimson), Scotland (red on gold), and the harp of Ireland.
Top Armour-clad knights used coats of arms to identify themselves to both friend and foe.

Centuries before the Vikings, the Romans chose the eagle as their totem. Cast or sculpted totems, mounted on poles, were carried by the Roman legions that conquered the known world. Emblems and badges evolved more rapidly in military circumstances than in civilian life, because war carried the greater urgency to communicate. By AD100, the Roman infantry marched behind a vexillum, a banner-like flag that was hung from a horizontal rod attached to a long pole. Usually red or purple, it might have been fringed along its lower edge, and often bore the number and symbol of the unit that carried it. 'Vexillology', a word meaning 'the study and collection of information about flags', is derived from the Latin *vexillum*.

The Romans introduced the dragon symbol into Britain (having adopted it from their central Asian enemies). A bronze dragon's head would be fixed to a pole, from which streamed a flag that writhed and curled in the wind like the dragon's tail (much like a modern windsock). Other early flags included the gonfalon with three or more tails, and triangular flags. By the time of the Norman invasion of Britain, most Western flag designs incorporated the Christian cross, although Harold, the Saxon king who was defeated in 1066, had a banner depicting a dragon, which he may have derived from Welsh tribes he had defeated. The Welsh war leader was traditionally known as *Pendragon*, or head dragon, and the dragon is still the heraldic symbol of Wales. Dragons also have Biblical associations with Satan (Revelation 12:9) and a great many Christian saints have achieved fame as dragon-slayers.

In the Middle Ages, various devices were used for identification. A knight (a member of the nobility or land-owning class) might choose an emblem by which he could be recognized in battle by his followers. This aid to recognition was needed because, once the visors of their helmets were closed, all knights looked pretty much alike.

Let's suppose our knight chose a beaver's head, which he fastened to the crown of his helmet. Let's suppose, too, that he survived a few decades of battle and was able to ride to war with four sturdy sons. They would also wear the beaver's head, but with additional emblems, say an oak leaf or a swan's feather, to distinguish one from the other.

Over time, the emblems by which a knight could be identified on the battlefield were transferred to his shield, while his followers decorated their own shields with a depiction of the emblem which, eventually, became the crest on the knight's coat of arms. It was called a 'coat' of arms because it was displayed not only on the shield, but was also painted or embroidered on the short surcoat the knight wore over his armour. In the 12th and 13th centuries there might be just one or two charges (see p18) to a shield but, over time, as families expanded through descent and marriage, it required careful study to distinguish one coat of arms from another.

Simplified versions of the coat of arms also began to appear on banners or flags, which had the advantage of being visible from a distance. Clear, bold patterns were essential for quick recognition in the confusion of battle, especially in windless conditions when the flag might droop, or in mist, twilight or at any time that visibility was poor. Foot soldiers, especially, relied on banners and flags to indicate when they should advance or retreat, or where the main thrust of the action was as, unlike mounted knights, they were not able to get a perspective on the battle.

Left *On the battlefield, flags and banners indicated when soldiers were to advance or retreat, so they had to be visible over a reasonable distance.*

DECIPHERING A COAT OF ARMS

A   Shield – the basic unit of a coat of arms

B   Supporters – figures which hold the shield

C   Crest – the element at the top, above the shield

D   Scroll (bearing a motto) – strip below the shield

E   Compartment – base on which the supporters stand

Above Detail from the flag of South Georgia and the South Sandwich islands.

Left The flags of British-administered territories, and the states of some Commonwealth countries, may show badges or heraldic coats of arms.

Top to bottom: South Georgia and the South Sandwich Islands, Western Australia, and Saskatchewan (Canada).

Flags and heraldry

Heraldry is a stylized and standardized way of telling the descent and achievements of an individual, a company, or a country. Coats of arms sometimes appear on flags, and flags on coats of arms. A coat of arms, correctly known as a heraldic achievement, may include a shield 'held' on either side by a supporter (a human or animal figure) standing on a compartment, or base. Above the shield is a crest, usually depicted on top of a metal helmet. There may be one or more scrolls bearing a motto, often in Latin or Medieval French.

An object on the shield, such as a glove, is termed a charge, and the shield is said to be 'charged with a glove'. A charge can be almost anything, including boars' heads, salmon, ships, ears of rye, or even a snake tied into a reef knot (in which position it is described as 'nowed'). Every object shown is of significance in the history of the family or organization on whose arms it appears.

In heraldry, only a limited range of tinctures – made up of metals and colours – are generally used. (Heraldry also utilizes furs, but these do not affect flags.) The metals are gold (known as or) and silver (argent). When metals are used on flags, or is usually depicted as yellow, and argent as white. The colours of heraldry are red (gules), blue (azure), black (sable), green (vert) and purple (purpure). Purple is rarely used and green is uncommon. Conventional heraldry has no standard colour charts to refer to when an achievement is being described, so gules, for example, may be carmine, vermilion, cerise or maroon. The same applies to the other tinctures. What matters is that the colour depicted should be unmistakably what it is intended to represent. When a charge is depicted in its natural colours, it is described as proper. This is very different to the art of creating a modern flag, where the chosen colours are carefully described using international standards of precise shades.

When it comes to flags, heraldic coats of arms or badges (simple devices to aid identification) are most frequently seen in the flag family of British-administered territories and states (see examples at left). The British Antarctic Territory flag, for example, shows the embellished coat of arms of the Falkland Islands Dependencies – with compartment, mantling (the material draped from the helmet), crest and supporters. By contrast, the flag of Western Australia shows simply the state emblem, or badge, of a black swan on a yellow disc. The flag of the Canadian province of Saskatchewan shows, in addition to a coat of arms, a badge in the form of the western red lily, the province's floral emblem.

Crosses and crescents

With the First Crusade (1096–99), Christian leaders from across Europe ceased fighting among themselves for long enough to attempt to carry the cross to the Holy Land – quite literally, as most of them had a large cross painted or embroidered on their surcoat. Each crusading nation had its own colour: red for France and Spain, white for England, blue for Italy, green for Flanders, while the Scots wore the saltire (X-shaped cross) of St Andrew. Although the crusaders' intentions were as varied as the outcome of their missions, a constant aim was to reconquer Palestine from the Muslims (then referred to as Saracens or Moors), with whose flags, symbols and emblems the people of Europe soon became thoroughly acquainted.

Islam prohibits the depiction of living beings, so Muslim imagery tends to feature inscriptions or geometric designs. The crescent was a frequent symbol, although it had been used in central Asia for centuries before the rise of Islam. Some Saracen flags carried an inscription in Arabic script: either a religious verse, or a means of identifying a particular leader. The influence on Western heraldry is unclear, but it does appear that the pole with a laterally attached flag was an Arab influence on the West.

Above Beginning in 1096, crusaders from across Europe set off under the sign of the cross to wrest the Holy Land from the Saracens.

A call to arms

Around 1150 heraldry began to develop principles which came to be applied to flags and coats of arms. The number of colours was limited to five and, to ensure optimal visibility at a distance, certain colour combinations were avoided. The use of one colour on another was prohibited unless the second colour was fimbriated (outlined with one of the metals). Fantastic creatures of legend that found their way into heraldic arms included the dragon, griffin, wyvern and unicorn, while newer motifs included crescents and Saracens' heads, heraldically called Moors' heads. There were several dozen versions of the cross, including the fylfot, the forerunner of the swastika. But designs that were satisfying on a rigid, painted shield did not always transfer successfully to flags.

Persons who were armigerous (entitled to use a coat of arms) were sometimes also entitled to carry a heraldic or armorial banner. Whereas a knight's coat of arms might be identical to his armorial banner, this

this was rarely the case with the arms of the more nobly born, or of rulers themselves. The royal standard or royal banner gradually evolved as a squarish flag of about 4:5 proportion. It frequently had a short fringe in the king's livery or national colours, with one or more decorative tasselled cords in the same colours.

The armorial banner or standard could be carried only by the person whose arms were depicted, so other flags, showing his personal devices such as a crest alone, were devised to be carried for him by his sons or esquires (young men who hoped to become knights themselves).

The evolution of modern flags

In the Middle Ages, royal banners gradually came to be associated with a particular territory rather than just a family or dynasty. Circumstances calling for their display were limited, however, until voyagers began to travel extensively and required distinctive flags that could identify their ships. Many of these early ensigns were armorial (based on a coat of arms), while others featured national colours.

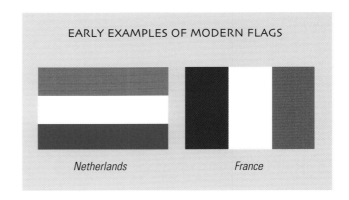

EARLY EXAMPLES OF MODERN FLAGS

Netherlands   France

Many countries' flag history begins with an emblem or symbol of their patron saint. England, for example, chose the red cross of St George for a flag, reserving depictions of St George slaying the dragon for other uses. In time, this latter image appeared on coins, medals and patronal banners, while the red cross on a white background remains the flag of England to this day (see p50).

The Dutch horizontal tricolour, the *Prinsenvlag* (Prince's flag) of the 16th century, is credited with being the first 'modern' flag design. With plain, uncomplicated stripes replacing intricate heraldic devices, the flag was both simple in execution and easy to distinguish. It was not long before the orange, white and blue colours were modified for use by the all-powerful Dutch East India Company, by the simple addition of the company's VOC monogram in the white band.

In the late 18th century, two new flags came into being that would resonate as symbols of freedom throughout the western world. Across the Atlantic, the newly independent United States of America asserted itself militarily and symbolically with a startlingly novel flag design. It is believed this was the first flag to depict stars, while the colours and pattern were unlike anything that had gone before.

The second strikingly different flag, that of revolutionary France, used the same colours of red, white and blue, but chose three vertical stripes, a pattern that soon became known as the *Tricolore*. By the time revolution revisited France in 1848, the idea of an independent nation-state, free from the tyranny of monarchy, was set to ignite a powerful ripple across Europe and South America. Ordinary people readily

Left *The French tricoloured cockade was chosen on 17 July 1789, three days after the storming of the Bastille. Red and blue were the colours of Paris, and white represented the royal house of Bourbon. The first tricolour flag, or* Tricolore, *was authorized on 24 October 1790.*

banners, and on huge drapes that festooned buildings in every town. The flag's career was short, but undoubtedly spectacular.

In South Africa, during the Anglo-Boer War (1899–1902), a light-hearted moment occurred when, in the early phases, Britain suffered a string of humiliating reverses and surrenders. The jubilant Boers joked that the English flag was really a plain white cloth, which was carrying simplistic design too far. In their view, their own republican flags were modern. The Transvaal, or Zuid-Afrikaansche Republiek, flew a *vierkleur* (four-coloured flag) comprising a horizontal red, white and blue tricolour, with a vertical green band at the hoist. Their sister republic, the Orange Free State, placed the red, white and blue tricolour in the chief canton, with a field of three orange and four white horizontal stripes.

Symbols of war and peace

Victory and conquest, or disapproval of an ousted regime, is sometimes expressed by banning an opponent's flag, particularly in times of war. Throughout history, there have been times when it has been illegal to display, or even to possess, certain flags. For instance, during the Nazi occupation of France during

Above *National pride, often embodied by the Stars and Stripes, was a strong motivating force for Americans during World War II.*

World War II, the discovery of a Free French flag with its patriarchal cross (cross of Lorraine) would have had severe consequences.

More recently, in the years before the African National Congress legitimately swept to power in South Africa, it was a criminal offence to display their flag. The burning of an opponent's flag, or even a representation of it, is frequently associated with war and conflict.

accepted the concept of a national identity, embodied in a common flag, in contrast with the banners and heraldic standards that were the preserve of the elite and the oppressor.

The right psychological moment, coupled with shrewd stage management, raised one national flag and emblem to unprecedented heights of public awareness in the 1930s. This was the flag of Nazi Germany, which revived the red, white and black colours of the former Imperial flag, but arranged them in a crisply modern design. Use of the ancient swastika emblem was actively encouraged on flags, badges and

Over time, various flags, shields and banners have achieved either fame or notoriety, not so much for their designs or any intrinsic qualities they possessed, but for the events or ideologies with which they were associated. Some are remembered and revered as symbols of good, while others will forever be associated with war or conquest. Very often, the way a particular flag is regarded depends on the personal standpoint of the viewer.

Military flags

Above *An ancient Roman vexilloid, a device fixed atop a staff, was probably the model for this modern recreation.*

Top *In this depiction of a military parade, the colours of various regiments are being carried behind the national flag.*

Military colours are a special type of flag that have played an important role in world armies for centuries. Historically, military colours were flags or standards carried to war and displayed on the battlefield but, with the changing nature of warfare in the 20th century, their role has become almost exclusively ceremonial. Until the early 20th century, virtually all military flags – other than the national flag – were army flags. The use of colours in most navies is recent, while air forces have developed only in the last hundred years.

Every military colour started out as a symbol of a particular group or military unit. It was a means of asserting corporate identity and of creating loyalty. Military groups were usually linked in a type of pyramid structure, with a sovereign or national leader at the top to whom the groups and the individuals owed loyalty. The colours, then, might symbolize a soldier's companions in the ranks, his officers and regiment and, ultimately, his country and its ruler. His loyalty was due to all of them, and his unit's colours became an object of veneration, to be shown the deepest respect.

To allow the colours to be seen from the greatest distance it became customary to fix devices, called vexilloids, on top of a pole. This first occurred in Roman times and each unit possessed a different one. Vexilloids were imbued with spiritual power, and recruits took their oath of allegiance while placing a hand on them. In action, the presence of the vexilloid indicated where the soldiers were to form up, advance or fall back. The loss of a vexilloid in battle was the greatest disgrace. Vexilloids may have been used in ancient Egypt, as images on pottery dated to 3000BC are thought to represent vexilloids depicting animals. In 104BC, it was ordered that an eagle was to be the only device carried on Roman army staffs. The Roman army later made use of a vexillum, or cloth square, attached to a horizontal rod near the top of the pole, and displaying the letters SPQR (*Senatus Populusque Romanus*, the 'Senate and People of Rome').

This format was later to be adopted in Nazi Germany: an eagle at the top of the pole above the letters NSDAP (for the National Socialist German Workers' Party, or Nazis) and a rectangular banner hung from a horizontal rod (although the banners represented political districts rather than regiments).

Early military flags

Flags, as we understand them today, probably weren't used militarily much before the 13th century. The authority for claiming their use at the Battle of Hastings in 1066 is the famous Bayeux Tapestry, which shows some 30 different personal flags of various shapes. The tapestry, however, was made some years after the battle, during which time the use and pattern of flags may have changed greatly.

German mercenary soldiers, or *Landsknechte*, were active in the 15th and 16th centuries. Each company of about 300 men had its own *Fahne* or standard. Its position on the battlefield marked the company's rallying place, and every soldier was expected to guard the standard with his life. In the English army (and, after 1707, when Scotland and England were united, in the British army) flags were used to mark the positions of senior officers on the field, and these flags gradually took on characteristics of the regiments they represented.

To be seen amid the dust and chaos of a battle, banners needed to be both large and bright. It is thought that those of the *Landsknechte* measured about two metres (22ft) square.

Colours and honours

The term 'colours' was first used to describe English military flags in the 16th century, 'by reason of the variety of colours they are made of'. Standardization was introduced in 1747, after which it was prescribed that each regiment of infantry (foot soldiers) should have two flags, which have since become known as the Queen's (or King's) Colour, and the Regimental Colour. The first symbolizes the loyalty owed to the country, and the second stands for the spirit and history of the regiment. The soldier who carried the colours was often a cadet officer, known as an ensign, after the flag or ensign.

In the British Army, the Queen's (or King's) Colour consists of the national flag (the Union Flag, often called the Union Jack), which also appears in the chief canton of some Regimental Colours. In the army of the USA, infantry regiments have two colours: the National and the Regimental. In the French and German armies, each infantry regiment carries only one colour.

The staff of a German colour has silver rings attached, on which are engraved the names of those killed in action while carrying the colour, and other commemorative information such as battle honours (a visible record of a campaign or action in which the regiment distinguished itself and received the right to use the name of the action). Battle honours are usually inscribed in scrolls on the Regimental Colour.

In Napoleonic times, French colours were carried on a staff topped with a wreathed eagle, and the flag itself became known as an 'eagle'. At the battle of Waterloo in 1815, two British cavalry regiments, the

Above *This World War II poster depicts the flags of the British, French and American forces who fought together for the liberation of Europe.*

First and Second Dragoons, captured a French 'eagle', which was later incorporated into the badge of each regiment. The badge of the Second Dragoons shows the eagle on a rectangle upon which is inscribed one of the principal battle honours, Waterloo.

Traditionally, in the British army, rifle regiments do not carry colours. When 'rifled muskets', were introduced early in the 19th century, they were more accurate than smoothbore muskets, and were issued only to those men who were capable of individual action against the enemy. Their speciality was skirmishing and reconnaissance, which entailed concealment, so colours would have been most inappropriate. One noteworthy change made at this time was that riflemen were dressed in dark green uniforms as a concession to camouflage, rather than the bright red coats of the line regiments.

Artillery regiments had no colours either, every gunner knowing that his position in battle was by the guns, which he had been trained to serve and never give up.

Cavalry (mounted regiments) carried elongated, narrow standards, called guidons, that tapered towards the fly, which was frequently split into two rounded 'tails'.

Above *At the Battle of Isandlwana, two British officers died trying to save their regimental colours from capture by the Zulu army. In military terms, the capture or taking of colours signifies defeat.*

During the Anglo-Zulu War fought in South Africa in 1879, a battalion of the British 24th Regiment, together with several hundred volunteers, was defeated at the battle of Isandlwana. In the midst of the chaos of the last moments of resistance, the British commander remembered the regimental colours and ordered two junior officers to carry them to safety. The officers were caught and killed by the Zulus at a river crossing, and the colours floated away down the stream, to be recovered later. Queen Victoria was greatly moved by the tale, and personally placed around the staff a silver wreath of immortelles (everlasting flowers) as a special honour.

The last occasion on which a British regiment carried its colours in action was in 1881, during the Anglo-Transvaal War, also fought in South Africa. The colours escaped capture only by being wrapped around the body of a soldier and covered with a coat. Thereafter it became the custom for regiments to 'lay up' their colours before proceeding on active service. This involves a ceremonial parade during which the colours are handed to a clergyman or other official for safe-keeping during the regiment's absence.

Colours may be laid up in a church or in a public building, such as a town hall. Retrieving the colours, on return from active service, also takes place with full ceremony. The colours are carried and guarded by a colour party, usually made up of a junior officer escorted by senior non-commissioned officers carrying rifles with bayonets fixed.

Periodically, a regiment may receive new colours to accommodate new battle honours or because the old colours have become fragile and unserviceable. Once colours have been replaced, the old ones are laid up and, on the principle of dust to dust, left to disintegrate. In practice, however, after a symbolic laying-up period of at least five years, old colours may be retrieved, perhaps for display in a regimental museum. While laid up they are on display, as a reminder to the public of the debt of duty and service that is owed to the country.

When the new colours are ready to be presented, usually by an important figure, such as a monarch or head of state, a ceremonial parade is ordered. The new colours are officially handed over and then laid on the piled drums of the regimental band to be blessed by the chaplain. On the first Sunday following this ceremony, the old colours are paraded through the ranks and then handed over for laying up and safekeeping. Laid up colours are never repaired or refurbished.

Airborne flags

When the first military aircraft went to war, some carried flags. These were usually the aircraft flown by the squadron commanders whom other pilots, in the absence of radio communications, had to watch closely for instructions. To be readily visible, small flags were attached to the ends of the wings, but it was soon found that the wing-tip vortices (powerfully swirling air currents coming off the wing tips) tore the flags to shreds, making the squadron commander's aircraft indistinguishable from the others. The first solution was to paint pennon-like flags on the fuselage, but this gave way to the elaborate system of alpha codes. The national flag was reduced, in most cases, to a tricoloured roundel (although the US Army Air Force, as it was called, settled for a white star on a blue disc).

Below *Clearly painted symbols on the fuselage enabled wartime pilots to quickly identify their squadron leader, or an enemy plane.*

Flags at sea

No-one knows when the first real flags were flown at sea, but they might have been preceded by patterns on the sails, either painted or sewn in contrasting colours. As regards the use of both flag and signal there can be fewer examples earlier than that of Theseus who, legend tells us, slew the fearsome Minotaur in its sinister labyrinth on the Mediterranean island of Crete. Theseus, the son of Aegeus, king of Athens, set out in a ship with black sails on a mission to destroy the monster that claimed regular tribute of young men and women, whom it devoured. Son and father agreed that if Theseus succeeded in his encounter with the Minotaur, he would return to Athens with his ship under a white sail. Weeks went by, and Aegeus, watching from a cliff, saw his son's ship returning, but with a black sail hoisted. In sorrow and despair, the old man killed himself – all because Theseus and his crew had forgotten to change sails. They had flown the wrong signal, raised the wrong flag.

Viking explorers were among the earliest mariners to carry images on their sails, later transferring these images to flags, which had their seafaring origin as multi-tailed flags (gonfalons) attached either to the mast or to a spar.

By the 10th century, many European ships mounted a metal cross or crucifix on the mainmast. Spain and Portugal placed large red crosses on the mainsail, causing Portuguese vessels, which pioneered many sea routes in the late 15th century, to become known as the 'caravels of Christ'. The cross was both a totem and, to some extent, a mark of nationality or royal ownership. Indeed, some of the earliest flags were those that went to sea.

Above *The pirate flag, or Jolly Roger, once brought fear into the hearts of sailors.*

Top *The 18th-century British ship* Royal Charlotte, *moored at Greenwich, flies the Red Ensign at the stern, the Union Flag from the mizzen mast and the King's Standard from the main mast.*

Flags have been used to identify friendly vessels and enemies alike. An attempted invasion of Britain from France in the 13th century was defeated in the Straits of Dover, giving the invaders no chance to land, and establishing a tradition of British sea power. Edward III (1326–77) became known as 'King of the Seas'. At sea, his ships had to be saluted by foreign vessels, which lowered their flag on approaching.

This custom has survived in the form of salutes between merchant ships at sea which, when passing, dip the national flag at the masthead. Another courtesy is to hoist a country's flag when entering its territorial waters, and keep it flying it for the duration of your stay. Naval ships at sea are generally exempt from the custom of dipping their national flag to ships of other nations. Lowering the ensign is a sign of submission, something no naval commander would like to contemplate.

Naval ships commanded by an officer ranked captain or lower traditionally fly a long, narrow commission pennant. If the commander is of higher rank, his rank flag may be flown. Ships returning to their home port after a long spell abroad fly a narrow paying-off pennant, up to 100m (330ft) long. Merchant ships sold out of service may also fly a paying-off pennant on their last voyage home.

Disguise and deceit

In wartime, the use of false colours was an accepted form of disguise. Flying false colours means using the flag of a neutral country in order to deceive enemy ships and gain an advantage. During World War I, when ship-to-ship radio was not widely available, British ships nearing waters known to be patrolled by German U-boats (submarines) were encouraged by the Admiralty to 'fly neutral flags, preferably American, in the Channel approaches'. Whereas an enemy U-boat might sink a British vessel on sight and without warning, it was expected to warn the ships of neutral nations. This meant the U-boat would have to surface, which was a disadvantage, especially if the supposedly neutral ship suddenly dropped the Stars and Stripes and ran up the White Ensign of the Royal Navy.

The law that allowed the use of false colours also prohibited a ship from opening fire while under false colours, hence the quick change of flags before shooting. Such armed decoys, known as 'Q-ships', were widely used in this war, and claimed many U-boats, more or less directly through flying a flag of deceit. Surrender in a sea battle was indicated by striking the national flag (rapidly hauling it down).

For centuries, pirates and privateers were among those who took advantage of neutral or friendly flags. Pirates were seagoing highway-men who robbed any ships, even those of their own country, for profit. A privateer usually had a commission from his country's government to attack and plunder the ships of certain nations for the benefit of his sovereign. A pirate ship would approach while flying the flag of a nation friendly to his intended victim, only at the last moment running up his pirate flag, often the legendary skull above crossed bones in white on a black field, although, in reality, pirate flags were rarely so simple. A privateer made the same approach but, like the Q-ships of a later era, would haul down the flag of deception and run up his country's flag before commencing hostilities.

Signals and signs

Historically, flags were used not only for identification, but also for signalling. Flag signals developed gradually from modest beginnings. The earliest (and for many years only) signal was a flag flown from the admiral's vessel, summoning his captains to the 'flagship'. The first signalling manual appeared in 1703 and stayed in use for 80 years. *A Signal Book for Ships of War* took over for several years more, until Admiral Lord Howe created a system in which each letter of the alphabet was assigned a number – the system that enabled Admiral Nelson to send his famous message before the Battle of Trafalgar in October 1805: 'England expects every man will do his duty'.

Nowadays, each letter is represented by a separate flag, which conveys a message, thus O means 'man overboard' and P 'we are about to sail'. Although modern communications have replaced older signal methods, commercial vessels still use the unambiguous messages conveyed by flags; such as N over C (I am in distress), Q (I am in good health and require inward clearance) and H (I have a pilot on board). Naval vessels transmit messages by means of code flags when it is important to maintain radio silence.

Flags flown on board today

International law requires all ships above a certain tonnage, both naval and merchant vessels, to fly their national flag. In maritime terms, this means the flag of the country in which the ship is registered. A ship that is owned in one country and registered in another is said to sail under a flag of convenience (which usually implies the country of registration has been chosen for economic reasons).

From bow to stern, a modern warship might fly a jack (a small version of the national flag) at the bow; a commission pennant at the head of the main mast, with a command flag below it if a flag officer is

Common symbols and colours

I t is usually much more than coincidence that the flags of certain countries – sometimes near neighbours, sometimes a world apart – share the same characteristics. Basic similarities are those related to particular colours, historic events, or religious symbols, as well as those that are derived from the flag of a colonizing power.

The language of colour

On flags, red is most frequently associated with strife, usually representing blood shed in a just struggle, such as for independence. Red also represents courage, hardiness and revolution. In the 19th century, the English poet Tennyson wrote of 'red ruin and the breaking up of laws', while Irish poet WB Yeats called red 'the colour of magic'. At the end of World War I (1914–18), a large proportion of the men of the German High Seas Fleet mutinied, and for a time every battleship in the harbour at Kiel flew a red flag at its masthead to indicate that it was under the control of a Sailors' Council. Their inspiration was the red flag of revolution that was first raised in Tsarist Russia in 1917 and had led to the signing of a truce with Germany. In newly created Soviet Russia, red was the colour of 'radicalism, socialism and revolution'.

By contrast, white is the colour of purity, peace and innocence. It may also represent snow. A plain white flag is the generally accepted signal of surrender. Blue can represent sea or sky, as well as freedom, justice, peace and patriotism. Green symbolizes the earth, agriculture and fertility. It is also the colour of Islam. Yellow, the colour of the sun and of

Above *By far the majority of flags use strong, vibrant colours, for easy visibility.*
Top *The red flag of the Communist Party of China resembles the flag of the former Soviet Union with its star omitted.*

gold, is often used to convey wealth and justice. Black represents determination, ethnic heritage and the overthrow of one's enemies.

When used together, red, white and blue are sometimes referred to as the Colours of Liberty, although there are no standard and consistent meanings for any colour used in flags across the world. Political alignments may be indicated through colours such as the Pan-African yellow, red, green and black.

In the 20th century, many newly independent nations opted for flags with plain colours and geometric designs, devoid of intricate objects, or decorated with only simplified charges, such as a star. Moving away from the confining laws of heraldic tradition was frequently an integral part of the passage towards democracy.

Stars shine for liberty

The first US flag (January 1776 – June 1777) is arguably the earliest modern national flag – one chosen by the people and representing them rather than the country's rulers. After the signing of the Declaration of Independence, this flag was succeeded by the first 'Stars and Stripes'. Both in design and in its usage by the common people, the US flag set precedents that were soon followed in other countries, as people began to rally around national flags in their search for civil liberties and democratic governments.

NATIONAL FLAGS PATTERNED AFTER THE STARS AND STRIPES

United States of America

Cuba

Liberia

Puerto Rico

Malaysia

Togo

A number of countries have used stars in their flag design. The flag of Liberia, which was established in 1822 as an African home for slaves liberated from bondage in America, is similar but, instead of the small stars of the US flag, the Liberian flag (p139) has a single, large star, and 11 stripes. Malaysia's flag (p90) has 14 stripes and, in the blue canton, a yellow crescent and star. Cuba (p116) and Puerto Rico (p117), which US military forces helped to liberate from Spain in 1898, have 'stars and stripes' flags with identical patterns, comprising broad stripes and a triangle at the hoist, set with a lone star. They are distinguished from one another by the arrangement of the colours. Togo (p140) has a similar design, with different colours.

The glory of union

One of the largest, and most obvious, flag families is that which includes the Union Flag of Great Britain (also known as the Union Jack). In 1606, When James VI of Scotland became James I of England, he proclaimed a new flag that combined the crosses of St George, England's patron saint (red right-angle cross on white), and St Andrew, the patron saint of Scotland (white diagonal cross on blue, see p50).

UNION FLAGS AT HOME AND ABROAD

Union Flag

Falklands

Hawaii

Use of this flag was more or less restricted to ships in the king's service. Merchant ships flew either St George's flag or that of St Andrew, according to choice. The first merchant ensign, a red field with St George's flag in the canton, was only formalized in 1634.

During the 19th century, at the height of the British Empire, the Union Flag covered the globe, but the days of colonial glory are past and many former British colonies, particularly in Africa, adopted unrelated flags at independence. Nevertheless, the Union Flag still appears in the chief canton of some 27 country, provincial or state flags, including one US state (Hawaii) and two Canadian provinces (on the flag of British Columbia it appears as a chief, extending the full width and one third of the depth – p111).

South and Central America – freedom from colonization

Much of South America was colonized by Spain and Portugal in the early 16th century, but by 1800 there was strong agitation for independence. Among the earliest revolutionary leaders was Francisco de Miranda, a Venezuelan who, in 1806, raised a flag that consisted of equal horizontal bands of yellow above blue above red. This has been interpreted as blue, representing the Atlantic Ocean, separating the New World (yellow) from Spanish tyranny (red).

Venezuela, Ecuador and Colombia all adopted versions of de Miranda's flag. Venezuela's flag (p127) has the same colours and divisions, plus an arc of seven small stars in the blue band.

In 1823, five Spanish provinces in Central America united in their resistance to colonial rule, forming the United Provinces of Central America. Their flag had a horizontal tribar of blue-white-blue with a triangular device at the centre, depicting five peaks (representing the five provinces) rising from the sea. Although the union lasted for only 15 years, the flag has remained, virtually unchanged, as the flag of Nicaragua (p114).

UNITED PROVINCES OF CENTRAL AMERICA

Nicaragua

Honduras

El Salvador

Guatemala

Costa Rica

Rican national coat of arms, on a white oval, is set on the red band, towards the hoist.

Two quite different emblems of freedom are depicted on many South American flags. The flags of Argentina (p131) and Uruguay (p130) feature a prominent golden radiant sun with the orb depicting a human face, known in heraldry as 'the sun in splendour'. On the Argentinian flag the sun commemorates the first mass demonstration in favour of independence (25 May 1810), when a bright sun broke through cloudy skies. Known as *sol de mayo*, or 'sun of May', this national symbol of Argentina represents liberty or freedom. A sun also appears on the flags of Bolivia and Ecuador.

A cap of liberty is depicted on the flag of Paraguay (p130) and the flag or coat of arms of several other South American countries. In heraldry, it is always red. In ancient Rome, a cap of red material was worn by freed slaves to indicate their new status as free people. It is also known as a Phrygian cap, from its use by freed slaves in Phrygia (an ancient country in Asia Minor). During the French Revolution the red cap of liberty became a symbol of resistance to royal authority.

FLAGS BASED ON DE MIRANDA'S FLAG

Venezuela

Ecuador

Colombia

The Honduras flag (p113) has the same tribar pattern, but with five stars on the central band, while that of El Salvador (p114) is similar to Nicaragua's. Guatemala's flag (p113) also has a national emblem at the centre, but has arranged the blue-white-blue as a vertical tribar.

Inspired by uprisings in France in 1848, the fifth of the former United Provinces, Costa Rica (p114), added a broad red band to its horizontal tribar of blue-white-blue. The Costa

From Islam to Pan-Arab

Various groups of countries use a limited range of similar colours, so that certain combinations become known as, for instance, Pan-Arab or Pan-African. The earliest Arab flags are thought to have consisted of religious inscriptions on a plain field of either a single colour or, sometimes, black and white, the colours of the Prophet Mohammed. Later, the green of the Fatimids, who were descended from the daughter of the Prophet, became one of the principal symbols of Islam. Other descendants, the Hashemites, chose red.

By the early 20th century, the combination of black, white, green and red was formally confirmed as representing Pan-Arabism rather than as any single national flag. The colours have been explained in the following terms: 'White is for our deeds, black for our battles, green for our fields and red for our knives'. The Pan-Arab colours were first raised as a flag during the Arab revolt against the tottering Ottoman (Turkish) Empire during World War I. When Turkey surrendered several weeks

Above *Red is a colour with strong associations. It was adopted by socialist and communist parties and the term 'red' has been used to denote someone with revolutionary leanings. The flag shown is that of the People's Republic of China, or 'Red China'.*

before the official armistice that ended the war, both Syria and Iraq, former provinces of the Ottoman Empire, chose traditional Pan-Arab colours for their new national flags.

A new set of Pan-Arab colours — red, white and black — introduced with the revolution that abolished the Egyptian monarchy in 1952, largely found favour with Arab countries that chose the republican system of government, such as Egypt (p136), Yemen (p73), Libya (p136) and Sudan (p145), while Syria (p71) and Iraq (p76) have modified their original choice. Monarchies, such as Kuwait (p75) and the United Arab Emirates (p74), adhere to the older colours, retaining the green.

Africa's Islamic states have tended to opt for the Pan-Arab colours, or for the Islamic emblem of the crescent and star on a plain field. Exceptions are the Comoros flag (p152), which includes stripes of different colours, and the Algerian flag (p135), which has a green and white field. The crescent and star emblem follows the distribution of Islam as the major religion in the Middle East and the Gulf, and an important faith in parts of Africa and Southeast Asia.

Independence in Africa

Flags of the independent states of Africa are a recent phenomenon. Well into the 20th century, the flags of the UK, France, Germany, Portugal, Spain, Italy and Belgium flew over their respective African colonies. Pan-African colours originated with Marcus Garvey (1887–1940), the Jamaican-born American black activist leader who led the Back-to-Africa Movement. Garvey established the Black Star Shipping Line to convey African Americans back to Africa, but this did not succeed. The colours Garvey chose were red, black and green. Later, yellow was borrowed from the flag of Ethiopia (p146), to give the full Pan-African colours, explained as 'Black for the people, red for the blood they have shed to become independent, and green for the fertile earth'. Yellow is variously said to stand for faith, peace and love.

Ethiopia, with its centuries-long history of national independence, was viewed by African people in the Americas as a new Promised Land. Marcus Garvey's followers borrowed the name of the last Ethiopian emperor, Ras Tafari (who took the name Haile Selassie when he was crowned), becoming known as Rastafarians.

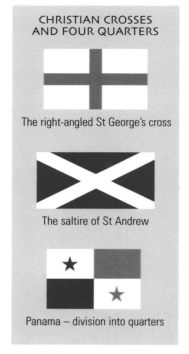

CHRISTIAN CROSSES AND FOUR QUARTERS

The right-angled St George's cross

The saltire of St Andrew

Panama – division into quarters

The first time full Pan-African colours were used in a national flag was in 1957, when the British West African colony of Gold Coast became independent as Ghana. The Ghanaian flag (p140) incorporated the Black Star of Garvey's ships. Other flags with three or more pan-African colours are Guinea (p138), Benin (p140), Mali (p141), Cameroon (p142), the Congo (p144) and Zimbabwe (p149).

Cross or quarter

A cross is the traditional symbol of Christianity and, reputedly, occurs in more than 300 design forms. Most cross designs consist of vertical and horizontal lines meeting so as to make four right angles, as in the cross of St George, but the saltire (or cross in saltire) is formed by the meeting of diagonal lines and resembles the letter X, as in the cross of St Andrew. These two forms are most frequently used for quartering a field on a flag or a heraldic shield.

However, the fact that a field is quartered does not necessarily imply the intention to depict a cross, as the flag of Panama (p115) shows.

The cross most associated with Christianity is the Latin cross, also known as the long or Passion cross. A cross shown on a number of steps or levels is called a cross Calvary. When the kings and leaders of Europe set out to conquer Palestine in the 11th century, each displayed some form of cross as a means of distinguishing himself to his own soldiers and allies. From this display, the expedition became known by the French word *croisade* (*croix* = cross) in English, crusade.

One of the most ancient and widespread crosses is the swastika, where each arm of the cross has an extension at right angles to the arm. Originally an eastern sun symbol, it is still used by hospitals and Buddhist organizations in Asia. In Germany, from 1935–45, it became infamous as the primary symbol of the Nazi regime and its principles. Neo-Nazis continue to use the swastika.

Scandinavian flags tended to follow the design of the Danish flag (p54), one of the oldest in the world. All have a plain field, and the quarters are not equal because the vertical component of the cross is set towards the hoist. Scandinavian flags incorporate only red, white or blue, except Sweden, which includes yellow.

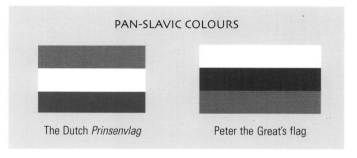

PAN-SLAVIC COLOURS

The Dutch *Prinsenvlag*

Peter the Great's flag

The flag of Portugal (p51) has borne some sort of cross since the 12th century, although other elements of design have been added. Originally the cross was blue on a white field, but it is now composed of an arrangement of five shields, retaining the colours of blue on white.

Unusual forms of the cross are the tau, or St Anthony's cross, which takes the form of the letter T; and the patriarchal cross, which features on the flag of Slovakia (p65). Also known as the Cross of Lorraine, it was the emblem of the Free French forces during World War II. The patriarchal cross has a second, narrower, pair of arms towards the top of the shaft.

From *Prinsenvlag* to Russian tricolour

The pan-Slavic colours (red, blue and white), used in one form or another by a number of countries, were derived from the Dutch *Prinsenvlag*, or prince's flag, a horizontal tricolour of red above white above blue. In 1697 Tsar Peter the Great of Russia spent several months travelling in western Europe to learn about shipbuilding techniques. He was impressed by the usage of flags in the Netherlands, especially its simple national flag which did not depict any heraldic symbols or other complex emblems.

Indeed, given his interests, it is possible that Tsar Peter acquired a copy of *Nieuwe Hollandse Scheepsbouw*, a volume on shipping published in Amsterdam just a few years prior to his arrival in Holland. This contained a comprehensive chapter of the flags of seafaring nations and their overseas trading companies. What is known is that Peter the Great designed his own variation of the Dutch flag for use by the Russian merchant navy, creating a horizontal tricolour of white over blue over red. This flew at the masthead of imperial Russia's commercial fleet until, together with the ornate eagle emblems of the ruling Romanovs, it was abolished in the wake of the Bolshevik revolution of 1917.

The flags of the old order were replaced by the yellow-on-red hammer and sickle of communism, which endured until the coming of democracy in the 1990s, after which the original imperial white-blue-red tricolour was restored as the national flag of the Russian Federation (p66).

FLAGS OF SCANDINAVIA

Denmark

Finland

Sweden

Norway

International organizations

Historically, treaties between countries concerned trade concessions or pacts of non-aggression and were often sealed by a marriage between high-ranking partners from either side. Improved communications and speedier travel have effectively shrunk the world to a global village, so modern treaties tend to be more pragmatic. Today, the visible seal of approval and acceptance, in place of the marriage, is the joint hoisting of both parties' flags.

At the headquarters of international organizations or associations it is common practice to fly the flag of the host organization in the senior position (first in a line, or at the 12-o'clock position in a circle), together with the national flags of the member states following in alphabetical sequence.

United Nations

The UN was founded in 1945, after the end of World War II, to establish and maintain international peace. The UN flag, adopted in 1947, has a light blue field on which is a map of the world within an olive wreath. Both blue and the olive branches symbolize world peace, and the map denotes global concern.

With 191 members, the United Nations is the world's largest and most influential international organization. In times of war, the UN may send soldiers and military equipment to the trouble zone, but the blue-bereted UN troops may engage only in self-defence and are primarily peacekeepers, not a fighting force.

Above The European Union flag, shown here in a banner format, maintains 12 stars regardless of the number of EU members.
Top Flags of member nations fly outside the European Union headquarters.

North Atlantic Treaty Organization

NATO was established in 1949 as a united military defence pact against the threat of increasing Soviet aggression. Member states are countries of western Europe and North America. Blue represents the Atlantic Ocean, the circle symbolizes unity, while the points of the compass denote the common direction the 19 member states have taken towards peace. The flag was adopted in 1953.

European Union

In 1955, the Council of Europe adopted a flag with a circle of gold stars at the centre. The design was adopted by the Council's successor, the European Union (EU), in May 1986. Originally, the intent was to show one star for each member nation, but it was finally decided to have an arbitrary number of stars on the flag as this would avoid the necessity of adding stars which, potentially, might have resulted in a total of 40 or more.

Commonwealth

Before World War I, the British Empire commanded over 25 per cent of the world's population and area. With the fall of many European thrones, the term 'British Commonwealth of Nations' came to represent the remaining empire, but was soon simplified to the Commonwealth. A voluntary association of countries, colonies or territories that were, or are still, ruled by Britain, the Commonwealth today includes some 54 states from across the world. The annual Commonwealth Heads of Government (CHOG) meeting is an important forum for discussions on global issues. The flag has a dark blue field with a globe, upon which no countries are depicted. The globe emits short gold lines, with a gap, to form the letter C.

Arab League

The Arab League flag has a green field with a central wreath of olive leaves, in white, enclosing a circular chain. Within the chain a crescent partially encloses the name of the organization, written in Arabic script. Green is the colour of Islam, of which the crescent is an emblem. The chain symbolizes strength and unity, while the wreath represents peace and security.

Association of Southeast Asian Nations

The flag was adopted in 1997, 30 years after the ASEAN was founded to promote economic cooperation and stability among the states of Southeast Asia. Red, white, blue and gold are the colours of the member states. The blue field represents sea, sky and friendship, and the central emblem, on a red disc outlined in white, represents 10 *padi* stalks (sheaves of harvested rice that has not yet been milled), one for each member nation.

Red Cross

A red cross couped (with arms shortened) on a white field has been the symbol of the International Committee of the Red Cross (ICRC) since the humanitarian organization was founded in 1863. The Red Cross concerns itself with human welfare in times of war, natural disaster, or humanitarian crisis. It has also played a role in successive Geneva Conventions on the conduct of war and the treatment of prisoners of war. An equivalent flag for use in Muslim countries displays a red crescent and was adopted in 1876, while a red Shield of David is depicted on the Israeli version.

FLAGS OF SOME INTERNATIONAL ORGANIZATIONS

United Nations

North Atlantic Treaty Organization

Commonwealth

Arab League

Association of Southeast Asian Nations

Red Cross

Flags in sport

When it comes to sports events, flags play many roles. At the opening ceremonies of most international and pan-national games, competitors parade under their national flags, while medal ceremonies become deeply emotional occasions as soon as the winning athletes mount the podium and their country's flag is raised and their anthem begins to play.

The flag of the International Olympic Committee (IOC) was designed in 1913. The white field symbolizes peace and friendship and the five rings, joined as a sign of unity, represent the five continents. A special, large version of the flag is hoisted at the opening ceremony of each Games and remains flying for the duration of the event.

Flags are also an important part of branding and marketing at major events, providing a strong visual image and serving as memorabilia for participants and spectators alike. Spectators often take national and/or team flags and banners to games, and wear clothing in their team's colours (English soccer leagues and American Superbowl are colourful examples of this). In hotly contested competitions, such as the European football (soccer) cup final, stadiums can become a noisy sea of waving flags.

At some sports meetings, flags are not restricted to the official versions. A national flag, for instance, may be overprinted with the portrait or name of a popular player or the badge of a favourite motor manufacturer. One of the more sincere forms of commitment to one's country is the national flag painted, often with great skill, on spectators' faces.

Above At least one colour in the Olympic flag can be found in each nation's flag.

Top Japanese football fans show support for their national team with a spirited display of flags, colours and banners.

Motor racing

In the hi tech world of Formula One (F1) motor racing, flags are an ideal way of communicating information to drivers on the track (an echo, perhaps, of the early days of motoring). In England, soon after the first motor vehicles, or horseless carriages as they were then called, took to the roads, the law compelled them to be preceded by a man on foot, waving a red flag to warn other road users of their approach. The law was repealed after a few years, but it is still commemorated by the annual London to Brighton vintage motor rally. The use of flags survives in motor sport because, although nowadays the drivers are in radio communication with their pits, there is no substitute for the instant on-track information provided by highly visible flags.

An official known as the clerk of the course is responsible for training and positioning a team of flag marshals around the circuit. Their role is to inform drivers of obstacles or hazards on the track ahead. Drivers who disregard flag signals endanger themselves and other competitors, and may be penalized. Some flags are always displayed waving. Others may be waved or held steady, with different meanings.

A stationary blue flag is a general warning that the car behind is about to lap and must be let through. When waved, it is an order to let the following car through at once, or risk a penalty. A stationary yellow flag means 'there is a hazard beside the track, do not overtake'; while a waved yellow flag signifies a more serious warning – that there is a hazard on the track, cars should not overtake, and must be prepared to follow an unusual line. Double yellow flags, waved, mean that the track is wholly or partially blocked: drivers must not overtake and must be prepared to stop. A yellow flag with red stripes indicates oil or water ahead. A green flag is always shown to indicate the end of the danger area controlled by the yellow flag. If a safety car is on the track, its presence is indicated by stationary yellow flags displayed together with a board on which are the letters SC.

A black and white diagonal flag is a first and only warning for 'unsportsmanlike behaviour'. A driver who does not obey it is likely to be shown a black flag, along with his number. He must then stop at his pits within one lap and report to the clerk of the course. The black flag thus invariably signifies either a penalty or a disqualification.

A red flag shown at the start/finish line and simultaneously at marshals' posts means that the race is stopped. Unlike the other coloured flags, the red flag is ordered directly by the clerk of the course – its display is not left to the discretion of individual marshals.

Perhaps the best-known of all flags used in motor racing is the black-and-white chequered flag which signals that the winner has passed the finish line and the race is over.

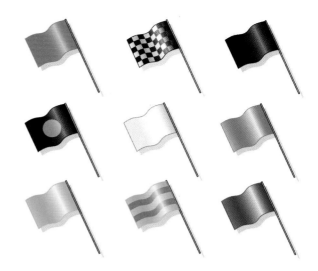

Above In motor racing, the marshal's flags convey a range of instructions and information to the drivers.

Below The chequered flag that signals the end of a motor race is perhaps one of the most famous sporting flags.

Field games

In games such as soccer (football), rugby and field hockey, line (touch) judges carry small flags to indicate where a ball has gone out of play, or to draw the referee's attention to infringements. (In American football, small squares of white cloth are used instead of flags.) It is not unusual for a linesman's call to be questioned by players and spectators alike!

Typically, the edge of the field of play is marked with flags at the corners, and sometimes also on the half and quarter lines. In the case of hockey, all flags except the corner flags are set back one metre from the line. Corner flags are typically triangular and attached to a flexible rod that can withstand violent collisions with players without either breaking or causing injury.

Golf clubs frequently fly both the national flag and the club flag during the hours of play. Each putting green has its own flag attached to a pole (the 'pin') that is removed when players aim for the hole. When

putting is over, the pole is replaced in the hole. These flags are usually braced by a rigid frame, and the colour of the flags of the first nine holes differs from the colour of the second nine. Other golf course flags may indicate areas that are out of bounds, or where the ground is under repair, usually shown as GUR.

In many sports, plain coloured flags are used as markers, either to indicate a route, as in cross-country running, or to mark a distance, such as the length of a jump, or the throw of a javelin or discus. Shooting and archery have the potential to be dangerous so, during both practice and competition, red flags are flown from the butts (the high earth banks behind the target) to warn bystanders to keep well away.

Below *Brazilian and English players are urged on by flag-waving fans as they wait in the tunnel prior to an international soccer match.*

Sailing

Yacht and powerboat clubs, whether at the coast or on inland lakes or dams, usually fly both the national and club flags from a mast at the clubhouse. Members' yachts may fly the club or national flag at the stern, with a small, triangular burgee (see p154) in club colours at the masthead, depending on the type of rig.

It is customary for skippers of cruising yachts to fly their national flag at the stern, especially when in a foreign port. It is also considered a courtesy to fly the national flag of the country you are visiting, and this is usually flown from the starboard spreader. The Q-flag is displayed when first entering a port, to indicate that all aboard are in good health, and you require inward clearance from the health authorities.

Flags conforming to the International Code of Signals are used at most levels of yacht racing (see p28). Coloured flags or variously shaped pennants are used, alone or together with sound signals, to indicate the run-up to, and start of, a race. Flags flown from the clubhouse (bridge), or from a start boat on the water, indicate ten and five minutes to go

Above *These yachts are 'dressed' with code flags and pennants for the opening cruise of the new sailing season. With modern communication methods, traditional signal flags are rarely used these days, but they continue to be flown on special occasions.*

before the start, the start itself and a recall, if any yachts were over the line ahead of the gun. If the finish line is at sea, a committee boat flying a blue flag will be situated on the line.

In yacht racing, frequently used signals include the C-flag, to show that the course has been changed, S to show it has been shortened, N to indicate that the race has been abandoned, and the answering pennant, or AP, to signal a postponement. Various yacht racing rules are also indicated by specific flags, such as the Z-flag, which is flown to show that Rule 30.2 is in effect. During racing, a yacht may declare a protest by raising a red flag.

Flags of the World

Flags are part of our world, part of the real world. They do not exist in a world of their own but were created to represent totemic emblems, kings, patron saints and deities, in order that they might be seen and known. Flags were also created to produce a particular effect, be it a sense of duty on the part of a subject, or fear in the heart of the foe. Ultimately though, our relationship with a flag is based on what the flag represents – not heraldically or in terms of design, but as a representative of those people who call it their own.

It is a two-way relationship: we accept our flag as symbolizing the honour, dignity, justice and strength of our country, but these are the same qualities that our country – and thus our country's flag – demands from us. Emblems alone have little power to inspire, console or frighten. They can only reflect the perceived qualities of those who hold the emblem or flag, as their own. Flags are what their people have made them.

Learning about flags and their stories is an exploration of the nations of our world, of the historical, political and cultural associations that bind us in harmony or enmity. It is also a story of ever-simplifying design. Dragons, lions and eagles still dignify some older flags, but the modern tendency is for clear-cut patterns and vibrant colours that say: 'Know me'.

World map

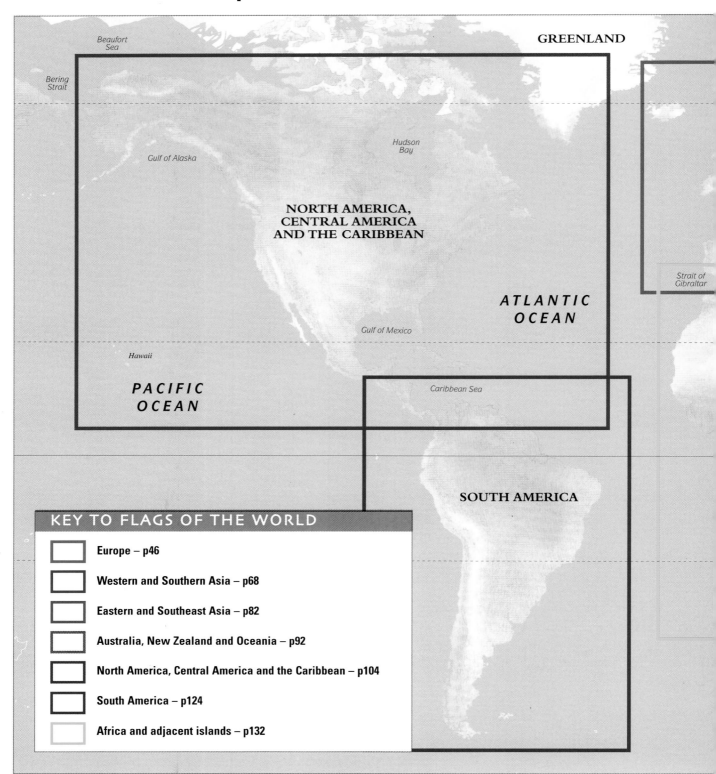

Beaufort Sea

Bering Strait

GREENLAND

Hudson Bay

Gulf of Alaska

NORTH AMERICA, CENTRAL AMERICA AND THE CARIBBEAN

Gulf of Mexico

ATLANTIC OCEAN

Strait of Gibraltar

Hawaii

Caribbean Sea

PACIFIC OCEAN

SOUTH AMERICA

KEY TO FLAGS OF THE WORLD

Europe – p46

Western and Southern Asia – p68

Eastern and Southeast Asia – p82

Australia, New Zealand and Oceania – p92

North America, Central America and the Caribbean – p104

South America – p124

Africa and adjacent islands – p132

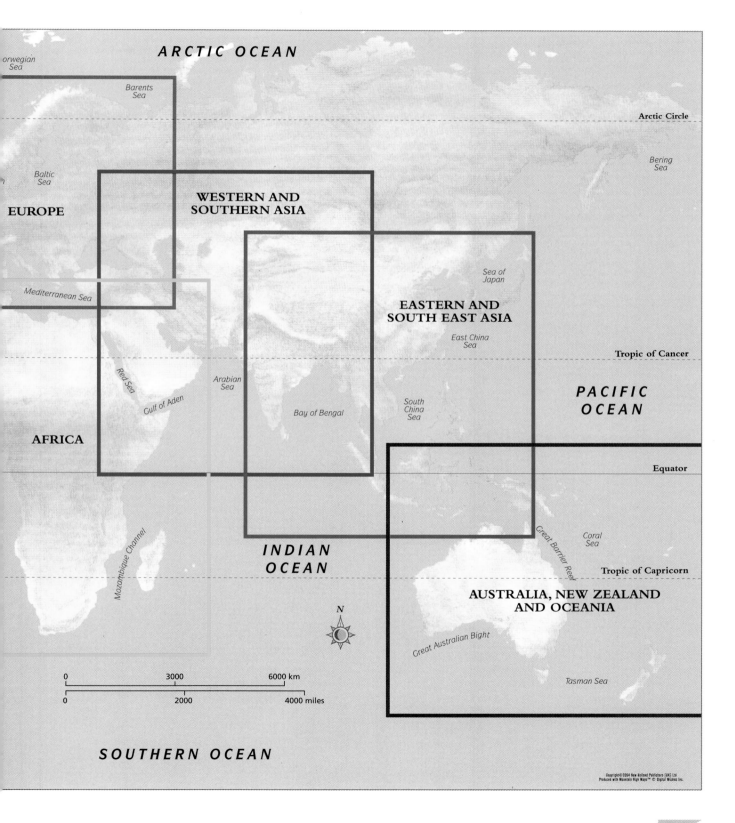

ARCTIC OCEAN

Norwegian
Sea

Barents
Sea

Arctic Circle

Bering
Sea

Baltic
Sea

WESTERN AND
SOUTHERN ASIA

EUROPE

Mediterranean Sea

Sea of
Japan

EASTERN AND
SOUTH EAST ASIA

East China
Sea

Tropic of Cancer

Red Sea

Arabian
Sea

PACIFIC
OCEAN

Gulf of Aden

Bay of Bengal

South
China
Sea

AFRICA

Equator

Mozambique Channel

Coral
Sea

Great Barrier Reef

INDIAN
OCEAN

Tropic of Capricorn

AUSTRALIA, NEW ZEALAND
AND OCEANIA

N

Great Australian Bight

Tasman Sea

0   3000   6000 km

0   2000   4000 miles

SOUTHERN OCEAN

Europe

From Portugal's Atlantic coastline to Russia's Ural Mountains, and from Norway's remote North Cape to the Mediterranean island of Crete, the 'Old World' of Europe presents a tight pattern of settlement where, over millennia, people of closely related cultural and ethnic origins have fought for the right to divide and rule in their own way.

Throughout Europe, the average distance from the sea is a relatively short 340km (210mi.). For centuries, the Mediterranean was the focus of cultural and trade development. Later, shore settlements along the Atlantic and North Sea coastlines came to play a greater role. From city-states and unsteady kingdoms, 15th-century explorers set out in their fragile craft to find a sea route to the east that could then only be reached by tedious journeys overland. They found the east, and a New World, and the culture the European colonists carried and imparted wherever they went has profoundly influenced the world ever since.

In the early centuries, despite the proximity of borders, there was little friendly contact between nations, while a host of different, though often related, languages presented an obstacle to amity. There were occasional instances of collaboration, such as the Crusades of the 11th and 12th centuries, which were undertaken with the, ultimately unsuccessful, objective of recapturing Jerusalem from Islam. For the most part, treaties kept an uneasy peace or, as happened in the early 20th century, ensured that a local incident, an assassination in Sarajevo in 1914, would engulf the entire continent.

Twentieth-century political alliances and politics, transformed into two world wars, brought about the destruction of long-ruling dynasties, the death by murder of millions of citizens, and a bloody realignment in preparation for the next war. The decline of empires saw the rise of communism, but Europe, the cradle of democracy, was also the birthplace of capitalism and the inventive spirit of the Industrial Revolution.

Following the fall of communism in the 1990s, Sarajevo again came to the fore, this time as a city besieged by Christian Serbs indulging in a bloody 'ethnic cleansing' of Muslims. UN, NATO and Russian troops brought a temporary lull but, in the Caucasus to the east, Russian troops launched an attack on the would-be independent republic of Chechnya. As in Bosnia, the UN and European Union (EU) attempted to mediate, producing an uneasy peace that was sporadically and viciously broken.

Although the European Union counts as members almost all the states of western Europe, as well as some in central Europe, the European Parliament, which meets in Strasbourg (France) and Brussels (Belgium), has still to overcome the suspicions of national parliaments and has not yet fully established itself.

Europe

Arctic Circle

Reykjavik ● ICELAND

0 500 1000 km

0 250 500 miles

GREENLAND

Baffin Bay

N

Davis Strait

Nuuk ●

Greenland Sea

ICELAND

Labrador Sea

FAROE ISLANDS
Thorshavn on Stromo ●

Norwegian Sea

SWEDEN

Gulf of Bothnia

FINL

NORWAY

Oslo ●

Stockholm ●

Hels

Gulf of Fin

T

ESTO

North Sea

Baltic Sea

LAT
R

DENMARK

Copenhagen ●

LITHUAN
V
RUSSI

IRELAND

Dublin ● *Irish Sea*

UNITED KINGDOM

NETHER-LANDS
Amsterdam ●

Berlin ●

POLAND

Warsa

Birmingham ●

Celtic Sea

London ●

English Channel

BELGIUM
Brussels ●

GERMANY

Prague ●
CZECH REPUBLIC

SLOVAK

LUXEMBOURG
Luxembourg ●
Paris ●

ATLANTIC OCEAN

FRANCE

Bern ●
SWITZERLAND

LIECHTENSTEIN
Vaduz ●

The Alps

Vienna ●
AUSTRIA

Bratislava ●

Budap

HUNGARY

SLOVENIA
Ljubljana ●

Zagreb ●
CROATIA

Belg

Bay of Biscay

PORTUGAL

SPAIN

Lisbon ●

Madrid ●

Andorra la Vella ●
ANDORRA

Barcelona ●

Monaco-Ville ● MONACO

SAN MARINO
San Marino ●

Vatican ●
VATICAN CITY
Rome ●

BOSNIA-HERZEGOVINA
Sarajevo ●

SERB
MONTE

Corsica (France)

Adriatic Sea

Sko
MACEDO
Tirana ●

N

Balearic Islands

Menorca
Mallorca
Eivissa
Formentera

Sardinia (Italy)

ITALY

ALBANI

GRE

0 250 500 km

0 100 200 300 miles

Strait of Gibraltar

Gibraltar City ●
GIBRALTAR

Mediterranean Sea

Sicily

Ionian Sea

MALTA ● Valletta

Mediterranean

Number of countries: 46

Largest country: Russia

Smallest country: Vatican City

Largest city: Moscow (Russian Federation)

Major cities: Amsterdam, Athens, Barcelona, Berlin, Birmingham, Brussels, Budapest, Copenhagen, Geneva, Hamburg, Istanbul, Kiev, London, Madrid, Manchester, Milan, Munich, Paris, Rome, St Petersburg, Vienna, Warsaw.

Highest point: Mt Elbrus (Elbruz), Caucasus, 5642m (18,517ft) – the highest point in Western Europe.

Lowest point: Caspian Sea shore, 28m/92ft below sea level.

Longest rivers: Ob-Irtysh, Asiatic Russia (5410km/3362mi.); Volga, European Russia (3685km/2290mi.).

Largest lake: Caspian Sea (371,000km²/ 142,200mi²).

UNITED KINGDOM

United Kingdom of Great Britain and Northern Ireland

Flag proportions: 1:2

Adopted: 1 January 1801

Capital: London

Area: 244,880km² (94,548mi²)

Population: 60 million

Language: English

Religion: Protestant, Roman Catholic

Currency: Pound

Exports: Machinery, vehicles, chemicals, foodstuffs, maps, manufactured goods.

The Union Flag's origins date back to 1277, when the banner of England's patron saint, St George (a red cross quartering a white field), was sometimes used as the flag of England. The white diagonal cross, or saltire, of St Andrew of Scotland dates back to at least 1385. Following the accession of James VI of Scotland to the throne of England (as James I), he chose a combined flag in 1606 for use as a jack on naval vessels, hence the origin of the name 'Union Jack'.

No change was made to the flag in 1707 when England and Scotland formed the United Kingdom of Great Britain, although possibilities were considered. The 1801 Act of Union established the United Kingdom of Great Britain and Ireland (later Northern Ireland). St Patrick's cross (a red saltire) was added as a counter-change (see p154) to St Andrew's cross, forming the present Union Flag which, in the heyday of the British Empire, was flown in most parts of the world.

Flags of the United Kingdom

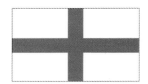

England: St George's Flag, in use since the 13th century.

Scotland: St Andrew's Flag, in use since the 14th century.

Wales
Approved in 1959.

Northern Ireland
Adopted May 1953.

IRELAND

Eire (Republic of Ireland)

Flag proportions: 1:2

Adopted: 29 December 1937

Capital: Dublin (Baile Átha Cliath)

Area: 70,283km² (27,148mi²)

Population: 4 million

Language: Irish, English

Religion: Roman Catholic, Protestant

Currency: Euro

Exports: Food, machinery and transport equipment, chemicals, manufactured goods.

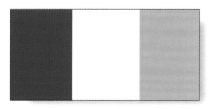

The 1916 Easter Rising, a rebellion against British rule, led to the formation of the Irish Free State in 1922, followed by independence from Britain in 1937. A green, white and orange tricolour was raised as the national flag of the Irish Free State (after 1949 the Republic of Ireland). The colours were worn in cockades (see p154) in sympathy with a French uprising that led to the restoration of the *Tricolore*, and also used by Irish nationalists in their 1848 struggle for freedom from Britain. Green represents the Catholic majority; orange the Protestant minority (supporters of William of Orange who, as William III, ruled Britain and Ireland from 1688–1702). White expresses union and peace between the two faiths.

PORTUGAL

Republic of Portugal

Flag proportions: 2:3
Adopted: 30 June 1911
Capital: Lisbon (Lisboa)
Area: 91,985km² (35,516mi²)
Population: 10,3 million
Language: Portuguese
Religion: Roman Catholic
Currency: Euro
Exports: Textiles, clothing, pulp and paper, wood, tinned fish, wine, cork, refined oil.

Portugal's lead in exploring the world beyond Europe in the 15th and 16th centuries is reflected in the armillary sphere, an old navigation instrument, depicted on the flag. The original shield of Portugal, from the reign of Alfonso Henriques in the 12th century, was white with five blue shields in the form of a cross, representing five Moorish kings defeated in battle in 1139. On each shield, five white dots represent the wounds of Christ. The red border with gold castles was added in the 13th century by King Afonso III. The red field was adopted to signify revolution, while green, the colour of hope, was the colour of Prince Henry 'the Navigator' who sponsored many early voyages of exploration.

SPAIN

Kingdom of Spain

Flag proportions: 2:3
Adopted: 24 December 1981
Capital: Madrid
Area: 504,750km² (194,884mi²)
Population: 41,2 million
Language: Spanish
Religion: Roman Catholic
Currency: Euro
Exports: Vehicles, machinery, electrical equipment, metals, foodstuffs, wine.

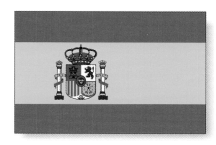

Red and yellow appeared on the flag of Catalonia (Cataluña) in the 13th century, and have appeared on other provincial flags, notably Castile and Aragon. These colours were used from 1785 to identify Spanish merchant shipping. A purple band was added when Spain became a republic in 1931, but the original flag was restored in 1939 under General Franco. Since then, the state flag has incorporated the national arms, in the yellow band, set towards the hoist. The quarters of the shield represent four regions of Spain: Castile, León, Aragon and Navarre. The shield is supported by the Pillars of Hercules, as Gibraltar and Jebel Musa were once known. The arms have changed many times, the last being in 1981.

GIBRALTAR

Gibraltar

Flag proportions: 1:2
Adopted: 1983
Capital: Gibraltar City
Area: 6.5km² (2.5mi²)
Population: 30,000
Language: English, Spanish
Religion: Roman Catholic
Currency: Euro, Gibraltar Pound
Industries: Financial sector, shipping services, tourism.

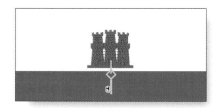

Known as 'the key to the Mediterranean', the unofficial flag of this British overseas territory shows a three-towered castle and golden key on a white field with a red band at the base. The arms, granted in 1502 by Spain's King Ferdinand, also feature a castle and key, symbolizing the security of Gibraltar and the fact that it controls access to the Mediterranean through the narrow Straits of Gibraltar. The same emblems feature on the badges of several British regiments who have served on 'The Rock', a strategic naval and air base.

Gibraltar has been under British control since 1713, yet Spain continues to claim sovereignty, despite referendums in favour of maintaining the status quo.

ANDORRA

Principality of Andorra

Flag proportions: 2:3
Adopted: July 1993
Capital: Andorra la Vella
Area: 468km² (177mi²)
Population: 70,000
Language: Catalan, French, Castilian, Portuguese
Religion: Roman Catholic
Currency: Euro
Industries: Tourism, banking.

The Principality of Andorra, high in the eastern Pyrenees, is one of the world's oldest states. The flag dates from around 1897, but its origin and symbolism are not documented. Neighbouring France and Spain have protected Andorra since the 13th century, and are represented by red and yellow (Spain) and blue and red (France).

The arms represent Spain's bishop of Urgel and the French Comte de Foix, under whose joint sovereignty Andorra was placed in 1278. The joint heads of state are still the bishop of Urgel and the president of France, represented by permanent delegates. Elements on the coat of arms recall the provinces of Catalonia and Béarn on which, historically, Andorra has been dependent.

FRANCE

Republic of France

Flag proportions: 2:3
Adopted: 5 March 1848
Capital: Paris
Area: 543,965km² (210,033mi²)
Population: 60 million
Language: French
Religion: Roman Catholic
Currency: Euro
Exports: Metals, chemicals, machinery and equipment, iron and steel, foodstuffs, wine.

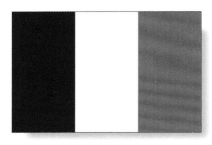

France's national flag, the *Tricolore*, has been in uninterrupted use since 1848. Blue and red are generally accepted as the colours of Paris. White, the colour of the royal House of Bourbon, is also associated with the Virgin Mary and Jeanne d'Arc, a 15th-century French heroine. The colours represent the ideals of the 1789 French Revolution: liberty, equality and fraternity. The *Tricolore* is flown with blue at the hoist. The vertical bands are of equal width, except at sea, when 'optical proportions' of 30:33:37 give the best visual effect.

The *Tricolore* is the official flag of France's Overseas Territories (such as Réunion and French Polynesia), some of which fly approved local flags alongside it.

MONACO

Principality of Monaco

Flag proportions: 4:5
Adopted: 4 April 1881
Capital: Monaco-Ville
Area: 1,95km² (0,75mi²)
Population: 33,400
Language: French, English, Italian, Monegasque
Religion: Roman Catholic
Currency: Euro
Industries: Banking, tourism, construction, consumer products.

Monaco, the second smallest state in the world (after the Vatican), forms an enclave in southern France. The steep territory is gradually being expanded by filling in the sea to reclaim more land. The flag, equal bands of red over white, takes its colours from the arms of the Grimaldi family, who have ruled the principality for over 700 years.

Monaco's flag is the same as the Indonesian bicolour (see p91), differing only in proportion.

BELGIUM

Kingdom of Belgium

Flag proportions: 13:15
Adopted: 23 January 1831
Capital: Brussels (Bruxelles)
Area: 30,518km² (11,778mi²)
Population: 10,3 million
Languages: Flemish, Walloon
Religion: Roman Catholic,
Protestant
Currency: Euro
Exports: Foodstuffs, livestock,
cut diamonds, iron and steel.

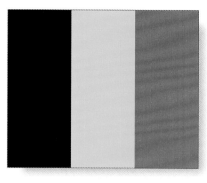

Belgium is a parliamentary democracy with a constitutional monarch. The vertical tricolour was almost certainly based on the French *Tricolore* and came into use with the founding of the independent Kingdom of Belgium in 1830. The colours appeared on the coat of arms of the Duchy of Brabant, a large province of the Low Countries (an area that encompassed Belgium, the Netherlands and Luxembourg).

The original arms of Brabant featured a gold lion rampant, its tongue and claws red, on a black field. A lion on a shield still features on the Belgian coat of arms.

LUXEMBOURG

Grand Duchy of Luxembourg

Flag proportions: 3:5
Adopted: 1848
Capital: Luxembourg
Area: 2586km² (999mi²)
Population: 446,000
Languages: French, German,
Letze-buergesch
Religion: Roman Catholic
Currency: Euro
Exports: Manufactured goods,
steel, electrical equipment.

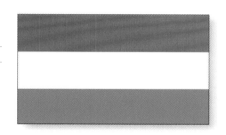

The horizontal tricolour of Luxembourg, Europe's last independent duchy, derived its colours from the 13th-century arms of the Grand Duke. Luxembourg was part of the Netherlands in the early 19th century, so the pattern and colours of the two flags are similar, although Luxembourg has a paler shade of blue. In the mid-20th century, Luxembourg formed an economic union with Belgium and the Netherlands (Benelux), setting the scene for the establishment of the European Union.

NETHERLANDS

Kingdom of the Netherlands

Flag proportions: 2:3
Adopted: 19 February 1937
Capital: Amsterdam
Area: 41,526km² (16,033mi²)
Population: 16 million
Language: Dutch
Religion: Roman Catholic,
Dutch Reformed Church
Currency: Euro
Exports: Dairy products, plants,
cut flowers, natural gas, petro-
chemicals, machinery.

The first horizontal tricolour of the Netherlands, known as the *Prinsenvlag* or Prince's flag, was raised in the 16th century (see p35). It had an orange band in honour of William the Silent, the protestant Prince of Orange, who rebelled against the Catholic Philip II of Spain, establishing an independent country in 1581. Red gradually replaced orange and, by the 18th century, was the confirmed colour.

Orange remains the Dutch royal colour and, on festive days connected to the royal family, an orange pennant is hoisted above the national flag.

DENMARK

Kingdom of Denmark

Flag proportions: 28:37
Adopted: 1625
Capital: Copenhagen (København)
Area: 43,075km² (16,631mi²)
Population: 5,4 million
Language: Danish
Religion: Lutheran
Currency: Danish krone
Exports: Machinery, electrical goods and equipment, animals, meat and meat products, metals.

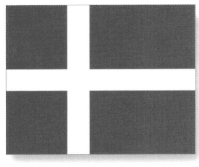

The Kingdom of Denmark dates from the 10th century, and the *Dannebrog*, or 'Danish cloth', is often claimed to be the oldest national flag. Although it can be officially dated to the second half of the 14th century, legend says that a vision of a white cross on a red field came to King Valdemar II during a crusade against the pagan Estonians in 1219. Spurred on by this sign from heaven, the Danes went on to win the battle. It was not until 1854, when private people were allowed to fly the flag, that it truly became national in character.

The Danish, or Scandinavian, off-centre cross was originally a conventional square-armed cross, but was amended so that the arm of the cross in the fly was extended. It is the model for the flags of all the Scandinavian countries.

GREENLAND

Greenland

Flag proportions: 2:3
Adopted: 6 June 1985
Capital: Godthaab (Nuuk)
Area: 2,175,600km² (840,000mi²)
Population: 56,000
Languages: Greenlandic (East Inuit), Danish, English
Religion: Lutheran
Currency: Danish krone
Exports: Fish and fish products.

The world's largest island, Greenland (Kalaallit Nunaat) was first inhabited by Eskimos from the North American Arctic. In about 982AD, the Viking explorer, Eric the Red, established settlements on the west coast. A self-governing overseas territory of Denmark since 1979, the flag's colours are the same as those of the Danish flag. Greenlanders call their flag *Erfalasorput*, 'our flag', or *Aappalaaroq*, 'the red'. As Thue Christiansen, the flag's designer, explains: 'the large white part of the flag symbolizes the icecap, with the white half-circle being the icebergs and pack ice. Red stands for the ocean, with our fjords represented by the red half-circle.' The circle also depicts the sun, which remains above the horizon during the brief summer months. The flag's 20th anniversary will be celebrated in June 2005.

FAROE ISLANDS

Faroes

Flag proportions: 8:11
Adopted: 5 June 1959
Capital: Thorshavn on Stromo.
Area: 1399km² (540mi²)
Population: 46,000
Languages: Faroese, Danish
Religion: Lutheran
Currency: Danish krone
Exports: Fish and fish products, handicrafts, stamps, ships.

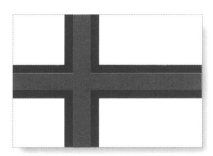

The people of the Faroe Islands (Føroyar) are descended from Viking settlers who arrived in the 9th century. The archipelago of 17 inhabited islands and one uninhabited island has been connected to Denmark since the 14th century and became a self-governing overseas administrative division in 1948.

The colours are similar to those of Norway's flag. Set on a white field, a red cross is fimbriated (narrowly bordered) in blue. Blue and red occur in traditional Faroese headdresses, while white represents sky, and waves breaking against the coast. The first flag, designed by Faroese students in Denmark, was only used on land but, during World War II, it became the ensign of the British-occupied Faroes, to distinguish their ships from those of German-occupied Denmark.

ICELAND

Republic of Iceland
Flag proportions: 18:25
Adopted: 17 June 1944
Capital: Reykjavík
Area: 103,000km² (39,758mi²)
Population: 288,000
Language: Icelandic
Religion: Lutheran
Currency: Krona
Exports: Fish, shellfish, animal feeds, nonferrous metals, iron and steel.

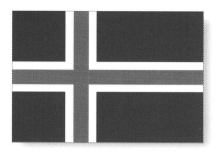

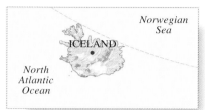

Fishing is the wealth of Iceland, which adopted its own flag only in 1915. Iceland's traditional colours are blue and white, for the sea and the ice, and the flag shows a white horizontal cross on a blue field, to which was added red for Denmark, from which many Icelanders' ancestors come. (Iceland and Norway's flags are identical in layout, and differ only in the placing of the colours.)

Iceland was under Danish occupation and influence from the 14th century and, from the 16th century, was represented in the arms of Denmark by, among other charges or objects, a stockfish crowned. The state flag depicts the national arms on a swallow-tailed flag.

NORWAY

Kingdom of Norway
Flag proportions: 8:11
Adopted: 17 July 1821
Capital: Oslo
Area: 323,878km² (125,050mi²)
Population: 4,5 million
Language: Norwegian
Religion: Lutheran
Currency: Norwegian krone
Exports: Petroleum, natural gas, fish products, metals, wood pulp and paper.

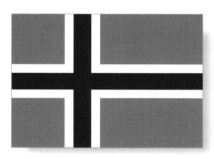

Norway was ruled by Denmark from 1380, during which time Norwegian ships flew the *Dannebrog*. The country was ceded to Sweden in 1814 and the current flag dates from 1821, when a member of the Norwegian parliament, Frederik Meltzer, suggested charging the Danish flag with a blue cross. Red, white and blue are the colours of the French revolutionary *Tricolore* and the flags of the USA and UK. In 1899, after a long struggle, Norway obtained the right to fly its flag without the 'union badge' which the Swedes had insisted on. After gaining independence in 1905, Norway retained that flag.

Although there are no legal requirements, Norwegian flags are often flown from white-painted poles, usually with a spike or ball terminal.

SWEDEN

Kingdom of Sweden
Flag proportions: 5:8
Adopted: 22 June 1906
Capital: Stockholm
Area: 449,964km² (173,806mi²)
Population: 8,9 million
Language: Swedish
Religion: Lutheran, Roman Catholic
Currency: Swedish krona
Exports: Wood, pulp and paper, machinery, motor vehicles, chemicals, iron and steel.

A royal decree of 1569 commanded that Swedish battle flags or banners were to depict a gold or yellow cross. The design of the national flag, a horizontal gold cross on a blue field, dates from soon after and was probably influenced by the *Dannebrog*. The colours come from the national coat of arms, which originated in the 14th century.

The arms consist of a blue shield quartered by a gold cross. Three gold crowns are depicted in the first and fourth quarters, and a lion in the second and third quarters. The shield is supported by two gold lions. The Royal Standard carries the coat of arms on a white square on a blue three-tailed flag. Similarities in the design of their flags are attributable to the close historical ties that exist between Denmark and Sweden.

FINLAND

Republic of Finland

Flag proportions: 11:18
Adopted: 1 January 1995
Capital: Helsinki (Helsingfors)
Area: 338,145km² (130,559mi²)
Population: 5,2 million
Languages: Finnish, Swedish
Religion: Lutheran
Currency: Euro
Exports: Metal, engineering, electronics, forestry.

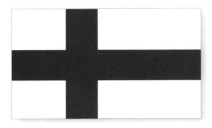

White is for the snow, and blue for the skies and many lakes of this Nordic country. Finland proclaimed its independence from Russia in 1917 and was recognized in 1920. Although the present flag was introduced in 1918, various combinations of blue and white had featured on Finnish flags for hundreds of years. In the land of the midnight sun, use of the flag is regulated by law, with the hours for flying it being from 08:00 to sunset, or 21:00 at the latest. Helsinki, Europe's northern-most capital, has 73 days of constant daylight in summer and 51 days of uninterrupted night in the winter.

The state flag and ensign carry the central motif from the Finnish arms, a gold lion rampant and bearing a sword, on a red field, at the junction of the arms of the cross.

ESTONIA

Republic of Estonia

Flag proportions: 7:11
Adopted: 8 May 1990
Capital: Tallinn
Area: 45,227km² (17,462mi²)
Population: 1,3 million
Language: Estonian
Religion: Christian (Lutheran and Orthodox)
Currency: Kroon
Exports: Foodstuffs, animal products, timber products, base metals, minerals, machinery.

A former Baltic province of imperial Russia, Estonia raised its flag of independence in 1918 after the Russians made peace with Germany. The horizontal tricolour of blue over black over white was designed in 1881 in colours representing Estonian folklore: blue for sky, faith and loyalty; black to commemorate a dark past of suffering, as well as the soil; and white for snow and for hope. When Soviet Russia occupied Estonia during World War II, the tricolour was banned. During the 'singing revolution' of 1987–88, when communism was clearly failing, the flag was openly displayed and it became the national flag of the Republic of Estonia in 1990.

Three gold lions on the coat of arms represent three eras of heroic struggle: in ancient times, during the 14th century and in the 20th century.

LATVIA

Republic of Latvia

Flag proportions: 1:2
Adopted: 27 February 1990
Capital: Riga
Area: 63,700km² (24,595mi²)
Population: 2,318,400
Language: Latvian
Religion: Christian
Currency: Lats
Exports: Wood and wood products, textiles, foodstuffs.

Although the constitution of this Baltic republic describes the flag as 'red with a white stripe', the colour is a distinctive shade unique to Latvia. There is some evidence that, in the 13th century, Latvian clans used a flag of somewhat similar design. The modern version, based on an old written document, was developed and used in the late 19th century and also from 1918–40, when Latvia was independent. A contemporary interpretation is that red is for 'the blood shed in the past' and white for truth, right and honour. Use of the flag was banned under Soviet rule, which commenced in 1940, but resumed when Latvia gained independence in 1990.

The arms of Latvia feature a griffin, a mythical winged beast representing a combination of strength and swiftness.

LITHUANIA

Republic of Lithuania

Flag proportions: 1:2
Adopted: 20 March 1989
Capital: Vilnius
Area: 65,300km² (25,170mi²)
Population: 3,5 million
Language: Lithuanian
Religion: Roman Catholic
Currency: Litas
Exports: Meat, dairy products, spirits, electricity, wood and wooden articles, iron and steel, TV sets.

Once Lithuania was free from Russian rule after World War I, it adopted the present flag, a horizontal tricolour of yellow above green above red, the colours of traditional Lithuanian cloth. Reoccupation by Russia in 1940 resulted in the flag being suppressed until full independence was gained in 1991. Yellow represents ripening wheat with its promise of freedom from hunger, green is for the country's forests and for hope, and red symbolizes courage in the cause of patriotism.

The arms of Lithuania incorporate a symbol of courage: a knight in white armour, brandishing a sword and mounted on a white horse, all on a red shield. The knight carries a blue shield marked with a double-armed or patriarchal cross.

POLAND

Republic of Poland

Flag proportions: 5:8
Adopted: 1 August 1919
Capital: Warsaw (Warszawa)
Area: 312,685km² (120,628mi²)
Population: 38,6 million
Language: Polish
Religion: Roman Catholic
Currency: Zloty
Exports: Machinery, textiles, chemicals, coal, copper, sulphur, steel, foodstuffs, wood, leather products, paper products.

The national flag consists of equal horizontal bands of white over red, while the civil ensign and diplomatic flag has a red shield at the centre of the white band. The use of red and white dates from the 13th century, but they became the national colours only in 1831.

The national arms are said to date from 1228. They depict a white eagle, crowned, on a red field, and have remained relatively constant despite a troubled history that saw Poland partitioned among Prussia, Russia and Austria. The eagle also retained its crown long after the fall of the Polish monarchy, although the crown was removed under communist rule (1945–89) and restored only after the fall of communism.

CZECH REPUBLIC

Czech Republic

Flag proportions: 2:3
Adopted: 30 March 1920
Capital: Prague (Praha)
Area: 78,864km² (30,449mi²)
Population: 10,3 million
Language: Czech
Religion: Roman Catholic
Currency: Koruna
Exports: Manufactured goods.

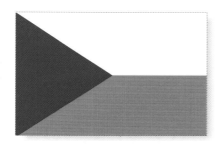

With the creation of Czechoslovakia in 1918, after the break-up of the Austro-Hungarian Empire following World War I, a blue isosceles triangle was added to the hoist to distinguish the flag from that of Poland. Czechoslovakia was composed of the crown lands of Bohemia, Moravia and part of Silesia, together with Slovakia, formerly part of Hungary. After the country was occupied by Germany in 1939, the flag was banned, and restored only in 1945 just before the communists came to power. When the Czech Republic and Slovakia separated in 1993, the Czechs retained the original flag, with its elements of the past. Red and white are derived from the heraldic emblem of Bohemia (a silver or white lion on a red field), while blue represents the state of Moravia.

GERMANY

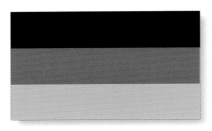

Federal Republic of Germany

Flag proportions: 3:5
Adopted: 23 May 1949
Capital: Berlin
Area: 357,028km² (137,849mi²)
Population: 82 million
Language: German
Religion: Protestant,
Roman Catholic, Muslim
Currency: Euro
Exports: Live animals, beer,
wine, foodstuffs, raw materials,
semifinished and finished goods.

The black-red-gold flag was adopted in 1848 for the anticipated union of German states. The colours reputedly appeared on the uniforms of the Prussian army that fought Napoleon at Waterloo in 1815. When the German Empire came into being in 1871, black, white and red were chosen. The black-red-gold flag was restored by the post-World War I Weimar Republic. When the National Socialist (Nazi) Party came into power in 1933, they reverted to red, white and black as the national colours, and decreed that the party flag should be the national flag. After World War II, the Weimar tricolour became the flag of the Federal Republic of Germany.

From 1949–90, West Germany was made up of 11 states (*Bundesländer*). Since reunification with East Germany this has increased to 16, each with its own state and/or civil flags.

SWITZERLAND

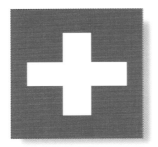

Swiss Confederation

Flag proportions: 1:1
Adopted: 12 December 1889
Capital: Bern
Area: 41,293km² (15,943mi²)
Population: 7,3 million
Languages: German, French
Religion: Roman Catholic,
Protestant
Currency: Swiss franc
Exports: Precision instruments,
pharmaceuticals, watches,
confectionery, electrical goods.

A white upright cross couped (cut short so the arms do not reach the edge of the field) on a red field is a relic of medieval times, when many European states flew a cross on a plain field. In the 13th century, the Schwyz canton (province) used a white cross on a red field, and this may have influenced the choice of flag for the confederation of Swiss cantons. The Swiss flag is square (1:1 ratio), unless used on ships, when it has 2:3 proportions. The national flag was introduced in 1848 as military colours and the proportions were regulated in 1852. The flag represents neutrality and refuge.

The flags of all 26 Swiss cantons originate from armorial banners based on the arms of the cantons, many of which date from the 14th and 15th centuries.

LIECHTENSTEIN

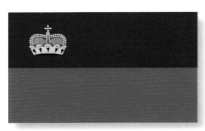

Principality of Liechtenstein

Flag proportions: 3:5
Adopted: 18 September 1982
Capital: Vaduz
Area: 160km² (62mi²)
Population: 34,000
Language: German
Religion: Roman Catholic,
Protestant
Currency: Swiss franc, Euro
Exports: Small machinery, dental
materials, stamps, ceramics,
precision instruments.

Liechtenstein was created as a Principality of the Holy Roman Empire in 1719. It has been independent since 1806. At the 1936 Berlin Olympic Games it was discovered that the flags of Haiti and Liechtenstein were identical, so in the following year a princely gold crown was placed in the chief canton of the Liechtenstein flag. There are two versions of the national flag, with the crown placed so as to be upright whether the flag is flown in the usual way or hung vertically, as is the custom in several central European countries.

The colours have been interpreted as blue for clear skies, red for embers in the hearth, and gold to signify that the people and the princely house are united in heart and soul. The Prince of Liechtenstein carries his coat of arms on the national flag, bordered with gold.

AUSTRIA

Republic of Austria

Flag proportions: 2:3
Adopted: 1 May 1945
Capital: Vienna (Wien)
Area: 83,859km² (32,377mi²)
Population: 8 million
Language: German
Religion: Roman Catholic, Protestant
Currency: Euro
Exports: Processed goods, food-stuffs, machinery and transport equipment, chemical products.

The Austro-Hungarian Empire was one of many monarchies that disappeared in the wake of World War I (1914–18) but the new republic retained a simple red-white-red tribar dating from at least 1230. According to legend, an Austrian duke was once involved in a fierce battle in which his surcoat (a tunic worn over armour) became liberally splashed with blood. When he removed his sword belt a white band was seen, and this honourable emblem became the basis of the national flag. Austria is divided into nine states or *Bundesländer*, each with its own flag.

The state flag is charged with a black heraldic eagle holding a hammer in one claw and a sickle in the other, as symbols of industry and agriculture respectively.

ITALY

Republic of Italy

Flag proportions: 2:3
Adopted: 18 June 1946
Capital: Rome (Roma)
Area: 301,302km² (116,332mi²)
Population: 56 million
Language: Italian
Religion: Roman Catholic
Currency: Euro
Exports: Wine, fruit, textiles, clothing, leather goods, wood, paper, machinery, motor vehicles, marble, chemicals.

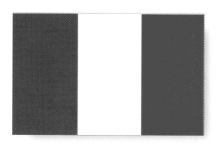

The ancient Romans were among the world's earliest flag-bearers. A collection of city-republics, kingdoms and papal states, Italy was temporarily united under French rule from 1796–1814, during which time the Italian tricolour was designed, reputedly by Napoleon. In 1861, when Victor Emmanuel II formed the Kingdom of Italy, the colours were retained, with the coat of arms of the House of Savoy added to the centre of the flag. The arms were removed in 1946 when the monarchy was abolished and Italy became a republic.

The Italian civil ensign carries a quartered shield bearing the emblems of four maritime states, Venice (the winged lion of St Mark), Genoa (St George's cross), Amalfi (Maltese cross) and Pisa (Pisan cross).

SAN MARINO

Most Serene Republic of San Marino

Flag proportions: 4:5
Adopted: 6 April 1862
Capital: San Marino
Area: 61km² (24mi²)
Population: 28,000
Language: Italian
Religion: Roman Catholic
Currency: Euro
Exports: Lime, building stone, ceramics, machinery, chemicals, wine, olive oil, textiles.

The Republic of San Marino, near the Adriatic Sea, is one of the oldest and smallest states in the world. Although the country dates from the 4th century, the flag was devised only in 1797. It comprises two equal horizontal bands (white over blue). White represents peace and the clouds surrounding Mount Titano, on which San Marino is built, while blue is for liberty and the sky. Although San Marino is a republic, the arms feature a crown, not representing a monarchy, but as a symbol of independence. They also depict three white towers on a blue field, each tower on the summit of a peak, and each with an ostrich plume rising from the top. The arms are placed at the centre of the flag for official purposes only.

MACEDONIA

Republic of Macedonia

Flag proportions: 1:2

Adopted: 6 October 1995

Capital: Skopje

Area: 25,713km² (9928mi²)

Population: 2 million

Language: Macedonian

Religion: Eastern Orthodox, Muslim

Currency: Denar

Exports: Manufactured goods, machinery, transport equipment, foodstuffs, tobacco.

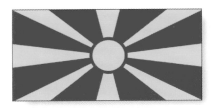

After centuries of Turkish rule, Macedonia was briefly part of Serbia (1913–19) before being incorporated into Yugoslavia. The Macedonian flag was the only Yugoslavian provincial flag under the communist regime (1945–91) that did not use Pan-Slavic colours, showing instead a gold-edged red star in the chief canton, on a red field. A controversial new flag, devised before independence in 1992, was abandoned after three years. The present flag displays a gold radiant sun on a red field, with eight rays, both diagonal and parallel to the edges of the flag, and broader at the ends than at the centre. Red and yellow come from the traditional Macedonian coat of arms, a golden lion on a red shield.

ALBANIA

Republic of Albania

Flag proportions: 5:7

Adopted: 7 April 1992

Capital: Tirana (Tiranë)

Area: 28,748km² (11,097mi²)

Population: 3 million

Language: Albanian

Religion: Muslim, Orthodox, Roman Catholic

Currency: Lek

Exports: Chrome, foodstuffs, bitumen, electricity, tobacco, crude oil, coal.

Myth says Albanians are descended from a black eagle. When Albania became an independent kingdom in 1912 after centuries of Turkish rule, the flag featured a double-headed eagle displayed in black on a red field. Albania backed Stalin after World War II, and a gold-edged star was placed above the eagle to symbolize the communist regime. The star was removed after the downfall of communism in Albania in 1992.

The Albanian arms also feature the black double-headed eagle on a red shield. An early version incorporated a gold warrior's helmet, recalling Iskander Bey, or Skanderbeg, an Albanian hero who led an uprising against the Turks in 1443.

GREECE

Hellenic Republic

Flag proportions: 2:3

Adopted: 22 December 1978

Capital: Athens (Athina)

Area: 131,957km² (50,949mi²)

Population: 11 million

Language: Greek

Religion: Greek Orthodox

Currency: Euro

Exports: Manufactured articles, clothing and accessories, olives and olive oil, vegetables, fruit, refined petroleum products.

Greece was part of the Ottoman Empire from the 14th century until 1829, and the flag recalls the struggle for independence from the Turks. The horizontal stripes (five blue, four white) echo the nine syllables of the patriots' motto, *Eleutheria i Thanatos*, 'Freedom or Death'; blue represents sea and sky, and white the justness of the Greek cause. Christianity is represented by a white cross in the chief canton. Periodic unrest after World War II saw the king ousted by an army coup in 1967, and the establishment of a democratic republic in 1973. Over the years, the shade of blue in the flag has been altered a number of times – the idea being to maintain the basic pattern while expressing change in the political regime of the country through alterations in the official colour.

CYPRUS

Republic of Cyprus

Flag proportions: 3:5
Adopted: 16 August 1960
Capital: Nicosia
Area: 5895km² (2276kmi²)
Population: 770,000
Languages: Greek, Turkish
Religion: Greek Orthodox, Muslim
Currency: Cypriot pound
Exports: Citrus fruit, potatoes, pharmaceuticals, clothing, cement, cigarettes.

Its strategic position in the Mediterranean means that Cyprus has a history of invasion and conquest. Part of the Byzantine Empire from AD395, it was taken by England during the Third Crusade (1191), annexed by the Ottoman Empire in 1571, fell under British rule in 1878, and became a crown colony in 1925. Since the 1960s, possession of Cyprus has been disputed between Greece and Turkey. In 1974 it was partitioned into the internationally recognized Greek Cypriot area and the Turkish Republic of Northern Cyprus.

Maps are rarely depicted on flags, but the island is depicted in dark yellow (for the copper first mined there in the third millennium BC). The white field symbolizes peace and hope, with crossed olive branches for conciliation. The flag is usually flown with the Greek national flag.

NORTHERN CYPRUS

Turkish Republic of Northern Cyprus

Flag proportions: 3:5
Adopted: 9 March 1984
Capital: Lefkosa (Nicosia)
Area: 3355km² (1295mi²)
Population: (see Cyprus)
Languages: Greek, Turkish
Religion: Islam (Sunni Muslim)
Currency: Turkish lira
Exports: Citrus fruit, potatoes, textiles.

Cyprus became a British crown colony in 1925. In the mid-1950s a guerrilla war, begun by Archbishop Makarios and General Grivas to seek *enosis* (union with Greece), led to both leaders being deported. Makarios returned as president of an independent Greek-Turkish Cyprus, but the Turks favoured a federal state in northern Cyprus. Grivas returned in 1971 and campaigned against Makarios' government. After Makarios was ousted in 1974, Turkish troops took control of the north, establishing a dividing line (now a UN buffer zone) and claiming about one-third of the island as a Turkish Cypriot area (recognized only by Turkey).

The flag of Northern Cyprus retains the white field of its southern counterpart, with the red crescent and star of Islam depicted between two horizontal red stripes.

TURKEY

Republic of Turkey

Flag proportions: 15:22
Adopted: 5 June 1936
Capital: Ankara
Area: 779,452km² (300,947mi²)
Population: 71 million
Language: Turkish
Religion: Muslim
Currency: Turkish lira
Exports: Clothing and textiles, foodstuffs, tobacco, leather, glass, refined oil, petroleum products.

Red has been the dominant colour in Turkish flags since the founding of the Ottoman Empire which, at its height in the 16th century, stretched from North Africa through the Levant to Hungary and the southern borders of Russia.

When the white star and crescent appeared on the red flag of the Ottoman Empire in 1793, it was already an established symbol of Islam. The star initially had eight points but a five-pointed version was used from the mid-19th century. The star is tilted so that one point touches an imaginary line joining the horns of the crescent. Full specifications for this, and all other flags used in Turkey, were drawn up in 1936.

BULGARIA

Republic of Bulgaria

Flag proportions: 3:5
Adopted: 27 November 1990
Capital: Sofia (Sofiya)
Area: 110,994km² (42,855mi²)
Population: 7,9 million
Language: Bulgarian
Religion: Eastern Orthodox, Sunni Muslim
Currency: Lev
Exports: Pork, poultry, tomatoes, cheese, wine, soda ash, poly-ethylene, ammonium nitrate.

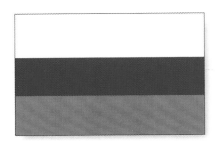

As part of the Ottoman Empire for almost 500 years, Bulgaria had no national flag. On becoming a principality in 1878, it adopted a horizontal tricolour of white over green over red, retaining this when Bulgaria became an independent kingdom in 1908. After the monarchy was abolished in 1946 and a people's republic proclaimed, a coat of arms was added to the white band. The arms (a lion rampant, the red star of communism and a cog wheel), were removed in 1990, after the fall of communism, and the flag reverted to the original tricolour. White represents peace, green stands for freedom and the emerging nation, and red the bravery of the people.

ROMANIA

Republic of Romania

Flag proportions: 2:3
Adopted: 27 December 1989
Capital: Bucharest (Bucuresti)
Area: 237,500km² (91,699mi²)
Population: 22,2 million
Language: Romanian
Religion: Romanian Orthodox, Greek Orthodox
Currency: Leu
Exports: Metals, textiles and clothing, minerals, machinery and equipment, foodstuffs.

The principalities of Wallachia and Moldavia broke from the Ottoman Empire in 1859, uniting as an independent kingdom under a blue-yellow-red vertical tricolour, still the national flag of Romania. Blue came from the Moldavian flag, yellow from Wallachia. Red, common to both, symbolizes Romanian unity. In 1867, the Royal Arms was added to the yellow band, where it remained (with several modifications) until it was replaced with a communist emblem in 1948. After the fall of the Caeusescu regime in 1989, the former coat of arms was restored, with amendments, but no longer appears on the flag. Romanian law provides for the punishment of any person found guilty of expressing contempt for the state insignia.

HUNGARY

Republic of Hungary

Flag proportions: 2:3
Adopted: 1 October 1957
Capital: Budapest
Area: 93,032km² (35,911mi²)
Population: 10 million
Language: Hungarian
Religion: Roman Catholic, Protestant
Currency: Forint
Exports: Raw materials, food-stuffs, semi-finished products, agricultural equipment.

The kingdom of Hungary was under Austrian control until 1848. When revolution broke out, Hungarian patriots hoisted a red-white-green tricolour, often with a central coat of arms. The colours were probably derived from the historical arms of Hungary, and the stripes inspired by the flag of revolutionary France. Red symbolizes strength, white stands for faithfulness, and green, hope. When Hungary became independent in 1918, the Hungarian arms were added, only to be replaced with appropriate Soviet emblems during the communist era (1949–90). Although restored with democracy in 1990, they no longer appear on the flag.

SLOVAKIA

Slovak Republic

Flag proportions: 2:3
Adopted: 1 September 1993
Capital: Bratislava
Area: 49,035km² (18,933mi²)
Population: 5,3 million
Language: Slovak
Religion: Roman Catholic, Protestant
Currency: Koruna
Exports: Manufactured goods, machinery, transport equipment.

Slovakia was under the dual monarchy of Austria-Hungary until 1918, when it became part of Czechoslovakia under the flag now used by the Czech Republic. When Slovakia was an Axis country (1939–45), the horizontal tricolour of white over blue over red was adopted. With the dissolution of Czechoslovakia in 1993, the Slovak arms were added off-centre on the flag to distinguish it from that of Russia.

The arms consist of a stylized blue image of mountains from which a white patriarchal cross (a cross with two high horizontal bars, the upper one shorter than the lower) rises against a red field.

MOLDOVA

Republic of Moldova

Flag proportions: 1:2
Adopted: 3 November 1990
Capital: Chisinau
Area: 33,700km² (13,000mi²)
Population: 4,2 million
Language: Moldovan
Religion: Romanian Orthodox, Moldovan Orthodox
Currency: Leu
Exports: Foodstuffs, machinery and equipment, textiles, clothing.

In 1940, parts of the historic principality of Moldavia were partitioned from Romania; the eastern portion becoming the Soviet republic of Moldova and the western part remaining with Romania. It has been independent since 1991.

The flag's colours are similar to those of Romania, but it is distinguished by the Moldovan arms in the central panel. The arms, based on those of the former principality of Moldavia, comprise a red and blue shield and an eagle displayed. The most prominent feature is the head of a wisent (aurochs or bison), an old Moldavian symbol of power and independence. The eagle clasps an olive branch, representing peace, and a mace, representing willingness to defend.

UKRAINE

Republic of Ukraine

Flag proportions: 2:3
Adopted: 28 January 1992
Capital: Kiev (Kyiv)
Area: 603,700km² (231,990mi²)
Population: 48 million
Language: Ukrainian
Religion: Ukrainian Orthodox
Currency: Hryvna
Exports: Grain, coal, oil, minerals.

Formerly part of Imperial Russia, Ukraine became an independent state in 1918 after the fall of the monarchy and the collapse of a short-lived Russian treaty with Germany. However, within a year, the country was under Soviet control, which lasted until 1991. The flag was banned during the Soviet era but permitted by the Nazis when they occupied Ukraine during World War II. After the war, it was banned again, to reappear as the national flag in 1991, when full independence was gained. The flag is said to resemble the Ukrainian landscape of golden wheat fields stretching to the horizon to meet the blue sky.

BELARUS

Republic of Belarus

Flag proportions: 1:2

Adopted: 7 June 1995

Capital: Minsk

Area: 207,600km² (80,134mi²)

Population: 10 million

Language: Belarussian

Religion: Belarussian Orthodox, Roman Catholic

Currency: Rouble

Exports: Machinery, chemicals, petrochemicals, iron and steel.

The patterned red-and-white vertical stripe along the hoist is derived from a woven pattern that appears on Belarussian national costume. The flag is horizontally divided into thirds, with two thirds red above one third green. Red recalls both sacrifice and victory under a red banner; first in medieval times at Grunwald and then against Fascist invaders in the 1940s. Green signifies spring and revival, and so is the colour of hope. When Belarus gained independence in 1991 the flag chosen was a red-white-red tribar which was first used in 1918. The present flag, which is similar to that of the former Soviet Byelorussia, was adopted in 1995. The national flag is usually flown from a staff painted in golden ochre.

RUSSIA

Russian Federation

Flag proportions: 2:3

Adopted: 11 December 1993

Capital: Moscow (Moskva)

Area:17,075,400km² (6,592,849mi²)

Population: 143 million

Language: Russian

Religion: Russian Orthodox, Christian, Muslim

Currency: Rouble

Exports: Minerals, metals, paper, gemstones, chemicals, timber, machinery, transport equipment.

Tsar Peter the Great visited the Netherlands in 1697 and, impressed by the Dutch tricolour, adopted it for the Russian merchant fleet, altering the order of the stripes to white, blue and red. This became the national flag in the 19th century but, after the Bolshevik revolution of 1917, the Red Flag with its communist emblems (hammer, sickle and star) was adopted. The tricolour reappeared in 1990 as communism faltered. Following the collapse of the Soviet Union in 1991, it emerged as the flag of the new state.

The Russian Federation comprises 21 republics, 49 provinces, six territories, ten administrative areas, two cities with federal status and one autonomous region.

The Commonwealth of Independent States

The Soviet Union was founded in 1922, shortly after the overthrow of the Russian monarchy. Almost 70 years later, in 1991, the leaders of Russia, Belarus and the Ukraine met in the Belovezhskaya Pushcha Nature Reserve (a UNESCO World Heritage Site) in Belarus to sign an agreement that established the Commonwealth of Independent States (CIS). A few weeks later, 11 of the 15 former Soviet Socialist Republics met in Alma-Ata, Kazakhstan, and signed the charter. The three Baltic republics (Latvia, Lithuania, Estonia) declined to join, opting for their separate independence. Georgia joined the commonwealth in December 1993.

The CIS charter stated that all members were independent states, thereby effectively declaring that the Soviet Union no longer existed. The headquarters of the CIS are in Minsk, the capital of Belarus (the former Soviet Republic of Byelorussia). The 11 original member states were Azerbaijan, Armenia, Belarus, Kazakhstan, Kyrgyzstan, Moldova, Russia, Tajikistan, Turkmenistan, Uzbekistan and Ukraine.

The CIS has been described as having few supranational powers, yet being more than a purely symbolic organization. It has co-ordinating powers in the spheres of trade, finance, legislation and security. The most significant issue for the CIS, due to occur in 2005, is the incorporation of member states into an economic union with a free trade zone.

GEORGIA

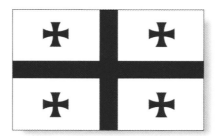

Republic of Georgia
Flag proportions: 2:3
Adopted: 14 January 2004
Capital: T'bilisi
Area: 69,700km² (26,900mi²)
Population: 5,3 million
Language: Georgian
Religion: Orthodox, Muslim
Currency: Lari
Exports: Iron and steel products, food, drink, machinery, textiles, chemicals.

The kingdoms composing Georgia were part of the Russian empire throughout the 19th century. However, Georgia enjoyed a brief period of independence from 1918–21, during which its national flag was dark red with a canton of black over white horizontal stripes. That flag was revived in 1991 after the collapse of the USSR when Georgia again became independent. In 2003, a popular revolution led by the National Movement against the government resulted in the adoption of its banner as the new national flag. This 'flag of five crosses', supposedly used by Georgians in the 12th century, emphasizes the Orthodox Christian faith of the majority of the population.

ARMENIA

Republic of Armenia
Flag proportions: 1:2
Adopted: 24 August 1990
Capital: Yerevan
Area: 29,800km² (11,490mi²)
Population: 3,8 million
Language: Armenian
Religion: Armenian Orthodox
Currency: Dram
Exports: Machinery, metal-working products, chemicals, petroleum products.

For several centuries Armenia was part of the Ottoman Empire. Following World War I it was briefly independent before becoming a Soviet republic in 1922. During the Soviet era, the horizontal tricolour of red above blue above orange was banned, but was raised again as the national flag of the republic of Armenia in 1991. Red represents the sun's energy and blood spilt during the struggle for independence, blue is for hope and the clear skies, and orange is for the blessing of crops at harvest.

AZERBAIJAN

Republic of Azerbaijan
Flag proportions: 1:2
Adopted: 5 February 1991
Capital: Baku (Bakí)
Area: 86,600km² (33,430mi²)
Population: 8 million
Language: Azeri
Religion: Muslim, Christian
Currency: Manat
Exports: Petroleum products, machinery, foodstuffs, textiles.

Azerbaijan's brief spell of independence, following the 1918 collapse of the Ottoman Empire, ended with annexation by Soviet Russia in 1920. The flag created to celebrate independence was prohibited by the new rulers, and only raised again as the national flag in 1991. It is a horizontal tricolour of blue above red above green. At the centre, entirely within the red band, are a white crescent and eight-pointed star, the emblems of Islam. Each point of the star represents one group of the Turkic peoples. Blue is their representative colour, green is for Islam and red for energy and progress.

Western and Southern Asia

Asia is the largest continent, with an area of 44 million sq km (17 million sq mi.), and any attempt to divide it must to some extent be arbitrary. Asia is also the highest continent, with many massive mountain ranges, including the Himalaya and Karakoram. Mount Everest, at 8850m (29,035ft) above sea level, is the highest mountain in the world.

At the western end of Asia, abutting Europe, is the Middle East, a region seldom far removed from the world's news. Here is land held sacred by many faiths, where areas of rich heritage are juxtaposed with modern settlements that are bitterly and bloodily contested. Here, too, ancient civilizations have left abundant evidence in the 'fertile crescent' along the rivers Tigris and Euphrates, extending from Syria to the Gulf.

Pan-Arab colours and Islamic emblems are prominent on the flags of most Middle East and Gulf states, where wealth is measured in the colossal oil reserves lying beneath the arid and sometimes frankly barren land. As in Europe, shared religions, history and ethnicity have not been proof against war, as the long struggle between Iraq and Iran, Iraq's invasion of Kuwait, and the resultant involvement of western powers in military conflict in the region so ably demonstrate.

Further afield, the partition of India that followed the withdrawal of British imperial power in 1947 was based on religion and resulted in the creation of Pakistan. This new, primarily Muslim country (India is 80 per cent Hindu) consisted of two separate territories, which led to the 1971 political separation of East Pakistan (now Bangladesh), situated around the Ganges delta.

Afghanistan once shared a legendary frontier with British India, but the Khyber Pass now crosses into Pakistan. The northern Afghan border was a source of tension for more than a century, ending with Russian invasion and, subsequently, an armed American presence. After the collapse of the Soviet Union in 1991, five of its former Asian states accepted membership of a new Commonwealth of Independent States (see p66).

The southern portion of the area being covered extends from Pakistan in the west, through India and the mountain states of Nepal and Bhutan, to Bangladesh, and protrudes some 3000km into the Indian Ocean as far as the island state of Sri Lanka.

Here are some of the most densely populated places in the world: Bangladesh has 849 people per sq km to India's 273, while the United States, by comparison, has 27. Some 18 principal languages are heard, in addition to many dialects.

Western and Southern Asia

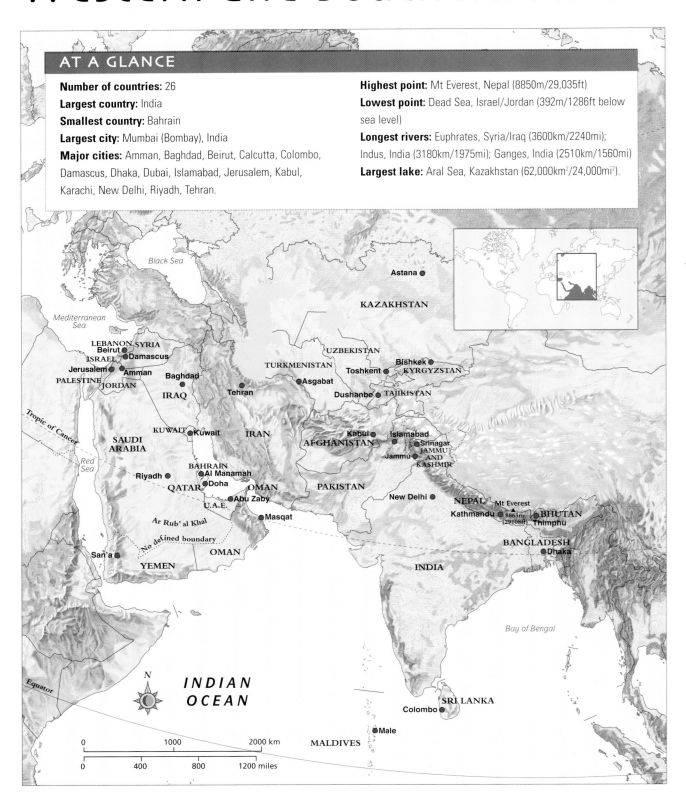

AT A GLANCE

Number of countries: 26
Largest country: India
Smallest country: Bahrain
Largest city: Mumbai (Bombay), India
Major cities: Amman, Baghdad, Beirut, Calcutta, Colombo, Damascus, Dhaka, Dubai, Islamabad, Jerusalem, Kabul, Karachi, New Delhi, Riyadh, Tehran.

Highest point: Mt Everest, Nepal (8850m/29,035ft)
Lowest point: Dead Sea, Israel/Jordan (392m/1286ft below sea level)
Longest rivers: Euphrates, Syria/Iraq (3600km/2240mi); Indus, India (3180km/1975mi); Ganges, India (2510km/1560mi)
Largest lake: Aral Sea, Kazakhstan (62,000km²/24,000mi²).

Black Sea

Mediterranean
Sea

Astana

KAZAKHSTAN

LEBANON SYRIA
Beirut
ISRAEL Damascus
Jerusalem
Amman
PALESTINE
JORDAN
Baghdad
IRAQ
Tehran

UZBEKISTAN

TURKMENISTAN
Asgabat

Bishkek
Toshkent KYRGYZSTAN

Dushanbe TAJIKISTAN

Tropic of Cancer

KUWAIT
Kuwait
IRAN

Kabul Islamabad
AFGHANISTAN Srinagar
Jammu JAMMU
AND
KASHMIR

SAUDI
ARABIA

Red
Sea

BAHRAIN
Riyadh Al Manamah
QATAR Doha
OMAN
Abu Zaby
U.A.E.
Masqat

PAKISTAN

New Delhi

NEPAL
Kathmandu Mt Everest
8863m BHUTAN
(29108ft) Thimphu

Ar Rub' al Khal

No defined boundary

San'a
OMAN
YEMEN

INDIA

BANGLADESH
Dhaka

Bay of Bengal

Equator

N

INDIAN
OCEAN

SRI LANKA
Colombo

Male

0   1000   2000 km

0   400   800   1200 miles

MALDIVES

SYRIA

Republic of Syria

Flag proportions: 2:3
Adopted: 3 April 1980
Capital: Damascus (Dimashq)
Area: 185,180km² (71,498mi²)
Population: 17,8 million
Language: Arabic
Religion: Muslim
Currency: Syrian pound
Exports: Crude oil, textiles, fruit and vegetables, cotton, phosphates.

Four hundred years of Turkish domination ended in 1920 when Syria became a French mandate. The French created two flags for Syria which were eventually replaced by a tricolour of green above white above black with three red stars in the centre, under which the country achieved independence in 1946. Each star represented a Syrian province. When Syria and Egypt formed the United Arab Republic (UAR) in 1958 the colours were changed to red, white and black, and only two stars were depicted. After briefly reverting to the earlier flag, Syria adopted the UAR flag with three stars instead of two, replacing it by a red-white-black flag bearing a gold central coat of arms which, in turn, was abandoned when the current flag was adopted.

LEBANON

Republic of Lebanon

Flag proportions: 2:3
Adopted: 7 December 1943
Capital: Beirut (Bayr't)
Area: 10,452km² (4036mi²)
Population: 4,3 million
Language: Arabic
Religion: Muslim, Christian
Currency: Lebanese pound
Exports: Paper, textiles, fruit, vegetables, jewellery.

The red bands in the Lebanese tricolour are each half the depth of the white band on which a cedar tree is represented in green. When Lebanon was mandated to France after World War I, the *Tricolore* was flown with a depiction of the cedar at the centre. Officially, the colours of the current flag are red, white and green and the cedar is not intended to be depicted 'proper' (lifelike, with brownish trunk and branches).

Cedars and Lebanon have been linked since the time of King Solomon, in the 10th century BC. The cedar is the symbol of the country's Maronite Christian community, supported by Biblical references such as Psalm 92:12: 'the righteous … shall grow like a cedar in Lebanon'. The cedar has come to symbolize immortality.

JORDAN

Hashemite Kingdom of Jordan

Flag proportions: 1:2
Adopted: 16 April 1928
Capital: Amman
Area: 89,206km² (34,443mi²)
Population: 5,4 million
Language: Arabic
Religion: Muslim, Christian
Currency: Jordan dinar
Exports: Phosphate, potash, fertilizers, fruit and vegetables, pharmaceuticals, textiles, soaps, plastics.

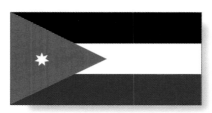

The Pan-Arab colours first flew in 1917 to rally forces to the Arab Revolt against Turkish rule. Jordan was mandated to Britain, but achieved a measure of independence in 1928 when the present flag was raised. The black, white and green bands represent the Arab Abbasid, Umayyad and Fatimid dynasties respectively. The red isosceles triangle at the hoist represents the Hashemite dynasty, whose descendants are the rulers of Jordan. The seven-pointed star at the centre of the triangle represents the unity of the Arab peoples in Jordan, as well as the seven verses that open the Koran and provide the basis for Islamic belief.

ISRAEL

State of Israel

Flag proportions: 8:11
Adopted: 12 November 1948
Capital: Jerusalem
Area: 21,946km² (8473mi²)
Population: 6,4 million
Languages: Hebrew, Arabic
Religion: Jewish, Muslim
Currency: Shekel
Exports: Citrus fruit, foodstuffs, machinery, chemicals, clothing.

The design of the flag predates the State of Israel by more than 50 years, although the *Magen David* (Star or Shield of David), was used for centuries as a symbol of Judaism. The outline of the six-pointed star is also known as the Seal of Solomon. Blue and white represent the *tallith* (Hebrew prayer shawl). The star, an ancient symbol associated with magical powers and defence against evil, has been used in countries as distant as Ethiopia, India and Nigeria. As a Jewish symbol, the star was first used on a flag in the 14th century, by the Jewish community of Prague. Flagpoles from which the Israeli flag is flown are sometimes painted blue for their lower third, and white for the remainder.

PALESTINE

Palestine Authority

Flag proportions: 1:2
Adopted: 1 December 1964
Capital: Jerusalem (disputed)
Area: 5860km² (2262mi²)
Population: 2,2 million
Languages: Arabic, English
Religion: Muslim
Currency: Jordanian dinar
Exports: Olives, fruit, vegetables, limestone.

Since Biblical times, occupation and imposed rule have been part of Palestine's legacy. After the Ottoman Empire collapsed in 1918, the Holy Land was mandated to Britain, beginning a conflict that, decades later, is still not resolved.

The present Palestinian flag was first used by the Arab National Movement in 1917, during a revolt against the Turks. It was readopted at the 1948 Palestinian conference in Gaza, and endorsed by the PLO in 1964. Green, the colour of Islam and fertile fields, is for the Fatimid dynasty of North Africa. Red, for sacrifice, represents the Hashemites, descendants of Mohammed, whose traditional black and white colours are also the symbols of mourning and remembrance. Black was used in battle and for revenge.

Israel and the Palestine Authority

When the Ottoman Empire collapsed after World War I, Palestine and Jordan were mandated to Britain in 1922 by the League of Nations. In 1947, a United Nations Special Committee on Palestine partitioned the land between Jordan and Israel.

The 1948 creation of Israel was bitterly opposed by Palestinian Arabs who had been calling for an independent homeland since the turn of the century. Several wars followed, including the Six-Day War of 1967, during which Israel occupied the West Bank of the Jordan River (Jordanian territory) and the Gaza Strip (Egyptian). These areas, considered as part of Palestine, are regarded by Israel as being of strategic importance

and Israeli settlements have been established in both, leading to the Palestinian description of them as 'occupied territories'.

The Palestine Liberation Organization (PLO) came into being in 1964 to bring about an independent state of Palestine. In 1993, the PLO and Israel signed a Declaration of Principles on self-rule for the West Bank and Gaza. After a five-year transition, Israel was to transfer powers to the Palestinian Authority (PA), established in 1994 and headed by former PLO leader Yasser Arafat.

Despite acts of terror on both sides, negotiations continued until the outbreak in 2000 of a second *intifadah* (holy war). Attacks and reprisals led to a hardening of attitudes, ending hopes of an early peaceful settlement.

SAUDI ARABIA

Kingdom of Saudi Arabia
Flag proportions: 2:3
Adopted: 15 March 1973
Capital: Riyadh (Al Riyad)
Area: 2,200,518km² (849,400mi²)
Population: 22 million
Language: Arabic
Religion: Muslim
Currency: Rial
Exports: Crude and refined oil, petrochemicals, wheat.

Green, the colour of Islam, is believed to have been the favourite colour of the Prophet Mohammed. On the Saudi flag, the Muslim statement of faith, or *shahada* ('There is no God but Allah, Mohammed is the Prophet of Allah'), appears in white Arabic letters, from the viewer's right to left, on both sides of the flag. Below the inscription, a straight-bladed, single-edged sword of typically Middle Eastern pattern represents justice. It depicts the sword of King Ibn Saud, who founded the kingdom in 1932 by uniting the kingdoms of Hejaz and Nejd. An absolute monarchy with no written constitution, Saudi Arabia is ruled in accordance with Islamic (*sharia*) law. Like many Gulf states, the country derives immense wealth from its oil reserves.

YEMEN

Republic of Yemen
Flag proportions: 2:3
Adopted: 22 May 1990
Capital: San'a
Area: 531,000km² (205,035mi²)
Population: 16,6 million
Language: Arabic
Religion: Muslim
Currency: Riyal
Exports: Petroleum products, cotton, manufactured goods, clothing, live animals, hides and skins, fish, rice, coffee.

North Yemen was originally part of the Ottoman Empire, while South Yemen was under British colonial domination until 1967. Although both countries expressed a desire to unite, the radical politics of the south and conservative politics of the north prevented unification. Even after a revolution in North Yemen, each republic maintained its own statehood and flag. South Yemen flew a red-white-black tricolour, with a blue triangle at the hoist and a red star for socialism. North Yemen also flew a red-white-black tricolour, but with a green five-pointed star at the centre. The unified flag, with the Pan-Arab red-white-black colours, represents the tricolour that had been basic to both territories.

OMAN

Sultanate of Oman
Flag proportions: 1:2
Adopted: 18 November 1995
Capital: Muscat (Masqat)
Area: 309,500km² (119,499mi²)
Population: 3 million
Language: Arabic
Religion: Muslim
Currency: Omani rial
Exports: Petroleum, metals and metal goods, textiles, animals.

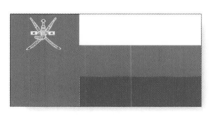

Oman's capital, Muscat, has been a trading post for centuries. Given its strategic location, it is not suprising that the country changed rulers many times in its history. Red has long been the dominant colour in the Gulf region. The Omani flag may be seen either as bands of white and green on a red field, or as a horizontal tricolour with a broad red band at the hoist. White is associated with a former imam (religious leader) of Oman, and represents peace. Green relates to the Jebel Akhdar highlands, or 'Green Mountains', in the north of the Sultanate. It is also the colour of Islam and of fertility. At the hoist is the emblem of the ruling dynasty: crossed swords and a gold *jambiyah* (traditional dagger with a curved blade).

UNITED ARAB EMIRATES

United Arab Emirates

Flag proportions: 1:2
Adopted: 2 December 1971
Capital: Abu Dhabi (Abu Zaby)
Area: 83,657km² (32,300mi²)
Population: 3,1 million
Language: Arabic
Religion: Muslim
Currency: Dirham
Exports: Crude oil, natural gas.

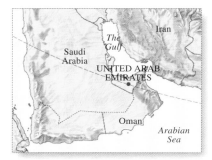

The United Arab Emirates (UAE), a federation of the emirates of Abu Dhabi, Ajman, Dubai, Fujairah, Sharjah, Umm al Qaiwain and Ras al Khaimah, was formed in 1971 from the Trucial States (a name given by the British for administrative purposes when the area came under a treaty in 1853). The seven hereditary emirs (sheiks) serve on the federal Supreme Council of Rulers of the UAE. Abu Dhabi is the capital and Dubai the chief port.

Although the traditional emirates' colours were red and white, Pan-Arab colours were adopted for the united flag (green for fertility, white for neutrality, black for the reserves of oil, and red for the original emirates' flags).

United Arab Emirates

Seven emirates (territories ruled by an emir or independent chieftain) known as the Trucial States, united in 1971 to form the independent United Arab Emirates under a flag of the Pan-Arab colours. The colours also have individual significance: green is for fertility, white for neutrality, black for the great reserves of oil, and red is the traditional colour of the emirates' flags. Some emirates still fly their original white and red flags together with the flag of the United Arab Emirates.

Abu Dhabi is the largest (67,350km²/26,000mi²) and richest of the emirates, with huge reserves of gas as well as oil. Some 80 per cent of oil exported from the UAE is from Abu Dhabi. Next in size, at some 3900km² (1500mi²), is Dubai, a prosperous trading centre for 160 years before the discovery of its oil. The other emirates are Sharjah, Ajman, Umm al Qaiwan, Ras al Khaimah and Fujairah.

Clustered on the Straits of Hormuz, an area once known as the Pirate Coast, the present emirates were a British protectorate until becoming independent in 1971. Today they are governed by a Supreme Council of Rulers, which includes all seven sheiks, who are heriditary emirs and absolute monarchs in their own emirates. Top positions are rotated and there are no political parties. Wealth is mainly in the form of oil revenues.

Abu Dhabi

Ajman

Dubai

Fujairah

Ras al Khaimah

Sharjah

Umm al-Qaiwain

BAHRAIN

Kingdom of Bahrain

Flag proportions: 3:5
Adopted: 16 February 2002
Capital: Manama (Al Manmah)
Area: 688km² (265mi²)
Population: 703,500
Language: Arabic
Religion: Muslim, Christian
Currency: Bahraini dinar
Exports: Oil and petroleum products.

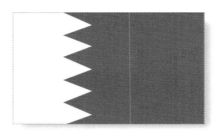

Bahrain comprises a group of islands in the Gulf, linked by a causeway to Saudi Arabia (at 25km/15,5 miles, the longest in the world). The unusual junction of colours in the flag, described heraldically as indented, has its origins in a treaty of 1820, whereby friendly states in the Persian Gulf undertook to border their flags with white, so that they could not be mistaken for pirate flags. Originally the line was straight but it was indented (serrated) in 1932 to distinguish the flag of Bahrain from those of its neighbouring territories. The five indentations of the flag stand for the five basic requirements of Islam. No fewer than nine legal articles describe and govern the use of the Bahraini flag.

QATAR

State of Qatar

Flag proportions: 11:28
Adopted: 1949
Capital: Doha
Area: 11,437km² (4416mi²)
Population: 610,500
Language: Arabic
Religion: Muslim
Currency: Qatari riyal
Exports: Petroleum.

The Al-Khalifa clan ruled both Qatar and Bahrain in the 18th and early 19th centuries under a plain red flag. A revolt in 1868 led to the independence of Qatar but, four years later, the Ottoman Turks established a protectorate in the area. After World War I, the British replaced the Ottomans and it is probably at that time that the national flag was established. However, there were many variations in the exact design and a standard pattern was not finalized until 1949. When Qatar became independent on 3 September 1971 no change was made in the national flag design, which recalls the flag of Bahrain, with which Qatar was long associated.

KUWAIT

State of Kuwait

Flag proportions: 1:2
Adopted: 24 November 1961
Capital: Kuwait (Al Kuwayt)
Area: 17,818km² (6880mi²)
Population: 1,9 million
Language: Arabic
Religion: Muslim, Christian
Currency: Kuwaiti dinar
Exports: Crude and refined oil, chemicals, fertilizer.

When Kuwait gained independence in 1961, after being under British rule since 1899, a flag in the Pan-Arab colours was adopted. The tricolour of green above white above red has a black trapezium at the hoist. An official explanation of the Pan-Arab colours stated that black symbolized the defeat of enemies, white was for purity, green for the fertile land and red for enemies' blood on Kuwaiti swords. An alternative explanation is that white is for honour, black is the sand raised by Kuwaiti horsemen in their battle for freedom, green is for the fields and red for gallantry.

IRAQ

Republic of Iraq
Flag proportions: 2:3
Adopted: 14 January 1991
Capital: Baghdad
Area: 438,317km² (169,247mi²)
Population: 25,5 million
Language: Arabic
Religion: Muslim
Currency: Iraqi dinar
Exports: Crude oil.

Iraqi flags have featured the Pan-Arab colours ever since the Arab Revolt of 1917. The basic pattern that is currently in use was devised in anticipation of a closer union with Egypt and Syria. Three five-pointed green stars were placed in a row in the central band of the horizontal tricolour of red above white above black. The union did not take place, but the design remained. The Islamic phrase, *Allahu Akbar* ('God is Great'), in green Arabic script, was added to the central band during the 1991 Gulf War.

IRAN

Islamic Republic of Iran
Flag proportions: 4:7
Adopted: 29 July 1980
Capital: Tehran
Area: 1,629,918km² (634,293mi²)
Population: 65,5 million
Language: Farsi
Religion: Muslim
Currency: Rial
Exports: Petroleum, crude oil, natural gas.

After the overthrow of the monarchy in 1979, the new Islamic Republic introduced a tricolour of green above white above red, with a red central device. The colours have been the national colours of Iran since the late 19th century. At the junction of the white band with the green and red are stylized Kufic inscriptions of the phrase *Allahu Akbar* ('God is Great'), repeated 22 times, because victory in the revolution occurred on the 22nd day of the 11th month of the Iranian calendar. The central device is composed of highly stylized emblems, including crescents and a sword, which together symbolize the five principles of Islam.

AFGHANISTAN

Islamic State of Afghanistan
Flag proportions: 1:2
Adopted: June 2002
Capital: Kabul
Area: 652,090km² (251,773mi²)
Population: 24,4 million
Language: Pashto, Dari
Religion: Muslim
Currency: Afghani
Exports: Fruit, nuts, carpets, wool, cotton, natural gas.

Afghanistan's frequent political changes have resulted in almost 20 flags since 1900. Following the ousting of the Taliban in 2001, the transitional government adopted a flag comprising a vertical tricolour of black (at the hoist), red and green. Black recalls flags previously flown in Afghanistan, while green is the colour of Islam. At the centre is the national arms. Enclosed within a wreath of grain are a mosque, showing the *mihrab* (recess in the wall that indicates the direction of Mecca), and a *minabar* (pulpit). Above the mosque is written the *Shahada*, or Muslim statement of faith ('there is no God but Allah, and Mohammed is the Prophet of Allah'). The inscription *Allahu Akbar* also appears.
(The flag depicted was correct at the time of going to print.)

TURKMENISTAN

Republic of Turkmenistan

Flag proportions: 2:3
Adopted: 3 March 2000
Capital: Ashkhabad (Asgabat)
Area: 448,100km² (186,400mi²)
Population: 5,6 million
Language: Turkmen
Religion: Muslim
Currency: Manat
Exports: Natural gas, cotton, electricity, petroleum and petroleum products.

Turkmenistan's unusual flag celebrates its culture. On a green field a white Islamic crescent is placed in the chief canton with the horns pointing to the hoist. Five five-pointed white stars represent new regions defined in the 1992 constitution. At the hoist, a multi-coloured vertical band depicts the hand-knotted carpets for which Turkmenistan is renowned. The five main *guls* (medallions) on the carpet represent traditional patterns, with the border *guls* depicting minor patterns. Turkmenistan gained independence in 1991 and declared a policy of neutrality in 1995, which was accepted by the United Nations. To symbolize this, in 1997, two olive branches, similar to those on the UN flag, were placed below the *guls*.

UZBEKISTAN

Republic of Uzbekistan

Flag proportions: 1:2
Adopted: 18 November 1991
Capital: Toshkent
Area: 447,400km² (172,741mi²)
Population: 26 million
Language: Uzbek
Religion: Muslim
Currency: Soum
Exports: Cotton, textiles, gold, machinery, foodstuffs.

The post-communist flag of Uzbekistan is a tricolour of blue above white above green, with a narrow red stripe at the junction of the colours. In the chief canton, all in the blue band, a white crescent and 12 five-pointed white stars are arranged in rows: three above four above five. The crescent, as a waxing moon, represents the new republic, with a star for each month of the year. Blue is for sky and water, white for peace, and green for fertility. The red stripes signify the life force of all people. Despite being a predominantly Muslim country, Uzbekistan's crescent is described in terms of growth rather than religion.

KAZAKHSTAN

Republic of Kazakhstan

Flag proportions: 1:2
Adopted: 4 June 1992
Capital: Astana
Area: 2,717,300km² (1,049,155mi²)
Population: 14,4 million
Language: Kazakh, Russian
Religion: Muslim, Christian
Currency: Tenge
Exports: Metals, mineral products, chemicals.

'National ornamentation' is the term used to describe the gold embroidery-like pattern at the hoist of Kazakhstan's flag that is reminiscent of features on the flags of Belarus and Turkmenistan. The field is light blue, for the vast skies of the Kazakhstan plains. On the field a steppe eagle, known locally as the *berkut*, flies horizontally with outstretched wings, a position referred to in heraldry as *volant*. Above the eagle, half framed by its wings, is a sun with short rays. Together they depict freedom and symbolize the aspirations of the Kazakh people.

TAJIKISTAN

Republic of Tajikistan
Flag proportions: 1:2
Adopted: 24 November 1992
Capital: Dushanbe
Area: 143,100km² (55,240mi²)
Population: 6,3 million
Language: Tajik
Religion: Muslim
Currency: Tajik rouble
Exports: Aluminium, cotton.

Red, white and green are the same colours as the flag of the former Tadzhik Soviet Socialist Republic. Red is a symbol of the sun and victory, green represents the fruits of the land, while white is the colour of cotton, the country's principal crop. Within the central white band is a gold crown below an arc of seven five-pointed stars. The crown denotes the country's sovereign independence. In Tajik culture, the number seven embodies all the human virtues. According to legend, heaven has seven orchards separated by seven mountains, each with a star at its summit. Together the symbols represent friendship between nations and unity of all classes.

KYRGYZSTAN

Republic of Kyrgyzstan
Flag proportions: 3:5
Adopted: 3 March 1992
Capital: Bishkek
Area: 199,900km² (77,180mi²)
Population: 5,1 million
Language: Kirghiz
Religion: Muslim
Currency: Som
Exports: Food, beverages, light industrial goods, nonferrous metals.

Although it declared independence in 1991, Kyrgyzstan only adopted its flag the following year. 'Kyrgyz' means red, and red is the colour associated with a traditional hero, Manas the Noble, who united the 40 tribes of Kyrgyzstan.

In the centre of the red field is a gold sun, a symbol of light and purity. The individual rays represent the tribes, while the lines across the sun represent the framework of a traditional Kyrgyz yurt, the tent in which nomadic peoples celebrate the virtues of home and family, the unity of space and time, and the very beginning of life itself.

PAKISTAN

Islamic Republic of Pakistan
Flag proportions: 2:3
Adopted: 14 August 1947
Capital: Islamabad
Area: 796,095km² (307,293mi²)
Population: 149 million
Language: Urdu
Religion: Muslim
Currency: Pakistan rupee
Exports: Cotton, textiles, clothing, leather, petroleum and petroleum products, rice, foodstuffs, live animals.

Pakistan became an independent Muslim state following the partition of British India in 1947. The green flag with a white star and crescent was designed by Mohammed Ali Jinnah who, as leader of the Muslim League, campaigned for Pakistan's independence and became its first governor general. Green is the colour of Islam, the white crescent signifies progress, and the five-pointed star symbolizes light and knowledge. The white vertical stripe at the hoist was originally said to stand for peace and prosperity.

INDIA

Republic of India

Flag proportions: 2:3
Adopted: 15 August 1947
Capital: New Delhi
Area: 3,165,596km² (1,222,332mi²)
Population: 1,050 billion
Languages: Hindi, English plus 14 other official languages.
Religion: Hindu, Muslim, Sikh, Christian
Currency: Indian rupee
Exports: Tea, textiles, clothing, chemicals, polished diamonds.

The horizontal tricolour of orange, white and green recalls the flag of the Indian National Congress (now the Congress Party), which was founded in 1885 to seek independence from British colonial rule. Saffron (orange) stands for Hinduism, courage and sacrifice, white for the hope of peace, and green for faith and chivalry. At independence in 1947, the flag was modified by the addition of a blue *chakra* (wheel) at the centre. Blue represents the ocean and sky. In Buddhism, the spinning wheel represents the inevitability of existence, and the 24 spokes of the wheel correspond with the hours in a day.

JAMMU AND KASHMIR

State of Jammu and Kashmir

Flag proportions: 23:32
Adopted: 24 October 1975
Area: Not applicable, as borders are disputed
Population: n/a
Capital: Muzaffarabad
Language: Urdu, Hindi
Religion: Muslim
Currency: Pakistani rupee
Exports: n/a

A disputed territory, Jammu and Kashmir was a state in British India ruled by a Hindu maharajah, although the majority of the population was Muslim. When India and Pakistan achieved independence in 1947, the maharajah acceded to India, and Muslims campaigned to bring the state under Pakistani rule. Most of Jammu and Kashmir has been integrated into India, but the dispute continues. The portion under Pakistani rule, often referred to as Azad ('free') Kashmir, has its own flag, government and constitution although it is not independent. Muslims are represented by the white crescent and star on a green background and Hindus by saffron. The four silver stripes stand for the snow-covered mountains of the area.

BANGLADESH

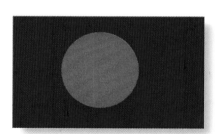

People's Republic of Bangladesh

Flag proportions: 3:5
Adopted: 25 January 1972
Capital: Dacca (Dhaka)
Area: 148,393km² (57,295mi²)
Population: 137 million
Language: Bengali
Religion: Muslim, Hindu
Currency: Taka
Exports: Jute and jute goods, tea, hides and skins, newsprint, fish, finished garments.

Bangladesh was established as the eastern province of Pakistan at the partition of India in 1947. It was substantially different in culture and language from West Pakistan, resulting in decades of resentment. Following a civil war that precipitated a massive refugee crisis, Bangladesh finally gained independence in 1971. On the flag, green is for the land, fertility and Islam. The red disc, set slightly towards the hoist, symbolizes the rising sun of independence after the blood-drenched struggle.

NEPAL

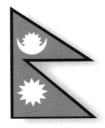

Kingdom of Nepal

Flag proportions: 4:3

Adopted: 16 December 1962

Capital: Kathmandu

Area: 147,181km² (56,831mi²)

Population: 25,2 million

Language: Nepali

Religion: Hindu, Buddhist, Muslim

Currency: Nepalese rupee

Exports: Carpets, clothing, hides and skins, grain, jute, oil seeds, ghee, potatoes, herbs.

The unique shape of the Nepalese flag is based on two triangular pennants once flown by rival branches of the Rana dynasty. The pennants are said to represent the Himalaya mountains and two religions, Buddhism and Hinduism.

Nepal is a monarchy and the crescent in the upper part represents the royal house, while the sun in the lower part is for the Rana family which, in the past, provided the hereditary prime minister. The sun and moon reflect the hope that the nation will endure. Crimson is the colour of the rhododendron, Nepal's national flower. It also stands for victory in war. The blue border signifies peace. Until 1962 the sun and moon were depicted with faces.

BHUTAN

Kingdom of Bhutan

Flag proportions: 2:3

Adopted: 1971

Capital: Thimphu

Area: 46,500km² (18,000mi²)

Population: 1,7 million

Language: Dzongkha, English, Nepali

Religion: Buddhist, Hindu

Currency: Ngultrum

Exports: Fruit, timber.

In local dialect, Bhutan means 'Land of the Dragon', and the dragon has been associated with the country since about 1200. Thunder was believed to be the sound of dragons roaring, and a religious sect, the Drukpas, claimed the 'thunder dragon' as their emblem. It is shown in white to symbolize purity and loyalty. Jewels clasped in its claws denote wealth, and the snarling mouth suggests the strength of the deities protecting the country. The field is diagonally divided to represent spiritual and temporal authority in Bhutan. Orange is for the Drukpa monasteries and Buddhist religious practice, while saffron is the colour of the reigning Wangchuk dynasty.

Buddhist prayer flags

Followers of the style of Buddhism practised in Nepal, Bhutan and Tibet use flags as a part of their worship. The flags, which hang in long strings in and around homes and monasteries, and near rivers, lakes and mountain passes, are said to bring happiness, long life and prosperity to the person who planted the flags, and to all those in the vicinity.

Prayer flags are regarded as offerings to the Buddhas and Bodhisattvas (divine beings) and the guardian spirits that inhabit sacred lakes and mountains. As the wind activates the flags, it carries the essence of the prayers printed on them to wherever it blows. Prayer flags also remind people to be mindful of Dharma (ideal truths, as taught by the Buddha) as they go about their daily business. The five colours represent the elements, and prayer flags are usually hung in the same order: yellow (earth), green (water), red (fire), white (cloud) and blue (sky).

Traditional cotton flags are printed with pictures of the deities, auspicious symbols, and invocations. Flags made of modern, more durable materials are also available.

SRI LANKA

Democratic Socialist Republic of Sri Lanka

Flag proportions: 1:2
Adopted: 7 September 1978
Capital: Colombo
Area: 65,610km² (25,343mi²)
Population: 19,4 million
Languages: Sinhala, Tamil
Religion: Buddhist, Hindu, Muslim, Christian
Currency: Sri Lankan rupee
Exports: Tea, clothing, textiles, gemstones, coconuts, rubber.

The gold lion clasping a sword, derived from the Sinhalese kingdom of Kandy, was the flag of Ceylon prior to 1815 when the island became a British colony. The lion signifies strength and nobility, the sword represents authority, crimson is for national pride, and the yellow border symbolizes Buddhism. After independence in 1948, the lion flag was flown again. In 1951, vertical bands of green and saffron were added to represent the minority Muslim and Hindu Tamil communities. In 1972, when Ceylon became Sri Lanka, four pipul leaves were added to the red panel. They represent the tree under which Gautama Siddhartha sat when he received enlightenment and became the Buddha, and stand for the Buddhist values of love, compassion, empathy and equanimity.

MALDIVES

Republic of the Maldives

Flag proportions: 2:3
Adopted: 26 July 1965
Capital: Male
Area: 298km² (115mi²)
Population: 281,000
Language: Divehi
Religion: Muslim
Currency: Rufiyaa
Exports: Marine products, clothing.

The 'Land of a Thousand Islands' was long a sultanate under British protection. In 1965 it achieved independence and altered its national flag by removing a vertical band at the hoist, made up of black and white diagonal stripes. The green central panel, with or without a white crescent, was added early in the 20th century. Green represents peace and prosperity, as well as palm trees, which are regarded as the islands' life source. Red is for blood shed for independence, and the white crescent is the symbol of Islam.

A plain red flag was used by many countries in the Indian Ocean area, including Oman, Zanzibar and the Comoros.

BRITISH INDIAN OCEAN TERRITORY

BIOT

Flag proportions: 3:5
Adopted: 4 November 1990
Capital: Diego Garcia
Area: 60km² (23mi²)
Population: 3500
Language: English
Religion: n/a
Currency: n/a
Exports: n/a

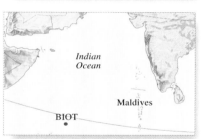

Situated 1900km (1180mi) northeast of Mauritius, the British Indian Ocean Territory (BIOT) comprises six main island groups in the Chagos Archipelago (some 2300 islands in total). It was established in 1965 to provide a joint US–UK military presence in the Indian Ocean. Diego Garcia, the largest, most southerly, and only inhabited island, is home to a large naval base. In 2000, a British High Court granted former residents, relocated to Mauritius and the Seychelles in the 1960s and 1970s, the right to return. Repatriation has been complicated by the US military lease on Diego Garcia.

The flag is based on the blue ensign, with the local badge in the fly. Blue and white wavy lines represent the ocean, the palm tree stands for the islands' natural vegetation and the Union Flag and crown symbolize British sovereignty.

Eastern and Southeast Asia

The Far East – far, that is, from the perspective of Europe, via a long sea voyage – includes China, Japan, Mongolia, Taiwan and Korea, an area about the same size as continental Europe. To many Westerners, it is almost as much the mysterious Orient as it was in the 13th century, when the Venetian explorer Marco Polo reached China after an overland journey of several years.

Population density is erratic, anything from 1,5 people per sq km in Mongolia to Macau's 30,000. Climate too is extreme, its principal feature being the monsoon rains that allow intensive planting on the coastal plains and inland valleys. The same broad region, however, includes the waterless and high-lying Gobi Desert.

The island cluster of the Philippines, between the South China Sea and the Pacific Ocean, is traditionally considered to be the transition point between the Far East and Southeast Asia. The latter region includes many islands and peninsulas, most of which are drained by large rivers, such as the Mekong and Irrawaddy. Southeast Asia comprises Vietnam, Cambodia, Laos, Thailand, Malaysia, Indonesia and Myanmar (formerly Burma).

Principal religions of the combined regions are Buddhism and Shintoism, although in South Korea Christianity and Buddhism each attract close to 50 per cent, while North Korea is largely atheist. Buddhism's prohibition on the slaughter of animals means that cattle-rearing plays only a small part in the economy, with much farming being only at the subsistence level.

There are many manufacturing centres here, the longest established, on average, being those of Japan which, ironically, has few natural resources such as oil or ores. Attempts to secure raw materials underlay militant Japanese expansion before and during World War II. The fighting did not end with Hiroshima, Nagasaki and military withdrawal; with peace in sight, the Soviet Union declared war on Japan, thereby laying the foundation for an enduring Communist presence in the north.

Colonial powers, notably France and Britain, came under fire from well-armed independence movements, some of them Communist backed. France withdrew from Indochina (Vietnam, Laos and Cambodia) while the Communist Chinese pushed the Nationalist Chinese from the mainland onto the island of Formosa (now Taiwan). The decade-long war in Vietnam severely disrupted the administration in neighbouring countries as well. In terms of a century-old treaty with China, the last British Union Flag in the region was lowered over Hong Kong in 1997, but the island's pragmatic administration has seen no loss of revenue.

Eastern and Southeast Asia

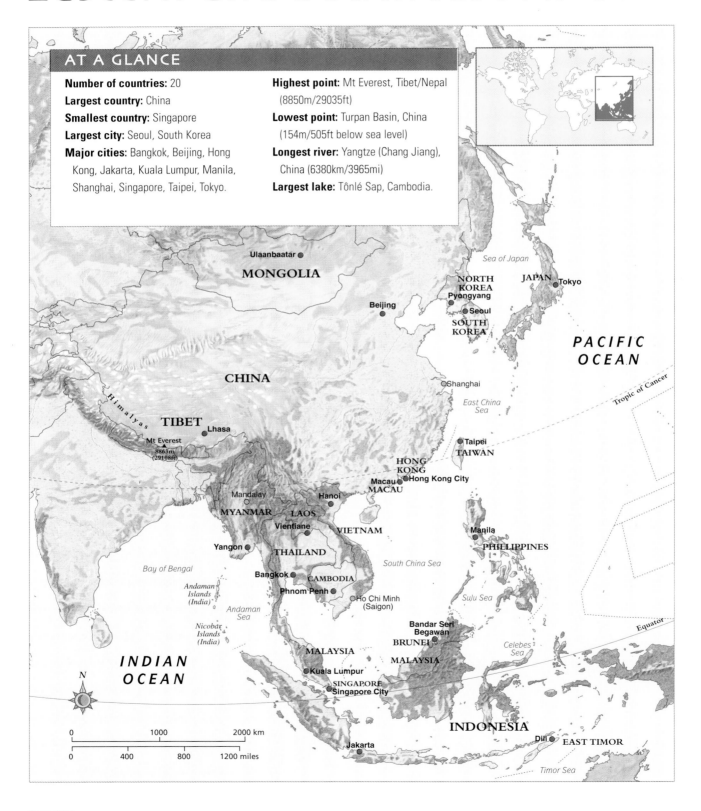

AT A GLANCE

Number of countries: 20
Largest country: China
Smallest country: Singapore
Largest city: Seoul, South Korea
Major cities: Bangkok, Beijing, Hong Kong, Jakarta, Kuala Lumpur, Manila, Shanghai, Singapore, Taipei, Tokyo.

Highest point: Mt Everest, Tibet/Nepal (8850m/29035ft)
Lowest point: Turpan Basin, China (154m/505ft below sea level)
Longest river: Yangtze (Chang Jiang), China (6380km/3965mi)
Largest lake: Tônlé Sap, Cambodia.

Ulaanbaatar

MONGOLIA

Sea of Japan

NORTH KOREA
Pyongyang

JAPAN
Tokyo

Beijing

Seoul
SOUTH KOREA

PACIFIC OCEAN

CHINA

Shanghai

East China Sea

Tropic of Cancer

TIBET
Lhasa

Mt Everest
8863m
(29108ft)

Taipei
TAIWAN

HONG KONG
Macau
Hong Kong City
MACAU

Mandalay

Hanoi

MYANMAR   LAOS

Vientiane

VIETNAM

Manila

PHILIPPINES

Yangon

THAILAND

South China Sea

Bay of Bengal

Bangkok

CAMBODIA

Andaman Islands (India)

Phnom Penh

Ho Chi Minh (Saigon)

Sulu Sea

Andaman Sea

Nicobar Islands (India)

Bandar Seri Begawan

Equator

BRUNEI

Celebes Sea

INDIAN OCEAN

MALAYSIA

MALAYSIA

N

Kuala Lumpur

SINGAPORE
Singapore City

INDONESIA

Dili
EAST TIMOR

0	1000	2000 km

0	400	800	1200 miles

Jakarta

Timor Sea

CHINA

People's Republic of China

Flag proportions: 2:3
Adopted: 1 October 1949
Capital: Beijing
Area: 9,572,900km²
(3,696,100mi²)
Population: 1,3 billion
Language: Mandarin Chinese
Religion: Atheist, Taoist,
Buddhist, Confucian
Currency: Yen
Exports: Mineral fuels, silk, satin,
cotton, footwear, machinery.

The Chinese flag was designed to be 'modest and majestic'. Red, the traditional colour of the Chinese people, also stands for communism. The large yellow star stands for communist ideology, while the four small stars represent the regions of China. Together, the stars echo the importance of the number five in Chinese philosophy. China's first national flag (1872), depicted the blue dragon of the Manchu (Ching) dynasty on a yellow field. Decades of struggle against European incursion led to the Boxer Rebellion of 1900, aimed at eliminating foreign domination. Clashes between nationalist and communist forces led to several flags being flown (see Taiwan p88) prior to the establishment of the People's Republic in 1949.

TIBET

Tibet

Flag proportions: 2:3
Adopted: c.1951
Capital: Lhasa
Area: 1,221,600km² (471,538mi²)
Population: 2 million
Language: Tibetan
Religion: Lamist (a form of
Mahayana Buddhism)
Currency: Yaun (Yen)
Exports: Wool, borax, salt, horn,
musk, herbs, furs, lapis lazuli.

The white triangle at the base of the flag symbolizes the snow-clad Himalaya in which this semi-autonomous region of China is situated. Two stylized snow-lions represent harmony between spiritual and temporal authority. They hold a gem symbolizing Buddhist philosophy, above which are three flaming jewels, representing Buddha, Dharma (the Doctrine), and Sangha (saints or guardians of the Doctrine). Behind the peak is a depiction of the sun, a symbol of freedom, prosperity and happiness. Its 12 rays symbolize the descendants of the original tribes of Tibet, and the colours symbolize the male and female deities that guard the flag. The gold border on three edges represents the spread of Buddhism's ideals.

MONGOLIA

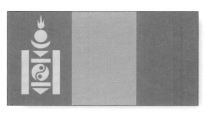

State of Mongolia

Flag proportions: 1:2
Adopted: 12 February 1992
Capital: Ulaanbaatar
Area: 1,565,000 km² (604,250mi²)
Population: 2,5 million
Language: Halh Mongol
Religion: Shamanist, Tibetan
Buddhist, Muslim
Currency: Tugrik
Exports: Minerals, metals, meat
and hides, livestock, wool.

Three vertical bands of red, blue, red have been used on the Mongolian flag since 1940, when the *soyombo* was added at the hoist. The national emblem of Mongolia, the *soyombo* has remote and mystical origins, incorporating elements of Buddhism and Lamaism. The uppermost symbol is a flame above a sun and crescent moon. Inverted triangles are ancient Mongol symbols for death. Horizontal panels indicate watchfulness, as do the two stylized fish which make up the Chinese yin-yang symbol. Two vertical columns express the old proverb that 'the friendship of two men is stronger than stone walls'. A star surmounting the emblem was removed in 1992 and the design of the *soyombo* was modified.

HONG KONG

Xianggang
Flag proportions: 2:3
Adopted: 1 July 1997
Capital: Victoria (Hong Kong City)
Area: 1092km² (421mi²)
Population: 7,4 million
Language: English, Cantonese
Religion: Confucian, Buddhist, Taoist, Christian, Muslim
Currency: Hong Kong dollar
Exports: Textiles, clothing, electronic goods and appliances, watches, cameras, plastics.

Formerly part of China, Hong Kong was occupied by Britain in 1841 and ceded by China in 1842. The Kowloon Peninsula was acquired in 1860 and the New Territories were secured under a 99-year lease from 1898. As a British crown colony, a blue ensign, depicting the local coat of arms, was flown. When the end of the leasehold approached, negotiations between Britain and China concluded in an agreement to transfer full sovereignty of Hong Kong to China in 1997 in exchange for an assurance that a capitalist economy and associated freedoms would be retained for at least 50 years. As a result, Hong Kong is now a special administrative region of China. Its new flag has a red field, on which is a stylized white flower of the bauhinia tree. The red stars within the five petals are derived from the Chinese flag and are intended to convey that Hong Kong is a part of China.

MACAU

Aomen
Flag proportions: 2:3
Adopted: 20 December 1999
Capital: Macao
Area: 25,4km² (9,8mi²)
Population: 470,000
Languages: Cantonese, Portuguese
Religion: Buddhist, Catholic
Currency: Pataca
Exports: Clothing, textiles, footwear, fuel, cement, machines.

Portuguese explorers established Macau as a trading and missionary post in 1537, and Portugal leased the tiny enclave from China in 1557. Macau was annexed in 1849 and, from 1887, was recognized by the Chinese government as a Portuguese colony, which it remained until it reverted to China in 1974 (although Macau remained under Portuguese administration until 1999). Macau is a special administrative region of China, operating under a similar 'one country, two systems' agreement as reached with Hong Kong.

The flag depicts, on a green field, a three-leafed lotus flower, representing the three islands of Macau. A stylized bridge and water below the flower indicate the inseparable contact with mainland China, while the golden colour of the five stars is derived from the Chinese flag.

JAPAN

Japan (Nihon/Nippon)
Flag proportions: 7:10
Adopted: 13 August 1999
Capital: Tokyo
Area: 377,727km² (145,852mi²)
Population: 127,2 million
Language: Japanese
Religion: Shinto, Buddhist
Currency: Yen
Exports: Electronic equipment, ships, motor vehicles, textiles, steel and nonferrous metals, chemicals.

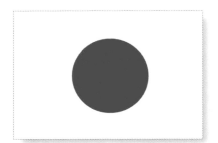

The red *Hinomaru* or 'disc of the sun' has been a Japanese symbol for more than 1000 years, and recalls the worship of Amaterasu Omikami, the Sun Goddess of the Shinto faith. The present national flag, with a red disc on a white field, was adopted after the restoration of the Meiji dynasty and the inauguration of Emperor Mutsuhito in 1867, which introduced an era of rapid change and westernization. The white field denotes purity and honesty, while red is said to stand for warmth and sincerity. Although Japan is known as the 'Land of the Rising Sun', the Japanese national flag has never depicted the sun with rays, although this pattern was adopted in 1889 as the naval ensign.

NORTH KOREA

Democratic People's Republic of Korea

Flag proportions: 1:2
Adopted: 9 September 1948
Capital: Pyongyang
Area: 122,762km² (47,402mi²)
Population: 24,8 million
Language: Korean
Religion: Officially atheist; but traditionally Buddhist, Confucian
Currency: North Korean Won
Exports: Minerals, metallurgical products, armaments, textiles.

From 1910 the flag of Japan flew over the annexed Korean peninsula. In 1948, the former kingdom was partitioned along latitude 38° North (the 38th parallel) into a communist north and democratic south. The flag adopted by North Korea expressed its newly acquired communist ideology with a five-pointed red star on a white disc, situated on a broad, horizontal red band bordered above and below by a narrow white stripe and a broader blue stripe. The flag retains the traditional Korean colours, with special prominence given to red, for the communist revolution. The white disc recalls the Chinese yin-yang symbol, which represents the opposing principles of nature (and also occurs, in a different form, on the flag of South Korea).

SOUTH KOREA

Republic of Korea

Flag proportions: 2:3
Adopted: October 1997
Capital: Seoul
Area: 99,274km² (38,332mi²)
Population: 48,6 million
Language: Korean, English
Religion: Christian, Buddhist, Confucian
Currency: South Korean Won
Exports: Electronics, textiles, clothing, ships, cars, iron, steel, telecommunications equipment.

The first national flag of Korea was established on 18 August 1882. Its basic design was re-established after Korea was liberated from Japanese rule in 1945, and there have been several minor modifications since then. White represents peace and purity, and is also the traditional colour of Korea. At the centre of the flag, the yin-yang symbol (*um-yang* in Korean) denotes the harmony that exists in natural opposites. The four groups of black bars, or trigrams, known as a *kwae*, derive from the *I-Ching* (Book of Changes), a Chinese divination system. The pattern of broken (yin) and unbroken (yang) bars illustrates principles of movement and harmony. Each trigram has a special meaning: the three intact bars at the upper hoist (top left) represent heaven and, moving clockwise, the others in turn depict water, earth and fire.

North Korea, South Korea and the DMZ

Following the failure of the Japanese occupation in 1945, the Korean Peninsula was divided more or less arbitrarily along the 38th parallel (38° North) into zones of temporary occupation, with the USA controlling the south and the Soviet Union the north. In 1948 this unnatural division was made permanent with the founding of the separate states of North Korea and South Korea.

The heavily mechanized, communist-led northern army invaded the south in 1950, resulting in a US-led military response by the United Nations. The war ended inconclusively in 1953, following which a demilitarized zone (DMZ) some 4km (2,5 miles) wide was created between the two countries which, having signed no peace treaty, are technically still at war. Tension along the DMZ has always been high, and has impacted upon diplomatic relations between the two Koreas. The situation is not helped by North Korea's nuclear capabilities, coupled with the country's fast-declining economy, chronic food shortages and extensive armed forces.

However, although their governments have been hostile for more than five decades, the common people of both North Korea and South Korea have expressed a strong desire for the eventual reunification of the peninsula by flying a single flag. Dating back to at least 1989, the flag is white with a representation in blue silhouette of the Korean peninsula. The flag was carried by a joint north/south team at the 2001 Sydney Olympics.

TAIWAN

Republic of China

Flag proportions: 2:3
Adopted: 28 October 1928
Capital: Taipei
Area: 36,179km² (13,969mi²)
Population: 23,3 million
Language: Mandarin Chinese
Religion: Buddhist, Taoist, Confucian, Christian
Currency: Taiwan dollar
Exports: Machinery, electrical equipment, metals, textiles, plastics, vehicles, sports goods.

The Taiwanese flag was the national flag of mainland China from 1928–49 (see also China p85), when Chiang Kai-Shek's Chinese Nationalist Party, or Kuomintang, was in power. After the communist victory in 1949, the nationalists retreated to the island of Formosa (now Taiwan) and established a government based on China's pre-1947 constitution. The white sun on a blue field, occupying the chief canton, is the flag of the Kuomintang. The blue background stands for liberty and justice; the sun represents equality and light with the 12 rays representing the hours of the clock, against which progress is constantly measured. The red field is for brotherhood and sacrifice, and for the Han Chinese, the dominant race in China.

VIETNAM

Socialist Republic of Vietnam

Flag proportions: 2:3
Adopted: 30 November 1955
Capital: Hanoi (Ha Nôi)
Area: 329,566km² (127,301mi²)
Population: 80,3 million
Language: Vietnamese
Religion: Buddhist, Taoist, Confucian, Roman Catholic
Currency: Dong
Exports: Rice, crude oil, coal, coffee, handicrafts, nuts, rubber, tea, tin, clothing.

Vietnam was part of French Indochina when Japan invaded in 1940. Following Japan's defeat, Vietnamese nationalists fought against the restoration of French colonial rule. In 1954, under the Geneva Convention, Vietnam was divided into communist North and pro-Western South, resulting in the Vietnam War (1964–76). After the fall of Saigon, the country was united as the Socialist Republic of Vietnam, under the flag of North Vietnam, which resembles that carried by Ho Chi Minh's resistance movement during the Japanese occupation. It consists of a five-pointed gold star at the centre of a red field. The points of the star represent the unity of the five groups of workers who built socialism. Red stands for revolution and for blood shed by the Vietnamese people.

LAOS

Lao People's Democratic Republic

Flag proportions: 2:3
Adopted: 2 December 1975
Capital: Vientiane (Viangchan)
Area: 236,800km² (91,400mi²)
Population: 5,4 million
Language: Lao
Religion: Buddhist, Traditional, Christian, Muslim
Currency: Kip
Exports: Electricity, timber (teak), plywood, coffee, gypsum.

Laos gained independence from France in 1953 and became a communist state in 1975, when the present national flag was introduced. It is unusual for being a communist flag without any star at all. The flag is divided into a broad horizontal blue band at the centre, flanked top and bottom by two red bands, half the depth of the blue. Red is for blood shed in the struggle for freedom during the civil war (1953–75) and blue for wealth. The white disc symbolizes the ruling Lao People's Revolutionary Party leading the country to prosperity. It is said to be based on the one in the Japanese national flag, used in recognition of Japan's work against western colonialism.

CAMBODIA

State of Cambodia

Flag proportions: 2:3
Adopted: 30 June 1993
Capital: Phnom Penh
Area: 181,035km² (69,898mi²)
Population: 13 million
Language: Khmer
Religion: Buddhist, Muslim
Currency: Riel
Exports: Timber, rubber, soya beans, sesame, rice, pepper.

Cambodia (Kampuchea) became a French protectorate in 1863. During most of World War II the country was occupied by Japan. Part of Indochina, Cambodia raised its own flag in 1949 when it achieved semiautonomy from France, before becoming independent in 1953. The present flag, dating from 1948, was reintroduced when the monarchy was reinstated in 1993, several other versions having been flown in the interim. The ancient temple of Angkor Wat, revered as the sanctuary of the Lord Creator of the world, is depicted in the red band. The temple buildings rest on a pedestal, representing the structure of the universe.

MYANMAR

Union of Myanmar

Flag proportions: 5:9
Adopted: 4 January 1974
Capital: Rangoon (Yangôn)
Area: 676,577km² (261,228mi²)
Population: 51 million
Language: Burmese
Religion: Buddhist, Christian, Muslim
Currency: Kyat
Exports: Teak, rice, pulses, gems, rubber, hardwood, base metals.

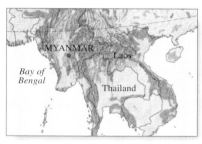

Burma became the Union of Myanmar in 1989, adopting a flag based on a symbol of resistance to Japanese occupation in World War II. Burma was a British colony until 1948 when it achieved independence. The resistance flag (a white star on a red field) was modified in 1948 by the addition of a dark blue canton and five small stars. The present design features a circle of 14 stars enclosing a 14-toothed pinion (cogwheel) and ears of rice, representing industry and agriculture respectively. Fourteen corresponds to the number of states in the country and the stars represent unity between them. Red signifies courage and decisiveness, white is for purity, and dark blue for peace and integrity.

THAILAND

Kingdom of Thailand

Flag proportions: 2:3
Adopted: 28 September 1917
Capital: Bangkok (Krung Thep)
Area: 513,115km² (198,114mi²)
Population: 62,5 million
Language: Thai
Religion: Buddhist, Muslim
Currency: Baht
Exports: Textiles, rice, tin, gemstones, rubber, electronic goods, tapioca, sugar, fish, machinery.

Thailand's flag was originally an expression of support for the Allied cause in World War I (most Allied flags used red, white and blue). The field is divided into horizontal bands, with the central blue band being one third of the depth of the flag. The bands of white and red above and below are each one sixth of the flag's depth. The colours symbolize the life-blood of the country (red), purity of the people and their Buddhist faith (white), and the monarchy (blue). The Thai people are proud of their culture and their flag, which is widely displayed.

MALAYSIA

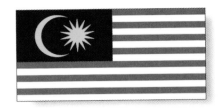

Federation of Malaysia

Flag proportions: 1:2

Adopted: 16 September 1963

Capital: Kuala Lumpur

Area: 329,758km² (127,317mi²)

Population: 23,4 million

Language: Bahasa Malaysia

Religion: Muslim, Taoist, Hindu, Christian

Currency: Ringgit

Exports: Palm oil, rubber, timber, petroleum, machinery, transport equipment, tin, textiles.

When Malaya changed its name to Malaysia in 1963, it adopted a flag closely resembling the US Stars and Stripes, with Islamic symbols. The seven red and seven white stripes symbolize unity within the federation, as do the 14 rays (points of the star) in the chief canton. The crescent and star together represent Islam, the principal religion. Blue represents Malaysian unity and affiliation to the Commonwealth. Yellow, the colour of the crescent and the star, is the traditional colour of Malaysian rulers. Malaysia comprises 13 states and two federal territories, Kuala Lumpur and Labuan.

SINGAPORE

Republic of Singapore

Flag proportions: 2:3

Adopted: 3 December 1959

Capital: Singapore City

Area: 641km² (248mi²)

Population: 4 million

Languages: Malay, Chinese, Tamil, English

Religion: Christian, Muslim, Taoist, Hindu

Currency: Singapore dollar

Exports: Electronics, machinery, vehicles, petroleum products.

Singapore (*Singa pura*, the 'lion city') was leased to the British East India Company in 1819. The flag was first used when Singapore received self-government from Britain in 1959, retained when it joined the Malaysian Federation in 1963 and formally adopted when the country gained independence within the Commonwealth in 1965. The flag is horizontally divided into equal bands of red over white, colours associated with the Malay people. Red represents equality and universal brotherhood, white stands for virtue and purity. The white crescent in the chief canton signifies that Singapore is a new and growing nation. The five five-pointed stars stand for equality, justice, democracy, peace and progress.

BRUNEI

State of Brunei Darussalam

Flag proportions: 1:2

Adopted: 29 September 1959

Capital: Bandar Seri Begawan

Area: 5765km² (2226mi²)

Population: 354,500

Language: Malay, Chinese, English

Religion: Muslim, Buddhist

Currency: Brunei dollar

Exports: Crude oil, natural gas.

Brunei, a small oil-rich state on the island of Borneo (part of Indonesia), is an absolute monarchy. The principal flag colour, yellow, is associated with the ruling Sultan, while the angled bands of black and white represent his chief ministers. At the centre of the flag is the state coat of arms in red. The twin-tailed flag and umbrella are royal symbols, while the upturned crescent represents Islam. The hands on either side signify government protection and promotion of the rights of the people. Two four-feathered wings symbolize the protection of justice, peace, tranquility and prosperity. The Arabic motto on the crescent translates as 'Always render service by the guidance of Allah', while the inscription on the scroll beneath it, *Brunei Darussalam*, means 'Brunei City of Peace'.

PHILIPPINES

Republic of the Philippines

Flag proportions: 1:2

Adopted: 16 September 1997

Capital: Manila

Area: 300,000km² (115,830mi²)

Population: 80 million

Language: Pilipino, English

Religion: Roman Catholic, Aglipayan, Muslim, Protestant

Currency: Peso

Exports: Electronics, timber, copra, fruit, seafood, chemicals, sugar, coconut oil.

When the Philippines gained independence from the USA in 1946, the flag raised had originally been used by nationalists during the struggle for freedom from Spain. The white triangle represents peace and purity, red is for courage (bravery), and blue for honour and ideals (patriotism). Within the triangle are an eight-rayed sun and three stars, all in gold. The stars represent the Philippine's main regions (Luzon, Visayas, Mindanao) while the sun stands for liberty, and represents the eight provinces that revolted against Spain. The flag is the only one in the world to change the way it is viewed. It is normally flown with the blue band on top, but when the country is at war, the red band is set uppermost.

INDONESIA

Republic of Indonesia

Flag proportions: 2:3

Adopted: 17 August 1945

Capital: Jakarta

Area: 1,917,525km² (740,356mi²)

Population: 214 million

Language: Bahasa Indonesia

Religion: Muslim, Hindu

Currency: Rupiah

Exports: Natural gas, oil, timber, rubber, coffee, tin, tea, palm oil, fishery products, coal, copper, pepper, manufactured products.

Indonesia, comprising over 13,600 tropical islands straddling the equator, was a Dutch colony from 1816 until 1945, when independence was proclaimed (it was not recognized by the Dutch until 1949). The government of 1945 was encouraged by Japanese opposition to Western colonialism and the flag was based on colours used by a 13th-century Indonesian empire. It comprises equal horizontal bands of red above white, sacred colours of the ancient empire, which were deliberately chosen by the nationalist movement of the 1940s. Officially called *Sang Dwiwarna* (exalted bicolour), the flag symbolizes the complete person, red being for the body and physical life, and white for the soul and spiritual existence.

EAST TIMOR

Democratic Republic of East Timor

Flag proportions: 2:3

Adopted: 20 May 2002

Capital: Dili

Area: 17,222km² (6649mi²)

Population: 949,000

Language: Portuguese, Tetum

Religion: Roman Catholic

Currency: US dollar

Exports: Coffee, cattle, crude oil, natural gas.

East Timor became independent from Indonesia in May 2002, when the flag of an interim UN administration was replaced with a flag dating from the country's 1975 transition from Portuguese colony to independent state, which was ended by invasion by pro-Indonesian militias. The black triangle at the hoist represents the dark periods of colonization, which endured for about 400 years. The yellow chevron or arrowhead depicts the struggle for independence and the hope of prosperity. Red is for blood shed for independence, a poignant association in view of the mass murders committed upon the East Timorese in 1999. White is for peace, and the five-pointed star is a light of hope for the nation's future path.

Australia, New Zealand and Oceania

Australia, the world's smallest continent, has an area of 7.68 million sq km (the continental USA covers 9.36 million sq km). In all this space, before European settlement, there lived perhaps a few hundred thousand native Australians, or Aborigines, and a range of animals, principally marsupials, the like of which had never been seen elsewhere. This is the greatest landmass of the territories of the Indo-Pacific region that are collectively known as Australasia and Oceania.

To the north of Australia is the vast scatter of islands once familiar to chartered trading companies and private adventurers as the East Indies – islands of silks and spices at the end of a gruelling trade route around the distant Cape of Good Hope. History and ethnicity are reflected in flags that carry, among other emblems, a pig's tusk, and the Union Flag of Great Britain. The mix of peoples is complex, deriving in part from the Asian mainland and in part from the three Pacific island groups known as Polynesia, Melanesia and Micronesia.

Most settlement patterns were established many centuries ago by indigenous or near-indigenous peoples who travelled across immense distances of ocean in open boats. For instance, Maori, a Polynesian people, settled New Zealand from the 10th century onwards. By contrast, the many Australians of Asian origin are much more recent, as a 'white Australia' immigration policy was abandoned only in the 1960s.

European colonization of the zone's many islands receded in the wake of World War II (1939–45), when the indigenous peoples, having been armed to resist Japanese invasion, began to seek independence for themselves. The war also resulted in a long-lasting American influence, most directly in the former United States Trust Territory of the Pacific Islands. Subsequent treaties include ANZUS (a mutual defence pact involving Australia, New Zealand and the USA), and the South Pacific Forum, a political and economic association of some 15 states, with its headquarters in Fiji.

During the past 50 years Australia has rapidly transformed its economy: 75 per cent of export earnings in 1947 were derived from agriculture, but farm-based earnings are now nearer to 20 per cent while the mining and manufacturing sectors have advanced. New Zealand's economy, thanks to its moist, warm climate, is still based primarily on agriculture, although the industrial sector is growing. Deposits of oil and minerals, including gold and silver, occur throughout Oceania, as in Papua New Guinea, which also exports rubber, timber and tropical fruits.

The sea remains a key to exploring the region, but nowadays it is mostly American-operated cruise liners that carry the prosperous and the privileged on leisurely journeys among the islands, making tourism an important source of foreign revenue for many of the smaller states and dependencies.

Australia, New Zealand and Oceania

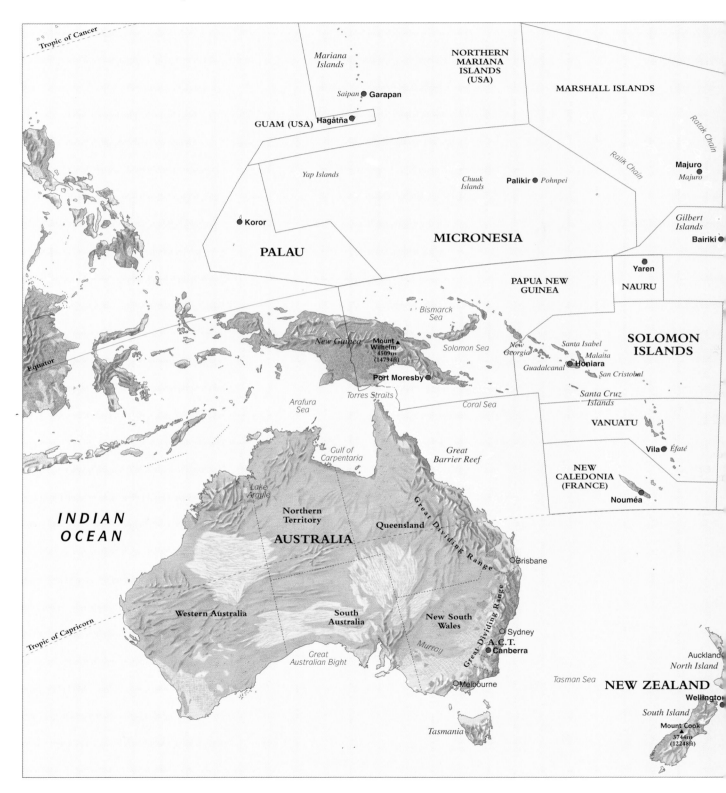

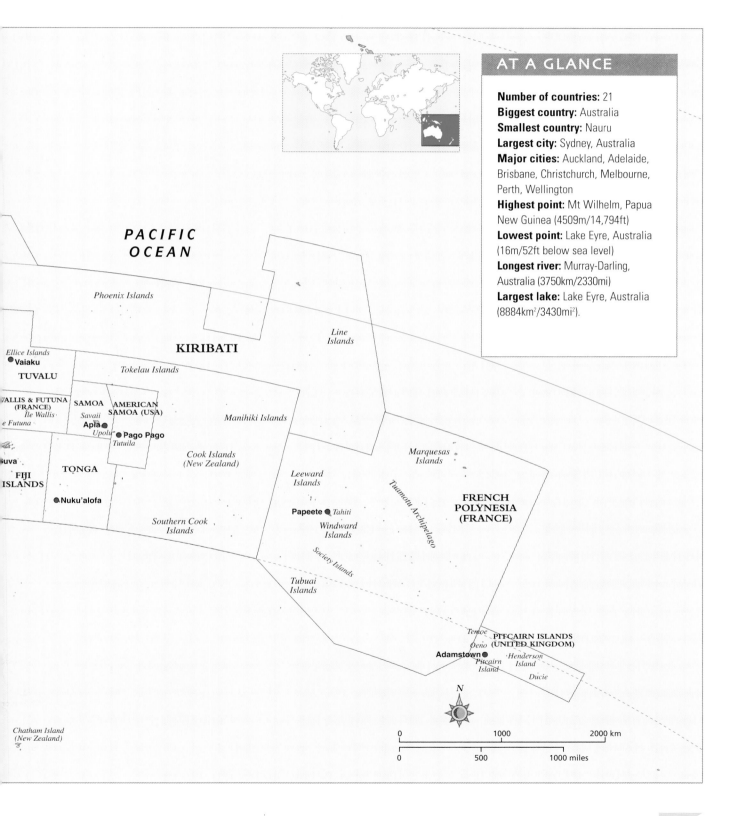

PACIFIC OCEAN

Phoenix Islands

Line Islands

KIRIBATI

Ellice Islands
● **Vaiaku**
TUVALU

Tokelau Islands

VALLIS & FUTUNA (FRANCE)
Île Wallis
e Futuna

SAMOA
Savaii
Apia ●
Upolu

AMERICAN SAMOA (USA)
● **Pago Pago**
Tutuila

Manihiki Islands

Marquesas Islands

uva
FIJI ISLANDS

TONGA

● **Nuku'alofa**

Cook Islands (New Zealand)

Leeward Islands

Tuamotu Archipelago

FRENCH POLYNESIA (FRANCE)

Papeete ● *Tahiti*

Windward Islands

Southern Cook Islands

Society Islands

Tubuai Islands

Temoe **PITCAIRN ISLANDS (UNITED KINGDOM)**
Oeno
Adamstown ● *·Henderson Island*
Pitcairn Island
Ducie

Chatham Island (New Zealand)

N

0   1000   2000 km

0   500   1000 miles

AUSTRALIA

Commonwealth of Australia

Flag proportions: 1:2

Adopted: 15 April 1954

Capital: Canberra

Area: 7,682,300km²
(2,966,368mi²)

Population: 20 million

Language: English

Religion: Christian, Muslim,
Jewish, Buddhist

Currency: Australian dollar

Exports: Metal ores and scrap,
coal and coal products, gold,
nonferrous metals, textile fibres.

Australia flies a version of the British Blue Ensign, with the Union Flag in the chief canton. The Southern Cross, a prominent southern constellation, is depicted at the fly. The large Commonwealth Star beneath the Union Flag represents the six states, Northern Territory and the external territories administered by the federal government. The shape, size and position of the stars was amended over the years until their final position was specified on 15 April 1954. The flag was the winning design in a 1901 competition that attracted 30,000 entries. Six submissions depicted a markedly similar pattern, and the prize money was shared among these entrants.

The British flag was first flown on Australian soil by the explorer Captain James Cook in 1778, and remained the official flag until 1954, after which the present Australian flag, which had previously flown alongside the Union Flag, was flown alone. It is possible that a future Australian flag design will dispense with the Union Flag.

Australian State flags

All state flags, other than those of the Northern Territory and the federal capital, Canberra (situated in Australian Capital Territory, or ACT), are based on the Blue Ensign and charged with the state badge in the fly. Some predate the national flag. The Northern Territory flag uses black and ochre to symbolize its Aboriginal heritage and desert environment. The ACT flag depicts Canberra's coat of arms alongside the Southern Cross in the city colours of gold and blue.

Australian Capital Territory
1993

Western Australia
1954

South Australia
1904

New South Wales
1876

Queensland
1959

Victoria
1901

Tasmania
1975

Northern Territory
1978

NORTHERN MARIANA ISLANDS

Commonwealth of the Northern Mariana Islands

Flag proportions: 20:39
Adopted: 25 October 1988
Capital: Saipan
Area: 457km² (117mi²)
Population: 80,000
Language: Chamorro, English
Religion: Roman Catholic
Currency: US dollar
Exports: Sugar, coconuts, coffee.

The Northern Mariana Islands, a self-governing incorporated United States territory, form part (with Guam) of the Marianas archipelago in the northwest Pacific. Raised in 1976, the flag has a large white five-pointed star in the centre of a blue field, representing the Pacific Ocean, which surrounds the islands with security and love. The star represents the many islands that make up the US Commonwealth territories. It is set upon a grey *latte* stone (a limestone column that supports traditional buildings), symbolizing the culture of the indigenous Chamorro people. In 1989 a wreath of flowers and shells was placed to encircle the original design. This circular head-wreath, comprising ylang-ylang, *seyur*, *ang'gha* and *teibwo* flowers, is another symbol of indigenous culture.

GUAM

Territory of Guam

Flag proportions: 22:41
Adopted: 9 February 1948
Capital: Hagåtña (Agaña)
Area: 549km² (212mi²)
Population: 164,000
Language: English, Chamorro
Religion: Roman Catholic
Currency: US dollar
Exports: Sweet potatoes, fish.

Guam, the largest of the Mariana Islands, is an unincorporated US territory and a major naval and air base. It was ceded to the US by Spain in 1898. The flag was designed in 1917 by the wife of an American naval officer, and the narrow red border was added in 1948. By tradition, it is always flown together with the US flag. The deep blue field represents the Pacific Ocean. The central oval shape, edged with red, is said to represent the slingshots used by the indigenous Chamorro people for hunting and warfare. Within the oval is a depiction of a coconut palm, the main crop. The tree, at the mouth of the Agaña River, has survived several typhoons and denotes tenacity and courage. The boat is a *proa*, a fast seagoing canoe that symbolizes courage and enterprise.

PALAU

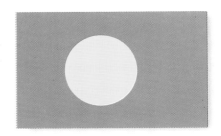

Republic of Palau

Flag proportions: 3:5
Adopted: 1 January 1981
Capital: Koror
Area: 488km² (188mi²)
Population: 20,000
Language: English, Palauan
Religion: Mostly Roman Catholic
Currency: US dollar
Exports: Copra, coconut oil, handicrafts, tuna.

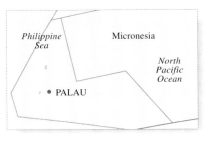

When Palau became a republic in 1981, it adopted a flag with a deceptively simple design, suggesting a full moon on the water or in the sky. However, when explained in terms of Palauan culture, the blue field is neither sea nor sky but represents the transition from foreign domination to independence and the freedom of self-rule. The gold disc is set slightly towards the hoist, and does indeed represent the moon, because full moon is regarded as the most favourable time for celebrations, planting or harvesting. It also signifies tranquillity, peace and love. Before independence, Palau was part of the US Trust Territory of the Pacific Islands and flew a version of the flag of the Federated States of Micronesia.

MICRONESIA

Federated States of
Micronesia

Flag proportions: 1:2
Adopted: 30 November 1978
Capital: Palikir
Area: 702km² (271mi²)
Population: 155,000
Language: English
Religion: Mostly Christian
Currency: US dollar
Exports: Copra, pepper, fish.

Situated in the northwest portion of Oceania, the Federated States of Micronesia are a collection of widely scattered islands in the Caroline group. Prior to independence in 1986, they were part of the US-administered United States Trust Territory of the Pacific Islands, whose flag was in the colours of the UN. The darker blue of the Micronesian flag represents the Pacific Ocean. Four white stars are arranged as a cross or the points of the compass, each star representing one of the island states that make up the federation, namely Chuuk, Kosrae, Pohnpei (Ponape) and Yap. (Two of the original six Trust Territories, Palau and the Marshall Islands, opted for separate independence.) Each state has its own flag, comprising a blue field charged with the state emblem.

MARSHALL
ISLANDS

Republic of the Marshall Islands

Flag proportions: 10:19
Adopted: 1 May 1979
Capital: Majuro
Area: 181km² (70mi²)
Population: 53,000
Language: Marshallese
Religion: Independent
Protestant Christian Church
Currency: US dollar
Exports: Coconut products, fish, shells, copra, handicrafts.

The long arms of the white star in the chief canton are said to depict a Christian cross, while the 24 points represent the Marshall Islands' municipalities. The twin stripes represent the parallel island chains of Ratak (sunrise, white) and Ralik (sunset, orange). The stripes widen and rise towards the fly, signifying growth and vitality. White is for peace and orange symbolizes prosperity and courage. Another interpretation is that the star and rising stripes depict the islands' position a few degrees north of the Equator. The dark blue field depicts the Pacific Ocean, across which the islands are scattered. The Marshall Islands were part of the US Trust Territory of the Pacific Islands from 1945–86, becoming self-governing in 1979 and gaining full independence in 1986.

PAPUA
NEW GUINEA

Independent State of
Papua New Guinea

Flag proportions: 3:4
Adopted: 1 July 1971
Capital: Port Moresby
Area: 462,840km² (178,704mi²)
Population: 4,7 million
Language: English
Religion: Protestant, Catholic
Currency: Kina
Exports: Gold, copper, oil, timber, coffee beans, copra, coconut.

The flag of Papua New Guinea (PNG) was designed by a local teacher, who chose red and black because of their widespread use in the country's indigenous art. The field comprises two right-angled triangles descending diagonally from the top of the hoist. The upper, red, triangle depicts, in gold, the *kumul* (bird of paradise) in flight, whose feathers were once used for ornamenting traditional headdresses. In the black triangle, five stars represent the Southern Cross as it appears over PNG, and also refer to a legend about five sisters.

NAURU

Republic of Nauru

Flag proportions: 1:2
Adopted: 31 January 1968
Capital: No official capital;
government offices situated in
Yaren district.
Area: 21,3km² (8mi²)
Population: 12,500
Language: Nauruan, English
Religion: Roman Catholic,
Nauruan Protestant Church
Currency: Australian dollar
Exports: Phosphates.

The royal blue field, symbolizing clear skies and a calm ocean, is divided by a horizontal gold stripe, representing the equator. The 12-pointed white star stands for the indigenous tribes of Nauru. The position of the star reflects the island's position one degree south of the equator. This tiny tropical island was called Pleasant Land by the Europeans who first visited it in 1798. Part of the German Empire from 1888, it came under Australian administration after 1918. During World War II the Japanese destroyed mining facilities and deported much of the population to Truk Atoll, 1600km (990mi) away. Nauru was a UN trust territory, jointly administered by Australia, New Zealand and the UK, from 1947 until independence in 1968.

SOLOMON ISLANDS

Solomon Islands

Flag proportions: 1:2
Adopted: 18 November 1977
Capital: Honiara
Area: 28,370km² (10,954mi²)
Population: 480,600
Language: English
Religion: Protestant, Catholic
Currency: Solomon Island dollar
Exports: Timber, fish, palm
products.

The Solomons comprise hundreds of islands in the Melanesian archipelago, including Guadalcanal (the largest), Malaita, San Cristobal, New Georgia and Santa Isabela. First sighted by Europeans in 1568, they became a British colony in 1883. Self-government was granted in 1976, independence within the Commonwealth in 1978.

The five five-pointed white stars stand for the five main groups of islands of this constitutional monarchy. The diagonal yellow stripe represents sunshine, while the blue and green triangles represent the sea and land. Japan occupied the Solomons for much of World War II.

VANUATU

Republic of Vanuatu

Flag proportions: 3:5
Adopted: 30 July 1980
Capital: Port-Vila
Area: 12,190km² (4706mi²)
Population: 200,000
Languages: English, French,
Bislama/Bichelama (pidgin)
Religion: Christian
Currency: Vatu
Exports: Copra, timber, cocoa,
coffee, kava, beef, seashells.

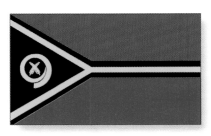

The golden Y-shape depicts the layout of the 70 islands of the Vanuatu archipelago. Gold is the colour of sunshine, black is for the indigenous Melanesian people, green for the natural wealth of the islands, and red for striving and sacrifice. A gold charge (object) set in the black triangle at the hoist depicts a curled boar's tusk, a symbol of prosperity, traditionally worn as a decorative pendant. Within the curve of the tusk are two crossed *namele* ferns, symbolizing peace. Europeans reached the islands in 1606, calling them the New Hebrides. Jointly administered by Britain and France from 1906, they escaped occupation by Japan in World War II. In 1980 the New Hebrides became Vanuatu, an independent republic within the Commonwealth.

NEW CALEDONIA

Territory of New Caledonia and Dependencies

Flag proportions: 2:3
Adopted: 5 March 1848
Capital: Nouméa
Area: 19,060km² (7359mi²)
Population: 211,000
Languages: French, plus 33 Melanesian-Polynesian dialects
Religion: Christian
Currency: Euro
Exports: Nickel ore, fish.

An overseas territory of France, this group of islands, 1400km (870mi) northeast of Brisbane, was settled by both Britain and France during the first half of the 19th century. It became a French possession in 1853 and served as a penal colony from 1864 until the early 20th century.

The status of the territory makes it legal for an approved flag to be flown alongside the *Tricolore*, but not on its own. The current local choice consists of a red field on which is depicted, in white, a flightless, crane-like bird, known locally as a *cagou*, which occurs only in New Caledonia.

TUVALU

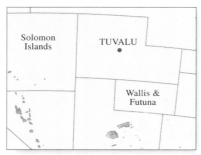

Tuvalu

Flag proportions: 1:2
Adopted: 11 April 1997
Capital: Vaiaku on Funafuti
Area: 24km² (9,5mi²)
Population: 11,300
Languages: Tuvaluan, English, Samoan
Religion: Christian
Currency: Australian dollar
Exports: Copra, fish.

Tuvalu flies a light blue version of the British Blue Ensign, perhaps to represent the clear waters of the Pacific Ocean. The nine five-pointed yellow stars represent the islands of the archipelago. When flying from a flagpole, with the fly pointing north, the stars on the flag are seen to be roughly occupying the geographical positions of the islands, which form a chain trending northwest to southeast. First reached by Europeans in 1795, the islands were a source of slave labour in the mid-19th century. A British protectorate from 1892, Tuvalu was part of the Gilbert and Ellice Islands from 1915–75, when the two groups separated to become Kiribati and Tuvalu respectively. Independence within the Commonwealth came in 1978.

WALLIS AND FUTUNA

Territory of the Wallis and Futuna Islands

Flag proportions: 2:3
Adopted: 5 March 1848
Capital: Mata-Utu on Ile Uvea
Area: 274km² (195mi²)
Population: 16,000
Language: French, Wallisian
Religion: Roman Catholic
Currency: Euro
Exports: Copra, chemicals, construction materials.

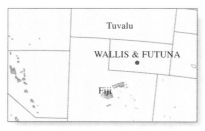

Wallis and Futuna is a French Overseas Territory, so the flag may only be displayed in conjunction with the *Tricolore*. The central white emblem on the red field is made up of four triangles with each base parallel to an edge and apex at the centre, resembling a modified Maltese cross (*cross pattée* – with triangular arms extending outwards). Three triangles represent three hereditary rulers, while the fourth denotes French sovereignty over this autonomous territory in the southwest Pacific, discovered by sailors in the 18th century. The emblem was probably introduced by French missionaries and retained when the islands became a protectorate in 1842. A white-bordered *Tricolore* occupies the chief canton. Red symbolizes courage, white the purity of high ideals.

FIJI

Republic of the Fiji Islands

Flag proportions: 1:2
Adoped: 10 October 1970
Capital: Suva
Area: 18,333km² (7078mi²)
Population: 812,000
Language: English
Religion: Christian, Hindu, Muslim
Currency: Fiji dollar
Exports: Sugar, canned fish, timber, ginger, molasses.

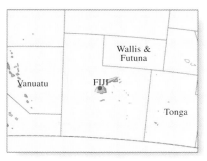

Originally inhabited by Melanesian and Polynesian people, Fiji became a British crown colony in 1874, achieved independence within the Commonwealth in 1970 and became a republic in 1987. The Fijian flag, one of the first to adopt a Blue Ensign with light blue, uses that colour to distinguish it from Australia and New Zealands' flags. The Union Flag is in the chief canton, with the shield from the republic's coat of arms at the fly. On the chief (the top third of the shield) is a crowned lion. Below the chief, the shield is quartered by St George's cross on a white field. The quarters show sugar cane, a coconut palm, a dove of peace and a bunch of bananas.

TONGA

Kingdom of Tonga

Flag proportions: 1:2
Adopted: 4 November 1875
Capital: Nuku'alofa
Area: 748km² (289mi²)
Population: 99,000
Language: Tongan, English
Religion: Christian
Currency: Pa'anga
Exports: Coconut products, clothes, vegetables, watermelon.

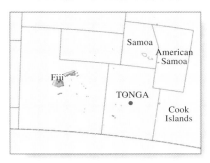

In 1862, King George Tupou I commanded that his country's flag should symbolize the Christian faith. The new flag was red with a red cross on a white canton. The King encouraged the spread of Christianity and the 1875 constitution states that the flag should be used for all time. Red is for the blood of Christ, white is for purity, and the cross is a Christian symbol. Tonga, a British protectorate from 1900, achieved independence as an hereditary monarchy within the Commonwealth in 1970. Early European visitors included Abel Tasman in 1643, but it was Captain Cook who bestowed the title, 'the Friendly Islands', in 1773. Of about 170 islands, 36 are inhabited.

SAMOA

Independent State of Samoa

Flag proportions: 1:2
Adopted: 26 April 1949
Capital: Apia
Area: 2831km² (1093mi²)
Population: 170,300
Language: Samoan, English
Religion: Protestant, Catholic
Currency: Tala
Exports: Palm products, timber, bananas, cocoa, beer, cigarettes.

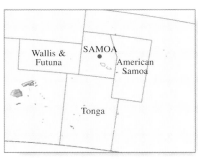

The present flag, granted in 1948 when Samoa was a territory of New Zealand, was jointly created by the kings of the rival kingdoms of Malietoa and Tamasese. It combined elements of their flags with the four-star Southern Cross of New Zealand, which appears in the chief canton. A small fifth star was added in 1949, making the constellation more like that of Australia. White stars stands for purity, while blue denotes freedom. Red, a traditional Samoan colour, is for courage. In 1962, Samoa (formerly Western Samoa) became the first Polynesian nation to be granted independence, as a constitutional monarchy within the Commonwealth. There are two main islands, Savai'i and Upolu, and two smaller islands.

AMERICAN SAMOA

Territory of American Samoa
Flag proportions: 10:19
Adopted: 17 April 1960
Capital: Pago Pago
Area: 195km² (75mi²)
Population: 70,000
Language: English, Samoan
Religion: Christian
Currency: US dollar
Exports: Canned tuna.

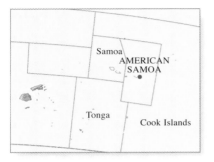

The flag is blue with an isosceles triangle based on the fly, its red-edged equal sides extending to a point midway along the hoist. At the fly, within the white triangle, is an American bald eagle in flight, a position described as *volant*. The eagle is 'proper' or in its natural colours. Its left claw clasps a staff (*fue*), a symbol of Samoan nobility and wisdom. In the eagle's right claw is a club used in ritual dances, representing the power of the chiefs. The symbolism of America's national bird clasping traditional icons of Samoan authority underlines the friendship between the USA and American Samoa, an unincorporated territory administered by the US Department of the Interior. The head of state is the US president, but the islands are ruled by an elected governor.

KIRIBATI

Republic of Kiribati
Flag proportions: 1:2
Adopted: 12 July 1979
Capital: Bairiki
Area: 717km² (277mi²)
Population: 95,000
Language: English
Religion: Christian
Currency: Australian dollar
Exports: Copra, seaweed, fish.

Kiribati's flag is identical to its coat of arms and is thus known as an armorial banner. Both show alternate white and blue horizontal wavy lines representing the Pacific Ocean. Rising from the sea is a gold radiant sun, above which flies a gold frigate bird (*Fregata minor*) symbolizing authority, freedom and command of the seas. Sun and bird are shown on a field of red. The rising sun also stands for the equator, which runs through Kiribati. The arms date from 1937 and were created for the former British colony of the Gilbert and Ellice Islands. The shield was incorporated into the British Blue Ensign but, with independence in 1979, the islands became Kiribati and Tuvalu respectively. Kiribati opted for amended arms for its flag, while Tuvalu chose its own set of symbols.

FRENCH POLYNESIA

Territory of French Polynesia
Flag proportions: 2:3
Adopted: 29 June 1985
Capital: Papeete (Tahiti)
Area: 4165km² (1608mi²)
Population: 220,000
Language: Tahitian, French
Religion: Roman Catholic
Currency: Euro
Exports: Cultivated pearls, coconut oil.

French Polynesia is an overseas territory of France, so the *Tricolore* is its official flag, although a local flag featuring the Polynesian colours (red and white) is recognized. In a central circle, within the white band, is a piragua (pirogue – a twin-hulled canoe that can be paddled or sailed), behind which is a gold radiant sun. Blue and white denote the wealth to be harvested from the sea, and piraguas are still used for fishing. Five rowers represent the *départéments* of French Polynesia: Tuamotu Archipelago, Marquesas and Tubuai islands, and the Society Islands, comprising the Windward Islands, *Îles du Vent*, (Tahiti, Moorea, Maio, Tetiaroa, Mehetia) and Leeward Islands, *Îles sous le Vent*, (Raiatea, Huahine and Bora-Bora).

PITCAIRN ISLANDS

Pitcairn, Henderson, Ducie and Oeno Islands

Flag proportions: 1:2
Adopted: 2 April 1984
Capital: Adamstown
Area: 47km² (18mi²)
Population: ±50
Languages: English, Pitcairnese
Religion: Seventh-Day Adventist
Currency: New Zealand dollar
Exports: Fruit, vegetables, stamps, curios.

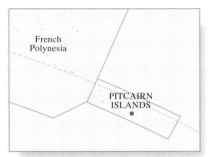

French Polynesia

PITCAIRN ISLANDS

The flag of this remote British overseas territory is the Blue Ensign with the Pitcairn Islands arms at the fly. The green triangle on the shield represents the rugged islands rising from the sea. The anchor, representing security, and a depiction of the Bible are references to HMS *Bounty*, as the Pitcairn community was founded after the famous mutiny in 1790. As a crest, a wooden Pitcairn wheelbarrow stands for vigour and industry. Also depicted is a branch of the miro plant, from which souvenirs are carved for sale to visitors. The territory, which includes Ducie and Oeno islands and the uninhabited coral atoll of Henderson Islands, lies some 3500km (2170mi) northeast of New Zealand and falls under the British high commissioner in that country.

NEW ZEALAND

New Zealand

Flag proportions: 1:2
Adopted: 12 June 1902
Capital: Wellington
Area: 270,534km² (104,454mi²)
Population: 4 million
Language: English, Maori
Religion: Christian
Currency: New Zealand dollar
Exports: Meat, dairy products, wool, fish, fruit, vegetables, wood, aluminium, machinery.

Pacific Ocean

NEW ZEALAND

Tasman Sea

New Zealand was discovered around 800AD by Polynesian navigators, who named it *Aotearoa*, 'Land of the Long White Cloud'. In 1642, Dutch explorer Abel Tasman sailed along the west coast, and in 1769 Captain James Cook claimed the country for the British crown. The first flag, chosen by Maori chiefs in 1834, consisted of a red St George's cross, with another cross and four stars on a blue field in the chief canton. After the Treaty of Waitangi in 1840, in which the Maori ceded sovereignty to Britain in exchange for guaranteed possession of their land, the Union Flag became the official flag. The present flag originated in 1869 as a Blue Ensign for maritime use only, but became the national flag in 1902. The Union Flag is in the chief canton; the Southern Cross on the fly is made up of four white-bordered red stars with five points, no two stars being the same size.

New Zealand overseas territories

Tokelau

Niue

Cook Islands

North America, Central America and the Caribbean

Originally only lightly populated by native Americans, the great northern continent was settled by Europeans (chiefly Spanish, French and British) from the mid-16th century. One of the earliest settlements, at St Augustine, Florida, was founded in 1565. The same mix of explorers and adventurers, seeking a westward route to India, encountered the Caribbean islands and the isthmus of Central America, where the Spanish influence remains dominant. In 1513 the Spaniard Vasco Núñez de Balboa crossed the isthmus and saw the Pacific Ocean. However, reaching the Pacific required either an arduous overland journey, or a sea journey that involved negotiating the southern tip of South America via the tempestuous Magellan Straits and Cape Horn, until the North-West Passage was opened up in 1904 and the Panama Canal began operations in 1914.

The heart of the region, in terms of both influence and population, is the United States. From the early 19th century, industrialization in Europe, as well as dynastic and social upheavals, led to a build-up of emigration to North America, principally to the USA, a flow of humanity that continued to within a few decades of the new millennium.

In 1994 the North American Free Trade Agreement (NAFTA) was implemented. The participants in this system of beneficial inter-dependence are the USA, Canada and Mexico, and the objectives are similar in principle to those in other parts of the world. Prospective benefits include the creation of new jobs, higher wages in Mexico, on-going environmental clean-ups and improved health. Whether or not NAFTA has improved the standard of life in this part of the global village is a matter of some contention.

The Stars and Stripes finds visual echoes in several flags, including that of Cuba, one of the battlefields of the Spanish-American War of 1898. The same conflict resulted in the American acquisition of Puerto Rico, with its colour-reversed version of the Cuban flag.

The flags of Central America share features that attest to a common history of colonization, revolution and liberation. Most of these countries, including Mexico, which shares a border with the USA, were profoundly influenced, ideologically, by revolutions in France in 1848 and earlier, and fought for their own liberation from conservative mother countries, an attainment too often followed by civil wars.

Colonization in the Caribbean depended on a plantation economy based squarely on slave labour and, even after emancipation, on frank exploitation. Most slaves on the islands, and in the southern states and territories of North America, were brought from West Africa, and their descendants and influence are still prominent today. While the islands explore alternative bases for their economies, such as tourism, mining, fishing and limited agriculture, most maintain grateful economic links with the former colonial power.

The French presence was most noted in the north, where Canada forms the northern border of the USA. This vast country stretches from the Atlantic in the east to the Pacific in the west. French influence was also marked in the southern USA, especially in conjunction with the territory known as the Louisiana Purchase.

In terms of area, Canada is slightly larger than the USA: 10 million sq km to 9.6 million sq km, but the population of the USA, at around 290 million, is about nine times that of Canada. After Russia, Canada is the second largest country in the world. Mexico measures some 1.9 million sq km and has a population of 105 million. Some of the island states of the Caribbean have a habitable area of only a few dozen square kilometres, while others, although small in total area, are spread over a number of separate land entities.

The countries whose flags are described in this section extend from several degrees north of the Equator to well into the Arctic Circle, and from around 55 to 170 degrees West.

North America

Central America and Caribbean

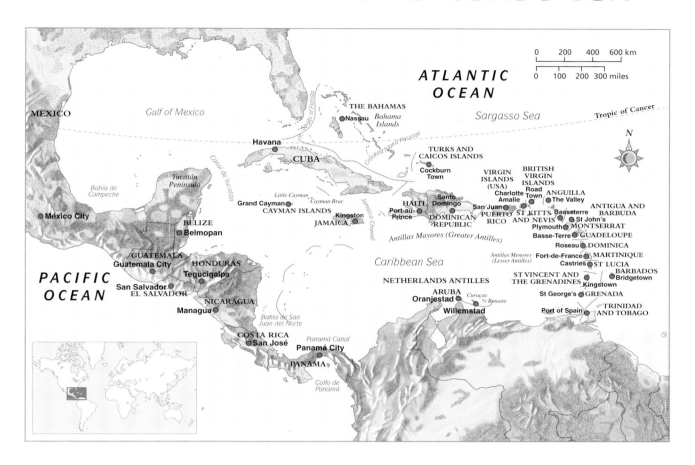

ATLANTIC OCEAN

0 200 400 600 km
0 100 200 300 miles

MEXICO

Gulf of Mexico

Straits of Florida

THE BAHAMAS

●Nassau *Bahama Islands*

Sargasso Sea

Tropic of Cancer

N

Havana

Canal de Yucatán

CUBA

Crooked Island Passage

TURKS AND CAICOS ISLANDS

Cockburn Town

VIRGIN ISLANDS (USA)

BRITISH VIRGIN ISLANDS

Road Town

ANGUILLA

Bahía de Campeche

Yucatán Peninsula

Little Cayman

Cayman Brac

Charlotte Amalie

The Valley

ANTIGUA AND BARBUDA

●México City

BELIZE
●Belmopan

Grand Cayman●

CAYMAN ISLANDS

Kingston

JAMAICA

HAITI

Jamaica Channel

Port-au-Prince

Santo Domingo

San Juan

PUERTO RICO

ST KITTS AND NEVIS

Basseterre

●St John's

DOMINICAN REPUBLIC

Plymouth MONTSERRAT

Basse-Terre● GUADELOUPE

Roseau● DOMINICA

Antillas Mayores (Greater Antilles)

Caribbean Sea

Antillas Menores (Lesser Antilles)

Fort-de-France● MARTINIQUE

Castries● ST LUCIA

BARBADOS

GUATEMALA
Guatemala City●

HONDURAS

●Tegucigalpa

NETHERLANDS ANTILLES

ST VINCENT AND THE GRENADINES

Bridgetown

PACIFIC OCEAN

San Salvador●

EL SALVADOR

NICARAGUA

●Managua

Bahía de San Juan del Norte

ARUBA

Oranjestad●

Curaçao

Bonaire

Willemstad

Kingstown

St George's● GRENADA

TRINIDAD AND TOBAGO

Port of Spain●

COSTA RICA

●San José

Panamá Canal

Panamá City●

PANAMA

Golfo de Panamá

NORTH AMERICA AT A GLANCE

Number of countries: 36

Largest country: Canada

Smallest country: St Kitts and Nevis

Largest city: Mexico City, Mexico

Major cities: Acapulco, Atlanta, Chicago, Dallas, Havana, Los Angeles, Managua, Montréal, Nassau, New York, Ottawa, Panama City, San Juan, San Salvador, Seattle, Toronto, Vancouver

Highest point: Mt McKinley, Alaska, USA (6194m/20,320ft)

Lowest point: Death Valley, California, USA (86m/282ft below sea level)

Longest river: Mississippi-Missouri, USA (6018km/3740mi)

Largest lake: Lake Superior, Canada (82,100km²/31,699mi²).

USA AT A GLANCE

Number of states: 50

Largest state: Alaska

Smallest state: Rhode Island

Capital: Washington DC (District of Columbia)

Ten largest US cities (in order of size): New York, Los Angeles, Chicago, Houston, Philadelphia, Phoenix, San Antonio, San Diego, Dallas, Detroit

Largest lake: Lake Superior (82,100km²/31,699mi²)

Longest river: Mississippi-Missouri (6018km/3740mi)

Highest point: Mt McKinley (Denali), Alaska, (6194m/20,320ft); Mt Whitney, California (4418m/14,494ft) is the highest point in the lower 48 states

Lowest point: Death Valley, Ca. (86m/282ft below sea level).

UNITED STATES OF AMERICA

United States of America

Flag proportions: 10:19
Adopted: 4 July 1960
Capital: Washington DC
Area: 9,6 million km²
(3,7 million mi²)
Population: 290 million
Language: English
Religion: Protestant, Roman Catholic, Jewish
Currency: Dollar
Exports: Machinery, motor vehicles, foodstuffs, aircraft, weapons, chemicals, computers, electronic goods.

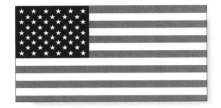

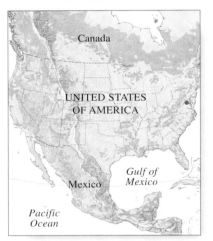

The USA grew from 13 colonies that, after years of tension, rose against the British government in April 1775. On New Year's Day 1776 a flag was raised. Called the Continental Colours, it had the British Union Flag in the chief canton and 13 horizontal stripes (variously red and white, or red, white and blue). On 14 June 1777 Congress adopted the first official flag, placing 13 white stars in the canton. In May 1795, when two more states joined the Union, two stars and stripes were added, making 15 of each. This version, known as the 'Star-Spangled Banner', was left unchanged until Congress passed the Flag Act of 1818 decreeing that while new stars might be added, the number of stripes was to revert to 13. The current Stars and Stripes has 50 stars, each representing a state, and 13 stripes, for the original colonies. The official date for adding a new star is 4 July. The last star was added in 1960, for Hawaii, which joined the USA in 1959.

The way the stars were used in the 1777 flag broke with traditional design and set a precedent for many nations' flags.

US State Flags

Date given is when the state joined the Union or ratified the Constitution.

Alabama
1819

Alaska
1959

Arizona
1912

Arkansas
1836

California
1850

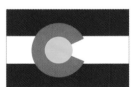

Colorado
1876

Connecticut
1788

Delaware
1787

District of Columbia
(Federal Territory)

Florida
1845

Georgia
1788

Hawaii
1959

Idaho
1890

Illinois
1818

Indiana
1816

Iowa
1846

Kansas
1861

Kentucky
1792

Louisiana
1812

Maine
1820

Maryland
1788

Massachusetts
1788

Michigan
1837

Minnesota
1858

Mississippi
1817

Missouri
1821

Montana
1889

Nebraska
1867

Nevada
1864

New Hampshire
1788

New Jersey
1787

New Mexico
1912

New York
1788

North Carolina
1789

North Dakota
1889

Ohio
1803

Oklahoma
1907

Oregon
1859

Pennsylvania
1787

Rhode Island
1790

South Carolina
1788

South Dakota
1889

Tennessee
1796

Texas
1845

Utah
1896

Vermont
1791

Virginia
1788

Washington
1889

West Virginia
1863

Wisconsin
1848

Wyoming
1890

CANADA

Canada

Flag proportions: 1:2
Adopted: 15 February 1965
Capital: Ottawa
Area: 10 million km² (4 million mi²)
Population: 31,5 million
Languages: English, French
Religion: Catholic, Protestant
Currency: Canadian dollar
Exports: Motor vehicles and parts, machinery, equipment, industrial goods and materials, forestry products.

In 1867, four Canadian provinces, Ontario, Nova Scotia, New Brunswick and Quebec, united to form the Dominion of Canada, but it was to be almost 100 years before this vast country flew its own flag. During that time it used a version of the British Red Ensign with the arms of Canada on a shield at the fly. When designs for a national flag were called for in the 1960s, a popular version (named Pearson's Pennant after its designer) had a sprig of three red maple leaves between blue bands. The version eventually approved shows a single stylized red maple leaf on a white square, between two vertical bands of red. White represents the snow that covers much of the country in winter; red is for energy and in memory of heroic sacrifices made by Canadian servicemen in the two world wars.

Canadian provinces and territories

Date given is date of entry into the Confederation.

Alberta
1905

British Columbia
1871

Manitoba
1870

New Brunswick
1867

Newfoundland and Labrador
1949

Northwest Territories
1870

Nova Scotia
1867

Nunavut
1999

Ontario
1867

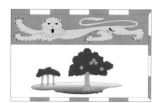

Prince Edward Island
1873

Quebec
1867

Saskatchewan
1905

Yukon Territory
1898

ST PIERRE ET MIQUELON

Saint Pierre and Miquelon

Flag proportions: 2:3
Adopted: c.1980
Capital: Saint-Pierre
Area: 242km² (93mi²)
Population: 7000
Language: French
Religion: Roman Catholic
Currency: Euro
Exports: Fish and fish products, crabs and lobster, animal feed.

There are eight islands in this French overseas territory off the southern coast of Newfoundland. The last remnant of France's North American empire, it was settled in the 17th century by Basque and Breton fisherman. The unofficial flag is rich in heraldry. A high-prowed galleon under full sail recalls French explorer, Jacques Cartier, who discovered the St Lawrence River in 1535. Blue depicts the Atlantic Ocean and the sky. The three emblems at the hoist commemorate the first colonists. In the chief canton, the Basque country is denoted by a green cross in saltire overlaid by a white cross, both on a red field. Brittany is represented by ermine, a fur, while Normandy is represented by two yellow lions *passant gardant*. Similar lions are depicted on the arms of England.

BERMUDA

Bermuda

Flag proportions: 1:2
Adopted: October 1967
Capital: Hamilton
Area: 54km² (21mi²)
Population: 64,500
Language: English
Religion: Christian
Currency: Bermudan dollar
Exports: Pharmaceuticals, flowers. Tourism and banking are important parts of the economy.

Bermuda, a self-governing British overseas territory, consists of some 138 coral islands in the Atlantic, about 20 of which are linked by bridges and causeways. An upmarket tourist destination and financial services centre, it enjoys one of the highest per capita incomes in the world. Many former British colonies fly a Blue or Red Ensign, usually 'defaced', that is, with the Union Flag in the canton and the badge of the colony at the fly. The Bermudan arms, granted in 1910, show a lion supporting a shield on which is displayed the wreck of the *Sea Venture*. The loss of this sailing ship off Bermuda in 1609, and the subsequent dispatch of assistance from the mainland colony of Virginia, led to British colonization of the islands.

United Provinces of Central America

In 1823, following their secession from the Mexican Empire, the Spanish provinces of Guatemala, Honduras, El Salvador, Nicaragua and Costa Rica formed the United Provinces of Central America (also known as the Central American Federation). The political union was more apparent than real, and by 1838 it had fallen apart.

The United Provinces adopted a common flag of two horizontal blue bands separated by a white band, all of equal width. While it might be believed that the blue-white-blue colours represented the isthmus of land bounded on each side by an ocean, the flag actually derived from that of Argentina (see p131), whose revolutionaries had tried to promote Central American independence.

Today, the flags of Honduras, El Salvador and Nicaragua retain the colours and pattern of the original flag, but each country has differentiated it in its own way. Costa Rica has put a red stripe in the middle, Nicaragua and El Salvador depict their coats of arms, Honduras has added five stars, and Guatemala has placed the stripes vertically.

All the flags, except that of Guatemala, have common elements on their coats of arms – mountains (or volcanoes) with a sea on each side, the cap of liberty, a rainbow, stars, and the inscription 'America Central'. The triangle symbolizes equality, while the white band represents the purity of the fatherland.

MEXICO

United Mexican States
Flag proportions: 4:7
Adopted: 23 November 1968
Capital: México City
Area: 1,972,550km² (761,602mi²)
Population: 105 million
Language: Spanish
Religion: Roman Catholic
Currency: Peso
Exports: Manufactured goods, crude oil and related products, agricultural products.

The flag has three equal vertical bands of green (at the hoist), red (at the fly) and white (in the centre, with the coat of arms). Within a wreath, an eagle perched on a cactus plant, clasping a snake in its beak and claw, illustrates the Aztec legend of the founding of Tenochtitlan (México City) in 1325. When Mexico adopted its flag in 1821, green represented religion, white was for independence, and red for unity between the Spanish and the ethnic people. Since Liberal reform in 1860, green has stood for hope, white for ethnicity, unity and purity, and red for the struggle for freedom and the blood of heroes. Green is also for natural resources.

The Mexican flag is distinguished from that of Italy (see p59) by the addition of the arms.

GUATEMALA

Republic of Guatemala
Flag proportions: 5:8
Adopted: 26 December 1997
Capital: Guatemala City
Area: 108,889km² (42,042mi²)
Population: 13,7 million
Language: Spanish
Religion: Catholic, Protestant
Currency: Quetzal
Exports: Coffee, sugar, bananas, cardamom.

In 1823, following the overthrow of the Mexican Empire, Guatemala joined five former Spanish provinces in the United Provinces of Central America (see opposite), before becoming independent in 1823.

The flag is a vertical tricolour of light blue, for justice and steadfastness, and white for purity. The civil flag is plain, but the state flag depicts the national arms. Crossed swords and rifles with fixed bayonets represent justice and liberty. A scroll, inscribed 'Libertad 15 de Septiembre de 1821', commemorates independence. A quetzal bird (*Pharomacrus mocinno*), which cannot live in captivity, symbolizes the nation's liberty. Success and victory are represented by two branches of laurel.

HONDURAS

Republic of Honduras
Flag proportions: 1:2
Adopted: 16 February 1866
Capital: Tegucigalpa
Area: 112,492km² (43,433mi²)
Population: 6,4 million
Language: Spanish
Religion: Roman Catholic
Currency: Lempira
Exports: Bananas, coffee, fruit, sugar, shrimp and lobster, lead, zinc, meat, timber.

Honduras was part of the great Mayan civilization whose city-states, centered on the Yucatán Peninsula and Guatemalan highlands, reached their zenith from about 300 to 900AD and endured until the Spanish conquest in the early 16th century. Discovered by Christopher Columbus, Honduras become a Spanish colony from 1526 until 1821, and was part of the United Provinces of Central America until 1838. The blue and white horizontal tribar derives from the United Provinces flag, with the five stars at the centre representing the former provinces. Blue represents sky and brotherhood, while white is for peace and purity.

EL SALVADOR

Republic of El Salvador

Flag proportions: 4:7
Adopted: September 1972
Capital: San Salvador
Area: 21,041km² (8124mi²)
Population: 6 million
Language: Spanish
Religion: Roman Catholic
Currency: Colón
Exports: Coffee, cotton, sugar.

El Salvador, tucked between mountains and the Pacific, is the smallest country in central America. The flag recalls the 1823 flag of the United Provinces of Central America. On a central white panel, behind a triangle representing the three branches of government (judicial, legislative and executive), are blue-and-white striped flags depicting the five provinces. Five volcanoes rise from the sea, and above their craters are a cap of liberty and a rainbow, the symbol of trust and hope. The arms are enclosed by a wreath tied in the national colours. The motto *Dios, Union, Libertad*, 'God, Unity and Freedom' (Liberty), is on a scroll beneath the triangle. The full name of the country encircles the arms.

NICARAGUA

Republic of Nicaragua

Flag proportions: 3:5
Adopted: 27 August 1971
Capital: Managua
Area: 130,682km² (50,456mi²)
Population: 5,6 million
Language: Spanish
Religion: Roman Catholic
Currency: Cordoba
Exports: Coffee, meat, cotton, sugar, seafood, bananas, chemical products.

Before the Spanish conquest, the Olmec, Maya and Aztec civilizations dominated Central America. The first European to reach Nicaragua, Gil Gonzalez de Avila, claimed the land for Spain in 1522. It remained under Spanish rule until 1821, then joined the United Provinces (see p112) until independence in 1838, hence the familiar blue-white-blue horizontal tribar of the flag. The arms are set within a triangle, the symbol of equality. Five volcanoes represent the members of the United Provinces, the sun and rainbow symbolize a bright future, and a cap of liberty stands for national freedom. Everything is encased within a circle made up of the name: Republica de Nicaragua, America Central.

COSTA RICA

Republic of Costa Rica

Flag proportions: 3:5
Adopted: 5 May 1998
Capital: San José
Area: 51,100km² (19,730mi²)
Population: 4 million
Language: Spanish
Religion: Roman Catholic
Currency: Costa Rican colón
Exports: Manufactured goods, coffee, bananas, sugar, cocoa.

Costa Rica signed a Declaration of Independence from Spain in 1821 and was part of the United Provinces from 1823–38. The wife of the president is said to have designed the flag in 1848 to embody the ideals of the French Revolution: freedom, equality and brotherhood, and the colours of the *Tricolore*.

The current flag has five horizontal stripes. The national arms are set within a white oval on the central red stripe, towards the hoist. Blue is for the sky, striving, intellectual thinking, perseverance and spiritual ideals. White is for happiness, wisdom and peace. Red is for the warmth, passion and generosity of the Costa Rican people, and their blood shed for freedom.

BELIZE

Belize
Flag proportions: 3:5
Adopted: 21 September 1981
Capital: Belmopan
Area: 22,965km² (8867mi²)
Population: 252,000
Language: English, Spanish
Religion: Roman Catholic,
Protestant
Currency: Belize dollar
Exports: Sugar, clothing, citrus
fruit, fish, bananas.

The Belize flag comprises a blue field with a narrow red border at top and bottom. The colours are those of the leading political parties. At the centre of the blue panel, on a white disk, are the national arms, set within a circle of 50 leaves as a reminder that the People's United Party introduced the flag in 1950. The arms were granted in 1907 to British Honduras, as the country was formerly known. They retain some of their original features, depicting tools used in forestry and ship-building, and a mahogany tree for the logging industry. Two supporters, a Creole and a Mestizo, signify both diversity and joint effort. The national motto, *Sub umbra floreo*, means 'I flourish in the shade'.

PANAMA

Republic of Panama
Flag proportions: 2:3
Adopted: 4 June 1904
Capital: Panama City
Area: 77,082km² (29,761mi²)
Population: 3 million
Language: Spanish
Religion: Roman Catholic,
Protestant
Currency: Balboa
Exports: Bananas, shellfish,
sugar, clothing, coffee.

When Panama's flag was created in 1903, it was baptized by Reverend Bernardino de la Concepción. The flag was designed by the then president, Manuel Amador Guerrero, and the first example was made by his wife. Panama's political affiliations are represented on the flag by blue (Conservatives) and red (Liberals). White symbolizes the hope for peace through closer understanding between political adversaries.

Another explanation is that blue depicts the Pacific Ocean and the Caribbean, while red is for blood shed by Panamanian patriots. The five-pointed blue star stands for the civic virtue of honest administration and the red star for lawful authority.

Panama Canal

'The land divided, the world united' is the slogan of the Panama Canal Authority, which operates this 'short cut' between the Atlantic and Pacific oceans. Panama was visited by Christopher Columbus in 1502, and in 1513, Spaniard Vasco Núñez de Balboa crossed the Darien isthmus and realized how narrow the land bridge was.

It was the mid-19th century before a canal was seriously considered. A French company began work in 1881 but poor planning drove them into bankruptcy. In 1901 the USA obtained the right to build a canal through Panama or Nicaragua. Panama, then part of Colombia, declared independence on 3 November 1903. The USA backed the new republic and, on 17 November, a treaty was signed granting the USA control of the Canal Zone in perpetuity, in return for a sum of US$10 million and an annual payment. The canal was built between 1904 and 1914. It extends for 64km (41mi) from Limón Bay, at Colón on the Atlantic, to Balboa on the Pacific (a total of 82km/51 miles including the access channels at both ends).

En route, ships pass through three sets of locks and traverse the man-made Gatún Lake and the narrow Gaillard Cut, a channel carved between sheer cliffs. The high-level Bridge of the Americas, on the Pacific end, keeps road traffic flowing along the transcontinental Pan-American highway.

The Panama Canal Zone is a neutral administrative territory guaranteed by a 1979 treaty. It extends for 5km (3mi) on either side of the waterway. After years of negotiations, the USA returned control of the canal to Panama on 31 December 1999.

BAHAMAS

Commonwealth of the Bahamas

Flag proportions: 1:2
Adopted: 10 July 1973
Capital: Nassau
Area: 13,939km² (5382mi²)
Population: 266,000
Language: English
Religion: Christian
Currency: Bahamian dollar
Exports: Oil products, chemicals, fish, rum, salt.

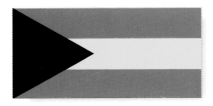

A former pirate base, the Bahamas was a British colony from 1783 to independence in 1973. Situated some 80km (50mi) southeast of Florida, it comprises 3000 islands, only 22 of which are inhabited. The black triangle at the hoist represents the energy, force and determination of the population, while the equal horizontal bands of blue, gold, blue symbolize the country's warm seas and sunny beaches. In a competition to design the flag, many entries depicted sunrise, which has been incorporated into the national arms.

Many merchant ships are registered in the Bahamas and fly the civil ensign – a red field quartered by a white cross, with the Bahamian flag in the chief canton.

TURKS AND CAICOS

Turks and Caicos Islands

Flag proportions: 1:2
Adopted: 7 November 1968
Capital: Cockburn Town
Area: 430km² (166mi²)
Population: 20,000
Language: English, French Creole
Religion: Christian
Currency: US dollar
Exports: Lobster, dried and fresh conch and conch shells.

This archipelago of 40 islands (eight inhabited) southeast of the Bahamas is a British overseas territory. Most smaller overseas territories (formerly crown colonies) use the British Blue Ensign, with the colony's arms or shield depicted at the fly. Some older ensigns show the arms on a white disc, but the arms are now mostly placed directly against the blue field. The arms of Turks and Caicos show a queen conch shell, once widely used for currency; a spiny lobster, the basis of a major industry; and a Turk's Head cactus, one of many plants unique to the islands, all on a yellow shield.

CUBA

Republic of Cuba

Flag proportions: 1:2
Adopted: 20 May 1902
Capital: Havana (La Habana)
Area: 114,524km² (44,237mi²)
Population: 11,8 million
Language: Spanish
Religion: Roman Catholic, Protestant
Currency: Cuban peso
Exports: Sugar, minerals, fish, tobacco, citrus fruit.

In 1849 a group of Cuban exiles approved a proposal from Miguel Teurbe Tolón for a flag to be used in the attempt to liberate their island from Spanish rule. There were other flag proposals in succeeding decades, but Tolón's design, inspired by the US Stars and Stripes, eventually became the national flag of Cuba. In an official description, the blue bars represent the three former provinces of the island, white is testimony to the purity of the ideal of independence, the triangle signifies liberty, equality and fraternity, and the star symbolizes freedom and independence, attained by spilling the blood of patriots, whose sacrifices are recalled by the red triangle.

Puerto Rico's flag (see p117) is similar to that of Cuba, but with reversed colours.

JAMAICA

Jamaica

Flag proportions: 1:2
Adopted: 6 August 1962
Capital: Kingston
Area: 11,425km² (4411mi²)
Population: 2,7 million
Language: English
Religion: Protestant, Roman Catholic
Currency: Jamaican dollar
Exports: Alumina, bauxite, sugar, bananas, beverages, tobacco.

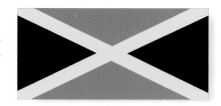

Yellow stands for sunshine and natural resources, black for the burdens borne by the people, and green for agriculture and hope for the future. An unofficial motto is the saying: 'Hardships there are, but the land is green and the sun still shineth'. Black, green and gold are Pan-African colours, and most Jamaicans are descended from black people who were brought from Africa as slaves.

Jamaica is a constitutional monarchy. A royal standard for HM Queen Elizabeth II, ruler of Jamaica, incorporates the red cross of St George on a white field. A ring of roses encloses a crowned 'E'. In each quarter of the cross is a pineapple, taken from the island's coat of arms, one of the oldest colonial arms, granted in 1661.

CAYMAN ISLANDS

Cayman Islands

Flag proportions: 1:2
Adopted: 24 November 1988
Capital: George Town
Area: 262km² (101mi²)
Population: 42,000
Language: English
Religion: Christian
Currency: Caymanian dollar
Exports: Turtle products. Tourism and offshore banking are the main revenue earners.

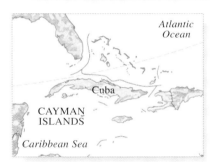

The low-lying Grand Cayman, Cayman Brac and Little Cayman islands were a pirate lair from the 17th century. Colonized by Britain, the Caymans were a dependency of Jamaica until they became a crown colony (now an overseas territory) in 1962. The flag is the Blue Ensign with the Cayman arms, granted in 1958, on the fly. Three stars represent the islands, the lion signifies the link with Britain; a turtle and a pineapple represent the local fauna and flora, and blue and white wavy bars depict the sea. A scroll bears the motto 'He hath founded it upon the seas', in tribute to the islands' origins.

PUERTO RICO

Commonwealth of Puerto Rico

Flag proportions: 2:3
Adopted: 24 July 1952
Capital: San Juan
Area: 9104km² (3515mi²)
Population: 3,9 million
Language: English, Spanish
Religion: Roman Catholic
Currency: US dollar
Exports: Chemicals, electronics, clothing, beverage concentrates, canned tuna, rum, medical equipment.

Claimed by Spain in 1493 after Columbus's second voyage to the Americas, the island became a colonial possession for 400 years, during which the indigenous population was nearly exterminated, and African slave labour introduced. The 1898 Spanish-American war resulted in the cession of Puerto Rico to the USA. Puerto Ricans were granted US citizenship in 1917 and, despite calls for US statehood, have repeatedly chosen to retain their commonwealth status.

Puerto Rico's flag resembles that of Cuba (see p116), with the colours reversed, as both were originally designed as anti-Spanish, pro-US emblems. The five-pointed star represents the country, and the triangle proclaims the republican ideals of liberty, equality and fraternity.

HAITI

Republic of Haiti

Flag proportions: 3:5
Adopted: 25 February 1986
Capital: Port-au-Prince
Area: 27,750km² (10,714mi²)
Population: 8,3 million
Language: French, Creole
Religion: Roman Catholic
Currency: Gourde
Exports: Manufactured articles, coffee, essential oils, sisal.

A French colony from 1697, Haiti proclaimed independence in 1804, following a rebellion the previous year. Haitian leaders in the independence struggle created a blue and red flag on 18 May 1803, by removing the white stripe from the *Tricolore*. The two stripes symbolized the black and mixed-race peoples of the country. In 1840 the stripes were made horizontal and the coat of arms placed at the centre. Haiti's arms include cannons and cannon balls, trumpets, a drum, and muskets with fixed bayonets, backed by six Haitian flags. A palm surmounted by a cap of liberty symbolizes independence. The weapons indicate a willingness to fight for freedom. The motto, *L'Union Fait La Force*, means 'Union Makes Strength.'

DOMINICAN REPUBLIC

Dominican Republic

Flag proportions: 5:8
Adopted: 21 August 1943
Capital: Santo Domingo
Area: 48,442km² (18,700mi²)
Population: 9 million
Language: Spanish
Religion: Roman Catholic
Currency: Peso Oro
Exports: Sugar, molasses, coffee, cocoa, tobacco, gold, silver, ferronickel.

In 1844, a group known as the Trinitarians, who were fighting to liberate their country from Haitian rule, changed the Haitian flag by quartering it with a white cross, to signify the Catholic faith, and altering the colours so the first and fourth quarters are blue, and the second and third quarters red. This is the civil flag, as flown by citizens on land and at sea, but for national and state use the coat of arms is placed at the centre of the cross. A shield, of the same pattern as the flag, is behind a trophy of Dominican flags supporting a crucifix and a Bible, open at St John's Gospel. Blue is said to stand for liberty, red is for the fire and blood of the independence struggle and the white cross is a symbol of sacrifice.

VIRGIN ISLANDS

Virgin Islands of the United States

Flag proportions: 2:3 or 3:5
Adopted: 17 May 1921
Capital: Charlotte Amalie
Area: 352km² (136mi²)
Population: 125,000
Language: English, Spanish
Religion: Christian
Currency: US dollar
Industries: Tourism is the mainstay of the economy.

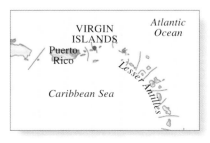

St Thomas, St Croix and St John, plus about 50 small islets, form an unincorporated territory of the USA, with residents electing a governor and legislature. From the 18th century, the Virgin Islands were owned by England and Denmark, but the USA purchased the Danish portion in 1917.

The emblem is partly derived from the US arms. It consists of a bald eagle on a white field, displayed *affronté* (showing its front), with its head turned to the side, and wings and legs spread. In its dexter (right) talon it clasps a laurel branch, and in its sinister (left) talon three arrows, representing the main islands. On its front is a shield with a blue chief (upper portion) and seven white and six red vertical stripes. The initials V and I, on either side of the eagle, stand for Virgin Islands.

BRITISH VIRGIN ISLANDS

British Virgin Islands
Flag proportions: 1:2
Adopted: 15 November 1960
Capital: Road Town
Area: 153km² (59mi²)
Population: 22,000
Language: English
Religion: Christian
Currency: US dollar
Exports: Rum, fruit, fresh fish. Tourism is the main industry.

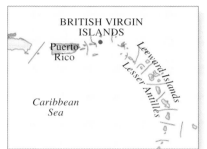

The Virgin Islands, the northernmost of the Leeward Islands in the Antilles, were discovered by Columbus in 1494. As they seemed innumerable, he named them after the followers of St Ursula who, with 11,000 virgin companions, was martyred during the Dark Ages. Settled by the Dutch in 1648, the islands were annexed by Britain in 1672. A self-governing overseas territory of the UK, the British Virgin Islands (BVI) comprise Tortola, Virgin Gorda, Anegada, Jost van Dykes and about 40 islets. The economy is closely linked to the nearby US Virgin Islands. Set on the Blue Ensign, the badge of the BVI, which dates from 1960, shows St Ursula holding a lamp. The 11 lamps alongside symbolize her followers. The Latin motto on the scroll reads *Vigilate* (be watchful).

ANGUILLA

Anguilla
Flag proportions: 1:2
Adopted: 30 May 1990
Capital: The Valley
Area: 102km² (39mi²)
Population: 13,000
Language: English, Creole
Religion: Christian
Currency: East Caribbean dollar
Exports: Lobster, fish, livestock, salt, concrete blocks, rum. Tourism and offshore banking are mainstays of the economy.

A British colony from 1650, Anguilla declared itself a republic in 1967, following a dispute against incorporation with St Christopher-Nevis. Since 1980, it has been a dependency (now an overseas territory) of the UK. The flag's design originated with a former Governor of Anguilla, and was submitted to London for approval before being put into use. When a British Red or Blue Ensign carries a depiction of a badge or coat of arms at the fly, the ensign is said to be 'defaced'. Anguilla's flag is the Blue Ensign defaced with a shield on which three dolphins leap on a white field (their interlocking circular design represents unity and strength) above a wavy turquoise base, symbolizing the Caribbean Sea.

ST KITTS AND NEVIS

Federation of St Christopher-Nevis
Flag proportions: 2:3
Adopted: 19 September 1983
Capital: Basseterre
Area: 261km² (101mi²)
Population: 39,000
Language: English
Religion: Christian
Currency: East Caribbean dollar
Exports: Sugar, manufactured products, postage stamps.

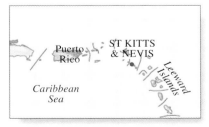

Named by Columbus in 1493, St Christopher (St Kitts) became Britain's first West Indian colony in 1623; Nevis was settled soon afterwards. Part of the Leeward Islands' Federation from 1871–1956, the islands formed a colony with the British Virgin Islands until 1960, were granted self-government in 1967, and gained independence within the Commonwealth in September 1983. The flag uses Pan-African colours (see p34), with green for the land's fertility, red for the struggle from slavery through colonialism to independence, yellow for year-round sunshine and black for the peoples' African heritage. Two white stars on the black diagonal band are said to represent the islands, but actually express hope and freedom.

ANTIGUA AND BARBUDA

State of Antigua and Barbuda

Flag proportions: 2:3
Adopted: 27 February 1967
Capital: St John's
Area: 442km² (171mi²)
Population: 69,500
Language: English
Religion: Christian
Currency: East Caribbean dollar
Industries: Tourism, construction, light manufacturing.

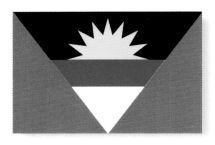

Antigua and Barbuda were British colonies from 1632 until independence in 1981. When the colony received self-government in 1967, a competition was held to design a new flag and more than 600 local people submitted entries. The winning designer, Reginald Samuel, described the flag as depicting a sun of hope rising in a new era, set against the background of the peoples' African heritage. The letter 'V' formed by the red triangles foretells victory, and red symbolizes the energy of the people. Blue represents the all-surrounding sea and white is for hope.

MONTSERRAT

Montserrat

Flag proportions: 1:2
Adopted: 1960
Capital: Plymouth (abandoned)
Area: 102km² (39mi²)
Population: 9000
Language: English
Religion: Christian
Currency: East Caribbean dollar
Exports: The economy has been severely hampered by volcanic activity since 1995.

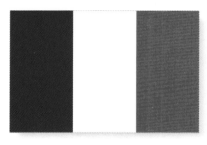

Montserrat, in the Leeward Islands, was named by Columbus in 1493 for an eponymous mountain in northeast Spain (*monte serrado*, jagged mountain). It became a British crown colony in 1871 and is now an overseas territory. The Blue Ensign is set with the island's badge at the fly. Comprising a shield on a white disc, it depicts a woman in an ankle-length garment, standing on a reddish-brown base (perhaps a beach) beneath a blue sky. Recalling the arrival of Irish immigrants in 1632, she holds a cross in her right hand and a harp in her left.

In July 1995, the Soufriere Hills volcano began erupting, resulting in widespread devastation. Major volcanic activity in 1997 forced the closure of air and seaports and the evacuation of many islanders.

GUADELOUPE

Department of Guadeloupe

Flag proportions: 2:3
Adopted: 5 March 1848
Capital: Basse-Terre
Area: 1780km² (687mi²)
Population: 440,000
Language: French, Creole
Religion: Roman Catholic
Currency: Euro
Exports: Bananas, sugar, rum. Tourism plays a key role in the economy.

A French possession since 1635, the Guadeloupe archipelago, in the Leeward Islands, consists of nine inhabited islands, the two largest being Basse-Terre and Grande-Terre. It shares one island, with the northern part, Saint-Martin, belonging to Guadeloupe and the southern portion, Sint Maarten, forming part of the Netherlands Antilles.

All French overseas departments fly the *Tricolore* as the official flag. However, a flag representing the department is permitted to be flown alongside the *Tricolore*. Guadeloupe's is horizontally divided, with the lower portion showing a radiant yellow sun and a green sheaf of sugar cane on a black or red field. The upper portion, which is one third of the flag's depth, has three yellow *fleurs de lis* on a blue field.

DOMINICA

Commonwealth of Dominica

Flag proportions: 1:2
Adopted: 3 November 1990
Capital: Roseau
Area: 754km² (291mi²)
Population: 70,000
Language: English, French patois
Religion: Roman Catholic
Currency: East Caribbean dollar
Exports: Bananas, soap, bay oil, vegetables, grapefruit, oranges.

A former French colony, Dominica was ceded to Britain in 1763, became a colony in 1805 and gained independence in 1978. The flag has a green field divided into four by a centred cross of equal stripes of yellow, black and white. Ten green five-pointed stars within a red disc represent Dominica's parishes, or administrative divisions. At the centre of the disc, a sisserou parrot (*Psittacus imperialis*) a bird unique to Dominica, symbolizes flight and the attainment of greater heights in fulfilling ambitions. Green depicts the lush vegetation of the land. The tri-coloured cross represents the Trinity; its colours are yellow for the Carib people and the sunshine, black for the dark, fertile soil and the island's African heritage, and white for rivers and the purity of hope.

MARTINIQUE

Department of Martinique

Flag proportions: 2:3
Adopted: 4 August 1766
Capital: Fort-de-France
Area: 1100km² (424mi²)
Population: 426,000
Language: French, Creole patois
Religion: Roman Catholic
Currency: Euro
Exports: Rum, refined petroleum products, bananas, pineapples.

Discovered by Spanish explorers in 1493, the volcanic island of Martinique became a French colony in 1635. It has been an overseas territory of France since 1972. As such, the official flag is the *Tricolore*, but local use is made of a blue flag quartered with a white cross that was flown by French ships prior to the 1789 Revolution. The flag was rediscovered around 1935 and has since become popular as a local symbol. In each quarter is a rearing snake extending its forked tongue, all in white. The sinuous body of the snake resembles the capital letter 'L', as the flag was that of the former French colony of St Lucia and Martinique and was flown by French merchant ships based on the two islands.

ST LUCIA

St Lucia

Flag proportions: 1:2
Adopted: 27 February 1979
Capital: Castries
Area: 617km² (238mi²)
Population: 156,000
Language: English
Religion: Roman Catholic
Currency: East Caribbean dollar
Exports: Bananas, copra, coconut products, tobacco, beverages.

First settled in 1605, St Lucia was the subject of dispute between Britain and France until 1814, when it was ceded to Britain. It gained independence in 1979. Against a blue field, representing the vast Atlantic Ocean, a yellow triangle overlies the base of a black isosceles triangle outlined in white. The triangles depict two local volcanic peaks, the Pitons, described as 'looking skyward – a symbol of hope'. Yellow is for sunshine, while black and white symbolize the island's dual African and European cultural heritage.

BARBADOS

Barbados

Flag proportions: 2:3

Adopted: 30 November 1966

Capital: Bridgetown

Area: 430km² (166mi²)

Population: 264,000

Language: English

Religion: Protestant, Catholic

Currency: Barbados dollar

Exports: Electrical components, chemicals, foodstuffs, cars and other durables.

Early British settlement, from 1627, was based on a sugar plantation economy. The former crown colony achieved self-government in 1961 and independence in 1966. Vertical bands of blue and golden yellow evoke the sandy shores of Barbados washed by the Atlantic Ocean. The central band bears a trident, which traditionally symbolizes control over the sea. The trident lacks its shaft, indicating the break with the past that came with independence. (The former colonial badge and seal depict the seated figure of Britannia with a shield and trident.)

ST VINCENT AND THE GRENADINES

St Vincent and the Grenadines

Flag proportions: 2:3

Adopted: 22 October 1985

Capital: Kingstown

Area: 389km² (150mi²)

Population: 120,000

Language: English

Religion: Christian

Currency: East Caribbean dollar

Exports: Bananas, other foods.

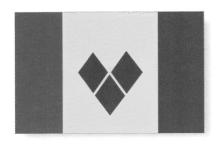

Occupied by Britain from 1762, St Vincent and the adjacent islands of the Grenadines achieved independence in 1979. The flag has a broad yellow vertical band between narrower bands of blue (at the hoist) and green. In the central band, three green diamonds form a 'V' for St Vincent. The diamonds and flag are popularly known as 'the Gems', from the islands' slogan, the 'Gems of the Antilles'. An official description states: 'the diamonds reflect the plural nature of the many islands in the group. Blue represents the sky and sea. Gold is for warmth, the bright spirit of the people and the golden sands of the Grenadines. Green represents the lush vegetation of St Vincent and the enduring vitality of the people.'

GRENADA

State of Grenada

Flag proportions: 1:2

Adopted: 7 February 1974

Capital: St George's

Area: 344km² (133mi²)

Population: 94,000

Language: English

Religion: Catholic, Protestant

Currency: East Caribbean dollar

Exports: Nutmeg, cocoa, mace, bananas, textiles.

Grenada was discovered by Columbus in 1498 and settled by France in 1650. A British colony from 1783, it achieved self-government in 1967 and independence in 1974. Sometimes called the 'Spice Island', Grenada proudly carries a depiction of a nutmeg on its national flag as it is the world's second largest supplier of this pungent spice. The red border symbolizes courage and harmony. Yellow is for the sun and for friendliness, and green for the natural vegetation and agriculture. Stars represent the parishes of Grenada, with the central star, on a red disc, depicting the capital, St George's.

TRINIDAD AND TOBAGO

Republic of Trinidad/Tobago

Flag proportions: 2:3
Adopted: 31 August 1962
Capital: Port of Spain
Area: 5124km² (1978mi²)
Population: 1,3 million
Language: English
Religion: Christian, Hindu, Muslim
Currency: Trinidad/Tobago dollar
Exports: Mineral fuels, lubricants, chemicals, manufactured goods.

Trinidad and Tobago were visited by Columbus in 1498 and colonized by Spain in 1532. Trinidad was ceded to Britain in 1802 and Tobago in 1814. Separate until 1889, they achieved independence within the Commonwealth in 1962, becoming a republic in 1976. The flag's designers explain the colours thus: 'Red ... represents the vitality of land and people, the warmth and energy of the sun, courage and friendliness. White is the sea, by which the islands are bound, the cradle of heritage, the purity of aspirations, and the equality of all men. Black represents the people's dedication. It is the colour of strength, unity, purpose and wealth of the land. The colours represent the elements earth, water and fire which encompass our past, present and future and inspire us as one united, vital, free and dedicated people'.

NETHERLANDS ANTILLES

Nederlandse Antillen

Flag proportions: 2:3
Adopted: 1 January 1986
Capital: Willemstad
Area: 960km² (370mi²)
Population: 216,000
Language: Dutch, English, Papiamento (local dialect)
Religion: Christian, Jewish
Currency: NA guilder
Exports: Petroleum products.

This autonomous territory of the Netherlands consists of five islands: Curaçao and Bonaire off the coast of Venzeuela, and Sint Maarten, Sint Eustatius and Saba in the Leeward Islands. The capital, Willemstad, is on Curaçao.

Each island has its own flag, but St Eustatius uses only the national flag (depicted here). Red, white and blue are the Dutch colours, and the Netherlands Antilles' flag has a white field quartered by a horizontal blue band, one third of the flag's depth, and a vertical red band. The two bands cross at the centre, blue on red, where an elliptical arrangement of five white five-pointed stars represents the islands. There were six stars until Aruba seceded in 1986 (see below).

ARUBA

Aruba

Flag proportions: 2:3
Adopted: 1 January 1986
Capital: Oranjestad
Area: 194km² (75mi²)
Population: 71,000
Language: Papiamento, Dutch, Spanish, English
Religion: Roman Catholic
Currency: Aruban guilder/florin
Exports: Animals and animal products, art and collectibles, machinery, electrical equipment.

Discovered by Spain in 1499, Aruba was claimed by the Dutch in 1636. It seceded from the Netherlands Antilles (see above) in 1986 to become an autonomous member of the Kingdom of the Netherlands. On a field of United Nations' blue are two yellow stripes close to the lower edge of the flag, with a red four-pointed star, outlined in white, in the chief canton. Blue depicts the sky and the Caribbean Sea, the star represents the main languages of Aruba, and the four corners of the earth from which its people have come to settle. The star is also Aruba itself, with its red soils fringed with white beaches. The yellow stripes symbolize the indigenous rain-flower, as well as the sun, tourism and mineral resources that are the mainstay of Aruba's economy.

South America

South America extends from the balmy Caribbean Sea, at about 10° North, to the storm-tossed Strait of Magellan and the majestic Cape Horn, at about 55° South latitude. East to west, its widest point is about five degrees south of where the equator cuts across Brazil and Ecuador. The total area amounts to some 17,8 million sq km (6,8 million sq mi). The continent's states are sometimes loosely referred to as Latin America, from its Spanish and Portuguese language origins. A few northerly states, though, inherited the French, English and Dutch languages.

Portuguese-speaking Brazil, covering an area of 8,51 million sq km (3,3m sq mi) and with a population of some 176 million, represents about half the people and the land of South America. For several decades in the 19th century, Brazil was an empire. Another South American country, Gran Colombia, no longer exists but its colours appear today in the flags of the former component countries — Ecuador, Venezuela and Colombia.

Many South Americans are a blend of Spanish, Portuguese, indigenous Indians, and African slaves (slavery was outlawed in Brazil only from 1871). The great ancient civilization of South America, that of the Incas, had their homeland in the Andes Mountains of Peru. Even today, more than 25 per cent of Peruvians speak the Amerindian languages of Quechua or Aimara rather than the official Spanish.

Many South American countries are well endowed with minerals, oil and natural gas. Agricultural products include coffee, cocoa, meat, fruit, wool and cotton. Despite healthy exports, most states are debtors and their populations comprise a few very wealthy and many very poor. In the north, the trade in illegal drugs, such as cocaine, continues to earn a significant amount of foreign currency.

Geographically, South America is dominated by the Andes range, extending north to south for some 7250km (4500mi), reaching its apex in the towering peak of Aconcagua (6960m/22,834ft) in the Argentinian Andes. Mighty rivers, such as the Amazon and Orinoco, flow eastward through the extensive equatorial rainforests which, vast as they are, are falling prey to slash-and-burn farming and over exploitation. South of the forest zone are the wide, temperate plains, or pampas, of Argentina — cattle country supreme. To the west, a narrow coastal plain of largely arid desert stretches from Peru to Chile.

Detached from the continent, but part of it, are the Falkland Islands, where the prospect of offshore oilfields led to conflict in 1982 between rival claimants, Argentina and Great Britain. Britain retains possession of the islands, called the Malvinas by Argentina, and of unpromising territory, principally research areas, still further south towards Antarctica.

South America

Panama Canal

Caracas

VENEZUELA

Georgetown

GUYANA

Paramaribo

Bogotá

SURINAME

Cayenne

FRENCH GUIANA
(FRANCE)

COLOMBIA

Equator

Quito

ECUADOR

Amazon

BRAZIL

PACIFIC
OCEAN

PERU

Lima

BOLIVIA

Brasília

La Paz

Sucre

PARAGUAY

São Páulo

Tropic of Capricorn

AT A GLANCE

Number of countries: 13

Biggest country: Brazil

Smallest country: Suriname

Biggest city: São Paolo, Brazil

Major cities: Bogotá, Buenos Aires,
Caracas, Quito, Lima, Montevideo,
Rio de Janiero, Santiago

Highest point: Aconcagua, Argentina
(6960m/22,834ft) – the highest peak
in the Western hemisphere.

Lowest point: Valdés Peninsula,
Argentina (40m/131ft below
sea level)

Longest river: Amazon (6516km/
4050mi)

Largest lake: Titicaca, Bolivia/Peru
(8340km²/3220mi²)

Asunción

CHILE

Cerro
Aconcagua

Santiago

6969m
(22834ft)

URUGUAY

Buenos
Aires

Montevideo

ARGENTINA

ATLANTIC
OCEAN

0   500   1000 km

0   250   500 miles

N

FALKLAND ISLANDS
(U.K.)

Falkland Islands
(U.K.)

Stanley

SOUTH GEORGIA
(U.K.)

Grytviken

ECUADOR

Republic of Ecuador

Flag proportions: 1:2
Adopted: 7 November 1900
Capital: Quito
Area: 270,670km² (104,551mi²)
Population: 12,3 million
Language: Spanish
Religion: Roman Catholic, Protestant
Currency: US dollar
Exports: Shrimps, bananas, coffee beans, cocoa beans, cut flowers.

An Inca kingdom before the Spanish conquest in the 16th century, Ecuador joined Gran Colombia (see below) in 1822, seceding from the federation in 1830 to form a republic. The flag is similar to Colombia and Venezuela's flags, but with the national arms at the centre. These incorporate a ship at the mouth of the Guayas River, representing trade and commerce; a sun of liberty; an axe and fasces (bundles of rods) as symbols of republicanism; four signs of the Zodiac, recalling the 1845 revolution; and the snow-capped Mt Chimborazo, surmounted by an Andean condor, signifying courage and freedom. The country takes its name from the equator, which runs through it.

COLOMBIA

Republic of Colombia

Flag proportions: 2:3
Adopted: 26 November 1861
Capital: Bogotá
Area: 1,141,748km² (441,020mi²)
Population: 44 million
Language: Spanish
Religion: Roman Catholic
Currency: Colombian peso
Exports: Coffee, petroleum, mineral products.

A Spanish possession from the 16th century, Colombia was liberated in 1819 by Simón Bolívar, a South American revolutionary leader. In 1822, Ecuador, Colombia and Venezuela formed the republic of Gran Colombia, whose flag is the basis of these nations' flags. Colombia became a separate republic in 1830. The flag is a horizontal tricolour of yellow over blue over red. The blue and red bands each occupy one fourth of the flag's depth, and yellow fills the upper half. Yellow stands for sovereignty and justice; blue for nobility, loyalty and vigilance, and red for courage, honour, and victory achieved by sacrifice. Yellow also represents universal liberty, blue the equality of all races, and red fraternity.

VENEZUELA

Republic of Venezuela

Flag proportions: 2:3
Adopted: 20 April 1936
Capital: Caracas
Area: 916,490km² (353,857mi²)
Population: 24 million
Language: Spanish
Religion: Roman Catholic
Currency: Bolívar
Exports: Petroleum and petroleum products, metals, natural gas, chemicals, motor vehicles, manufactured goods.

Columbus explored the area in 1498 and it was settled by Spain in 1520. The original flag, an equal tricolour of yellow over blue over red, was created by Francisco de Miranda, who freed the country from the Spanish province of New Granada in 1806. Following a rebellion against Spanish rule in 1811, led by Simón Bolívar, Venezuela was part of the republic of Gran Colombia from 1819 until independence in 1830. The present flag, originating from 1864, incorporates seven five-pointed white stars at the centre of the blue band. Each star represents a Venezuelan province that supported the fight against Spain. Blue represents liberty, red represents courage, and yellow is for the original federation of states.

GUYANA

Cooperative Republic of Guyana
Flag proportions: 3:5
Adopted: 20 May 1966
Capital: Georgetown
Area: 214,969km² (83,000mi²)
Population: 861,000
Language: English
Religion: Christian, Hindu, Muslim
Currency: Guyana dollar
Exports: Sugar, gold, bauxite, rice, timber, rum, shrimps.

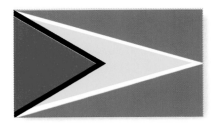

Guyana was ceded from Holland to Britain in 1814, becoming a British colony until independence in 1966, then a republic within the Commonwealth from 1970. The flag, known as the 'Golden Arrow', has five symbolic colours. Green is for agriculture and forestry, white for the perennial rivers, black for the people's endurance, red for the zeal and vigour of a young country, while the golden arrow itself represents mineral wealth. The designer of the flag, Whitney Smith, chose green because more than 90 per cent of the country is covered with fields or forests, once the domain of the Arawak, Carib and Warrau Indians.

SURINAME

Republic of Suriname
Flag proportions: 2:3
Adopted: 25 November 1975
Capital: Paramaribo
Area: 163,820km² (63,278mi²)
Population: 454,000
Language: Dutch
Religion: Hindu, Catholic, Muslim, Protestant
Currency: Suriname guilder
Exports: Aluminium, alumina, shrimps, bananas, plantains, rice, timber, wood products.

After the colony of Dutch Guiana gained independence as Suriname in 1975, it faced a series of coups before order was restored and democratic elections held in 1991. Red and green were the colours of Suriname's main political parties at the time of independence, while the yellow five-pointed star suggests unity and points towards a golden future. Although Suriname is home to people of several ethnic groups, notably those of Indonesian, Indian and African descent, a single star was chosen to represent unity and hope. The colours have been interpreted as representing fertility (green), justice and freedom (white) and progress and spiritual renewal (red).

FRENCH GUIANA

Département of Guiana
Flag proportions: 2:3
Adopted: 5 March 1848
Capital: Cayenne
Area: 89,150km² (34,420mi²)
Population: 187,000
Language: Creole, French
Religion: Roman Catholic
Currency: Euro
Exports: Timber, shrimps, gold, rum, rosewood essence, clothing.

Settled by France in 1604, Guiana became a French possession in 1817, a *département* in 1946 and an administrative region in 1974. It was once notorious for its offshore penal colonies, notably Devil's Island (est. 1852), but the shipment of convicts ceased after 1945. The European Space Agency launches communication satellites from Kourou. Fishing and forestry are important industries.

Much of the territory now in French Guiana was contested by France and Brazil. In the late 19th century, some French businessmen sponsored the 'republic' of Independent Guyana. The venture failed, although their flag (red and black stripes with a white star) briefly flew over the settlement at Counani.

PERU

Republic of Peru

Flag proportions: 2:3
Adopted: 25 February 1825
Capital: Lima
Area: 1,285,216km² (496,225mi²)
Population: 26,7 million
Languages: Spanish, Quechua
Religion: Roman Catholic
Currency: Nuevo sol
Exports: Copper, fish meal, zinc, gold, refined oil products.

Peru's flourishing Inca Empire was vanquished by the Spanish conquistador Pizarro who, in 1533, executed Atahualpa, the last Inca emperor. Peru became Spain's headquarters in South America and was the last country to receive independence, in 1826, after liberation by General José de San Martín, known as *El Liberador* (the Liberator). For his flag, he chose red and white to represent the Inca Empire and the rising sun. San Martín saw white as standing for peace and progress; red as symbolizing courage and endeavour. On the arms are symbols of the animal, vegetable and mineral kingdoms. The palm and laurel wreaths around the shield are symbols of peace.

BRAZIL

Federative Republic of Brazil

Flag proportions: 7:10
Adopted: 12 May 1992
Capital: Brasília
Area: 8,511,996km² (3,287,893mi²)
Population: 176 million
Language: Portuguese
Religion: Christian
Currency: Real
Exports: Soya, iron, manganese and other ores, coffee, orange juice, tobacco, cocoa beans.

A former Portuguese colony, Brazil became a kingdom in 1822, under King (later Emperor) Pedro I, and a republic in 1889. The blue sphere depicts the sky as seen from Rio de Janeiro at independence on 15 November 1889. Each star represents a state. The latest, added in 1992, makes 27 (with the Federal District). The constellations are accurate, and the size of the stars does not reflect the importance of the state. The motto, *Ordem e Progresso*, 'Order and Progress', is inscribed on a white band representing the equator. Green symbolizes the vast Amazon rainforest which covers much of the country, and yellow the rich mineral resources.

One of the world's tallest flagpoles, in the capital, Brasília, flies a national flag measuring 70 x 100m (230 x 320ft).

BOLIVIA

Republic of Bolivia

Flag proportions: 2:3
Adopted: 14 July 1880
Capitals: Sucre, La Paz
Area: 1,098,581km² (424,165mi²)
Population: 8,5 million
Language: Spanish
Religion: Roman Catholic
Currency: Boliviano
Exports: Timber, zinc, gold, tin, natural gas, jewellery.

Bolivia was part of the Inca Empire until it was conquered by Spain in 1538, becoming part of Peru. It stayed under Spanish rule until liberation by Simón Bolívar in 1825. By 1851, earlier versions of the flag had given way to the red-yellow-green horizontal tricolour used today. Red is for courage, yellow for mineral resources and green for fertility. At the centre of the state flag the unusually full coat of arms comprises an oval enclosing symbols of the country's wealth, surrounded by weapons and banners in the national colours, surmounted by a condor with wings raised.

Bolivia has two capitals, Sucre and La Paz (the seat of government and the highest capital city at 3600m/11,800ft).

PARAGUAY

Republic of Paraguay

Flag proportions: 3:5

Adopted: 27 November 1842

Capital: Asunción

Area: 406,752km² (157,042mi²)

Population: 5,9 million

Language: Spanish

Religion: Roman Catholic

Currency: Guaraní

Exports: Oil seeds, cotton, wood and timber products, hides, skins and meat.

The flag of Paraguay, a former Spanish colony that gained independence in 1811, is unique for having an obverse (facing side) that is different to the reverse. Both sides have horizontal bands of red over white over blue. The colours, influenced by the *Tricolore,* represent patriotism and justice (red), unity and peace (white), and liberty (blue). On both sides, a central white disc is enclosed within thin blue and red circles. The obverse disc contains the state arms: a five-pointed yellow 'Star of May', recalling the date of independence, within a wreath of palm and laurel branches tied with red, white and blue ribbon, surrounded by the words *Republica del Paraguay.* The reverse bears the seal of the national treasury, a lion guarding a cap of liberty, and the motto *Paz y justicia* ('Peace and justice').

URUGUAY

Republic East of the Uruguay

Flag proportions: 2:3

Adopted: 11 July 1830

Capital: Montevideo

Area: 176,215km² (68,037mi²)

Population: 3,4 million

Language: Spanish

Religion: Roman Catholic, Protestant, Jewish

Currency: Uruguayan nuevo peso

Exports: Textiles, meat, hides and skins, cereals, footwear.

The golden 'sun in splendour' and the stripes are adapted from the flags of Argentina and the USA respectively. The sun, a symbol of freedom, known in South and Central America as 'the Sun of May' (*Sol de Mayo*), occupies the chief canton, while the field's equal horizontal stripes (five white and four blue) represent Uruguay's provinces. A Spanish colony until 1814, the territory was subsequently disputed by Argentina and Brazil, and annexed to both individually before gaining independence in 1830.

Uruguayan naval ships fly a flag of equal horizontal bands of blue-white-blue, with a diagonal red band rising from the hoist to the fly. This was once the flag of José Artigas, who led the movement for separation from Spain.

CHILE

Republic of Chile

Flag proportions: 2:3

Adopted: 18 October 1817

Capital: Santiago

Area: 756,945km² (292,258mi²)

Population: 15 million

Language: Spanish

Religion: Roman Catholic, Protestant

Currency: Chilean peso

Exports: Agricultural products, wine, minerals, manufactured goods.

The first European to reach Chile was the Spanish explorer Ferdinand Magellan who, in 1520, sailed though the strait that now bears his name. Santiago, the capital, was established in 1541 and Chile remained under Spanish rule until independence in 1818. The 'lone star' Chilean flag was designed by Charles Wood, an American who fought alongside General José de San Martín to liberate Chile from Spain. Blue is for clear skies, white for the snow of the Andes, and red for the blood shed in the struggle for freedom. The white star is to guide the country towards progress and honour.

ARGENTINA

Republic of Argentina

Flag proportions: 2:3
Adopted: 12 February 1812
Capital: Buenos Aires
Area: 2,780,092km² (1,073,859mi²)
Population: 36,5 million
Language: Spanish
Religion: Roman Catholic, Protestant
Currency: Peso
Exports: Beef, cereals, oils, fruit, fish, wine.

In 1810, Manuel Belgrano led mass demonstrations in support of liberation from Spain. He used a blue and white cockade (ribbon) to commemorate the 25 May uprising, when the clouds over Buenos Aires cleared to reveal the sun in a blue sky. The cockade became official in February 1812 and the colours were soon adopted as a flag. Independence was achieved in 1816. In 1818, a golden radiant sun, *Sol de Mayo* or 'Sun of May', was added to recall the 1810 uprising. The sun is depicted with a face (known in heraldry as the 'sun in splendour'), from coins in use in Argentina at the time. It also features on the arms, along with the red cap of liberty.

Argentina has disputed claims to the Falkland Islands (see below) and parts of Antarctica.

FALKLAND ISLANDS

Islas Malvinas

Flag proportions: 1:2
Adopted: 1948
Capital: Stanley
Area: 12,173km² (4700mi²)
Population: 3000
Language: English
Religion: Christian
Currency: Falkland pound
Exports: Wool, hides, meat. The sale of squid fishing rights is a major source of revenue.

The Falkland Islands' version of the Blue Ensign was granted in 1948. Set within a circle are the arms on a shield. On the blue upper part, or chief, is a ram, underscoring the role wool plays in the island's economy. The wavy bands of blue and white on the base suggest the sea, on which is the *Desire*, the flagship of explorer John Davis, who discovered the islands in 1592. Stars on the ship's sail represent the Southern Cross.

East and West Falkland, and about 200 adjacent islets, are an overseas territory of the UK. After the 1982 war between Britain and Argentina over sovereignty, new port and airport facilities were opened in the capital, Stanley.

SOUTH GEORGIA AND THE SOUTH SANDWICH ISLANDS

South Georgia

Flag proportions: 1:2
Adopted: 2003
Main port: Grytviken
Area: 3903km² (1506mi²)
Population: No permanent pop.
Language: English
Religion: N/a
Currency: N/a

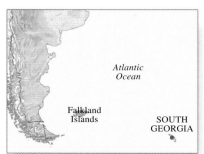

South Georgia and the South Sandwich Islands, some 1000km (600mi) southeast of the Falklands, were visited by Captain Cook in 1775 and annexed by Britain in 1908. The British Antarctic Survey has a base in Grytviken and a station on nearby Bird Island, but the South Sandwich Islands are uninhabited. The islands are administered from the Falklands, and a badge was granted to commemorate liberation after the 1982 war against Argentina. The blue and silver diamond pattern on the shield is described in heraldry as 'lozengy azure and argent', while the green wedge is known as a 'pile'. A lion rampant holds a flaming torch, symbolizing exploration. The supporters are a penguin and a seal.

Africa and adjacent islands

The former 'dark continent', covering an area of about 30 million sq km (12 million sq miles), extends from the southern shores of the Mediterranean, at about 35° North, to Cape Agulhas, in South Africa, at almost 35° South. Natural resources include timber, gold and other rare metals, and diamonds, discovered first in South Africa but also found in Namibia and Botswana. There are large offshore oil reserves in Angola. Oil is also found in Nigeria, while the unpromising Sahara Desert conceals large deposits too. The continent's relatively late development is attributable to Africa's vast size and largely inhospitable terrain over which transport was formerly all but impossible.

Africa was the last major zone to be colonized and exploited by the 'old world' civilizations of Europe. Portugal established tentative settlements along the newly discovered sea route to India in the early 16th century. By that time, outposts of the Turkish Ottoman Empire in North Africa were already more than 200 years old. But it was the 19th century that generated what became known as 'the scramble for Africa', in which territory was eagerly claimed by, among others, Spain, Belgium, Germany, Italy, France and Britain.

British territory reached its maximum extent in the mid-20th century, after two world wars deprived Italy and Germany of their territorial claims. A wave of independence began in the 1950s and, by 1994, 'the last colony' – independent, white-ruled South Africa – had accepted a black-majority government, finally ending 'outsider' rule over Africa.

Patterns of colonization may be traced by the dominant European language of Africa's countries, such as the Anglophone swathe from the Cape of Good Hope to Cairo. One unwelcome aspect of European-imposed borders was the disruption of traditional and ancient patterns of trade and settlement. For many countries, the legacy of colonization in Africa was fragmentation, coupled with bitter competition for basic resources such as land and water.

The flags of independent Africa rarely reflect the continent's colonial past. One of the ways by which the African people have asserted their Africanness is through their countries' distinctive new flags. Pan-African colours have replaced earlier designs that borrowed heavily from the colonial powers, while some flags of the new generation still feature the emblems of Marxism, and even depict the weapons carried by resistance movements now adjusting to the role of political parties.

An association of African states, the Organization of African Unity (OAU), was founded in 1963 to combat colonialism and promote African unity. By 2001 there were no longer any African colonies and the African Union (AU) was established to enhance the economic, political and social integration and development of all African people.

A new initiative is an acknowledgement by African leaders of the pressing need and duty to eradicate poverty and set their countries on a path of sustainable growth and development, while at the same time participating actively in the global economy and body politic. The South African-led NEPAD (New Partnerships for African Development) is one part of a development policy known as the African Renaissance.

The continent faces many challenges, such as recurring drought (virtually endemic in the Horn of Africa), flood and famine, and the rampant spread of diseases such as malaria (the biggest killer), AIDS and tuberculosis. Many ethnic hostilities have yet to be resolved, other than by war or the slaughter of civilians, in such places as the DRC, Rwanda, Liberia and Nigeria.

Africa and adjacent islands

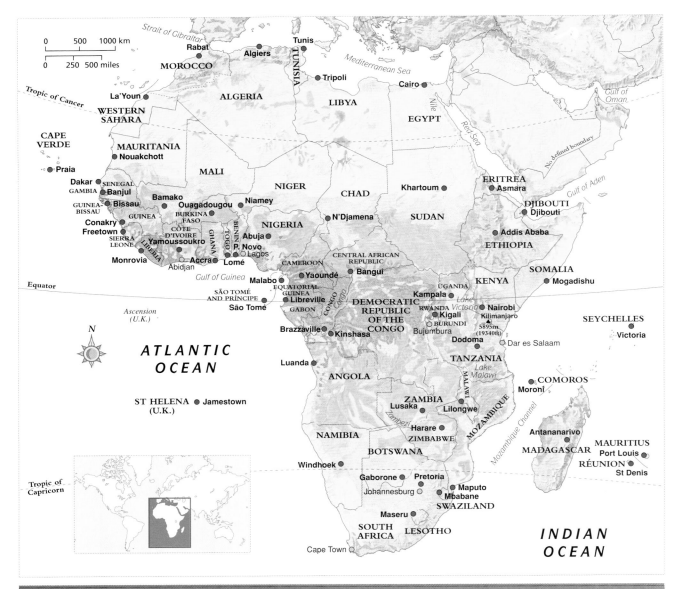

0 500 1000 km
0 250 500 miles

Strait of Gibraltar
Rabat
Tunis
Algiers
MOROCCO
TUNISIA
Tripoli
Mediterranean Sea
Cairo
Tropic of Cancer
La'Youn
WESTERN
SAHARA
ALGERIA
LIBYA
EGYPT
Gulf of Oman
CAPE
VERDE
MAURITANIA
Nouakchott
Red Sea
Nile
No defined boundary
Praia
MALI
NIGER
CHAD
Khartoum
ERITREA
Asmara
DJIBOUTI
Gulf of Aden
Dakar
SENEGAL
GAMBIA
Banjul
Bamako
Niamey
N'Djamena
SUDAN
Djibouti
GUINEA-
BISSAU
Bissau
Ouagadougou
GUINEA
BURKINA
FASO
NIGERIA
Addis Ababa
Conakry
Freetown
CÔTE
D'IVOIRE
GHANA
BENIN
TOGO
Abuja
P. Novo
ETHIOPIA
SIERRA
LEONE
Yamoussoukro
LIBERIA
Accra
Lagos
Monrovia
Abidjan
Lomé
CAMEROON
CENTRAL AFRICAN
REPUBLIC
SOMALIA
Gulf of Guinea
Malabo
Yaoundé
Bangui
KENYA
Mogadishu
Equator
EQUATORIAL
GUINEA
UGANDA
SÃO TOMÉ
AND PRÍNCIPE
Libreville
Kampala
*Lake
Victoria*
Nairobi
SEYCHELLES
São Tomé
GABON
DEMOCRATIC
REPUBLIC
OF THE
CONGO
RWANDA
Kigali
BURUNDI
Kilimanjaro
5895m
(19340ft)
Victoria
*Ascension
(U.K.)*
N
Brazzaville
Kinshasa
Bujumbura
Dodoma
Dar es Salaam
**ATLANTIC
OCEAN**
Luanda
TANZANIA
*Lake
Malawi*
COMOROS
Moroni
ANGOLA
ST HELENA
(U.K.)
Jamestown
ZAMBIA
Lusaka
Lilongwe
MOZAMBIQUE
Mozambique Channel
Antananarivo
MAURITIUS
Port Louis
RÉUNION
St Denis
NAMIBIA
Harare
ZIMBABWE
MADAGASCAR
Zambezi
*Tropic of
Capricorn*
Windhoek
BOTSWANA
Gaborone
Pretoria
Johannesburg
Maputo
Mbabane
SWAZILAND
Maseru
SOUTH
AFRICA
LESOTHO
**INDIAN
OCEAN**
Cape Town

AT A GLANCE

Number of countries: 56 (including the Indian and Atlantic ocean islands)

Biggest country: Sudan

Smallest country: Seychelles

Largest city: Cairo, Egypt

Major cities: Abidjan, Accra, Algiers, Abuja, Bamako, Brazzaville, Cape Town, Dakar, Dar es Salaam, Durban, Johannesburg, Kinshasa, Lagos, Lusaka, Luanda, Maputo, Mombasa, Nairobi, Port Louis, Port Said, Pretoria, Tunis, Tripoli, Windhoek, Yamoussoukro

Highest point: Mt Kilimanjaro, Tanzania (5895m/19,340ft)

Lowest point: Lac' Assal, Djibouti (156m/512ft below sea level)

Longest river: Nile, Uganda/Sudan/ Egypt (6825km/4241mi)

Largest lake: Victoria, Kenya/Uganda/ Tanzania (69,500km²/26,834mi²).

MOROCCO

Kingdom of Morocco
Flag proportions: 2:3
Adopted: 17 November 1915
Capital: Rabat
Area: 458,730km² (177,192mi²)
Population: 30 million
Language: Arabic
Religion: Muslim
Currency: Dirham
Exports: Phosphates, minerals, seafoods, citrus fruit, tobacco, clothing.

The red field proclaims the descent of Morocco's royal family from the Prophet Mohammed. Red was also used by the sherifs, or governors, of the Holy City of Mecca and the imams (religious leaders) of Yemen. At the centre of the flag, in green, is a pentagram (five-pointed star). Known as the 'Seal of Solomon', it is an ancient symbol of life and health. The Seal is voided, or depicted in outline, to show its construction. It was added to the flag, which for centuries had been plain red, when the French imposed a protectorate over the country. As a sign of mourning, the Moroccan flag has been tied around the mast rather than unfurled at half-mast.

WESTERN SAHARA

Sahrawi Arab Democratic Republic
Flag proportions: 1:2
Adopted: 27 February 1976
Capital: Laayoune (El-Aaiún)
Area: 266,800km² (103,011mi²)
Population: 262,000
Language: Arabic
Religion: Sunni Muslim
Currency: Moroccan dirham
Exports: Phosphates.

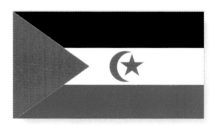

Morocco annexed most of Western Sahara (formerly Spanish Sahara) in 1976. Mauritania claimed the rest but relinquished it in 1979 under pressure from the Polisario Front liberation movement. A guerilla war contesting Moroccan sovereignty ended in 1991 with a UN-brokered cease-fire, but the territory remains in dispute. The flag, in Pan-Arab colours, comprises a horizontal tricolour of equal bands of black, white and green with a red equilateral triangle at the hoist. In the white band are the Islamic crescent and star in red. Red represents the blood shed in the struggle for independence, black is for the period of colonization, white is for peace, while green, the colour of Islam, stands for progress.

ALGERIA

Democratic and Popular Republic of Algeria
Flag proportions: 2:3
Adopted: 3 July 1962
Capital: Algiers (Al-Jazair)
Area: 2,381,741km² (919,595mi²)
Population: 32,7 million
Language: Arabic, French
Religion: Sunni Muslim
Currency: Algerian dinar
Exports: Crude oil, refined petroleum products, natural gas concentrates, olive oil, wine.

The flag is vertically divided into two equal bands of green and white, with green at the hoist. At the centre is a five-pointed red star within a red crescent, which faces towards the fly. Green is the traditional colour of Islam, while the crescent and star are symbols of the faith. White stands for purity and red symbolizes liberty and the sacrifices made in its attainment. The horns of the crescent are unusually long, to contain good fortune and happiness. Algeria was a French colony from 1830 until it achieved independence in 1962.

TUNISIA

Tunisian Republic
Flag proportions: 2:3
Adopted: 3 July 1999
Capital: Tunis
Area: 164,150km² (63,378mi²)
Population: 9,7 million
Language: Arabic, French
Religion: Muslim
Currency: Tunisian dinar
Exports: Clothing, textiles, crude oil, fertilizers, olive oil, fruit, leather, footware, fish products, machinery, electrical equipment.

Tunisia was part of the Ottoman (Turkish) Empire from 1574 until 1881, when the country became a French Protectorate. Independence was granted in 1956 and Tunisia became a republic in 1957. In the 19th century, Tunisia wanted to assert its autonomy and, in 1835, the national flag on which the current design is based was adopted. The crescent and star are Islamic symbols, but the crescent alone was used in North Africa centuries before Islam arose. The waxing crescent moon is said to bring good fortune.

LIBYA

Socialist People's Libyan Arab Jamahiriya
Flag proportions: 1:2
Adopted: 20 November 1977
Capital: Tripoli
Area: 1,759,540km² (679,358mi²)
Population: 5,5 million
Language: Arabic, Italian, English
Religion: Sunni Muslim
Currency: Libyan dinar
Exports: Crude oil, refined petroleum products, chemicals.

This is the only national flag consisting of a single colour. When the United Kingdom of Libya gained independence from Italy in 1951, the flag consisted of horizontal bands of red, black and green, with a white crescent and star at the centre, representng the Libyan provinces of Fezzan, Cyrenaica and Tripolitania. In 1969, following a successful military coup led by Colonel Muammar al Qaddafi, the crescent and star were removed and the colours changed to red, white and black. The present flag was adopted in 1977, after Libya quit the tri-national Federation of Arab Republics (with Egypt and Syria) to become an Islamic Socialist state. Green is the traditional colour of Islam.

EGYPT

Arab Republic of Egypt
Flag proportions: 2:3
Adopted: 4 October 1984
Capital: Cairo
Area: 1,002,000km² (386,900mi²)
Population: 68 million
Language: Arabic
Religion: Sunni Muslim
Currency: Egyptian pound
Exports: Crude oil, cotton goods, refined petroleum, aluminium, oranges, potatoes.

Red, white and black are the Arab Liberation colours. The flag was used in 1952 by the liberation movement that deposed the king of Egypt. Red is for the struggle, white for the revolution, and black for the end of oppression. When Egypt joined the United Arab Republic in 1958, the flag was charged with two green stars. When the Federation of Arab Republics was formed in 1972, the Hawk of Quraish replaced the stars. In 1984 the flag reverted to that of the 1952 liberation struggle. On the white band is a stylized gold eagle 'displayed, wings inverted' (spread with wing tips down) known as the 'Eagle of Saladin', after the legendary 12th-century sultan of Egypt.

Under Egyptian law, 'abusing' the national flag, or the flag of another country, is a punishable offence.

MAURITANIA

Islamic Republic of Mauritania

Flag proportions: 2:3
Adopted: 1 April 1959
Capital: Nouakchott
Area: 1,030,700km² (398,000mi²)
Population: 2,7 million
Language: Arabic
Religion: Muslim
Currency: Ouguiya
Exports: Fish, fish products, iron ore.

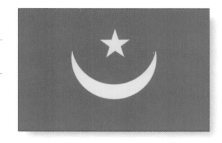

Yellow and green are Pan-African colours while green, additionally, is the colour of Islam. The green field of the Mauritanian flag has been described as symbolizing hope, while yellow represents the sands of the Sahara Desert.

On this flag, the crescent and star emblem are unusual in that the crescent is depicted pointing upward. The same pattern is repeated on the national seal of this Islamic republic, together with other elements.

SENEGAL

Republic of Senegal

Flag proportions: 2:3
Adopted: September 1960
Capital: Dakar
Area: 196,720km² (75,954mi²)
Population: 10 million
Language: French, Senagalese, Arabic
Religion: Muslim
Currency: CFA franc
Exports: Fish, refined oil products, chemicals, groundnuts.

With the exception of the green star at its centre, the Senegalese flag is identical to that of Mali (see p141), as the two former French colonies were briefly united. The Pan-African colours of green, yellow and red were first used by Ethiopia and Ghana, and the star is said to represent unity and hope. In Senegal the colours also represented the three political parties that merged to form the *Union Progressiste Sénégalaise*, or Senegalese Progressive Union, of President Leopold Senghor. The star represents light and knowledge, and occurs frequently in African symbolism.

THE GAMBIA

Republic of the Gambia

Flag proportions: 2:3
Adopted: 18 February 1965
Capital: Banjul
Area: 11,294km² (4363mi²)
Population: 1,4 million
Languages: English, local patois
Religion: Muslim
Currency: Dalasi
Exports: Groundnuts, groundnut oil and cake, cotton lint, fish, hides and skins.

A former British colony, The Gambia obtained self-government in 1963, achieved independence as a consitutional monarchy within the Commonwealth in 1965, and became a republic in 1970. The flag adopted at independence was designed by Mr L Tomasi. There is more than one interpretation of the colours, but none are political. The simplest description is that the blue band represents the River Gambia as it flows through the green equatorial forests and the red soils of the savannah. The country, the smallest on the African continent, lies on either side of the Gambia River.

CAPE VERDE

Republic of Cape Verde

Flag proportions: 10:17

Adopted: 25 February 1992

Capital: Praia

Area: 4033km² (1557mi²)

Population: 450,000

Language: Portuguese

Religion: Roman Catholic, Protestant

Currency: Cape Verde escudo

Exports: Fish, salt, volcanic rock, bananas.

Cape Verde, an archipelago of ten volcanic islands off the coast of West Africa, was settled by the Portuguese in the 15th century. When Cape Verde gained independence in 1975, there was a move towards linking it with Guinea (now Guinea-Bissau), and so they initially used similar flags. There was insufficient support for this, and the current flag came into being after the first multiparty elections brought a new government to power in 1992. The circle of yellow stars depicts the ten main islands in unity and without domination. A circle has no beginning or end, thus there is no dominant position. Blue is for the Atlantic Ocean and for the sky, red is the road to progress and reconstruction and the effort that must be expended to follow it, and white is for peace.

GUINEA

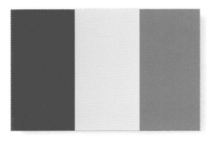

Republic of Guinea

Flag proportions: 2:3

Adopted: 10 November 1958

Capital: Conakry

Area: 245,857km² (94,926mi²)

Population: 9 million

Language: French

Religion: Muslim

Currency: Guinean franc

Exports: Bauxite, alumina, gold, diamonds, coffee, fish.

Guinea was part of a Muslim empire, centred on Mali, which flourished until the 15th century. Colonization by France, Britain and Portugal established the slave trade by the mid-15th century. In 1958, French Guinea became independent as Guinea, adopting the red-green-yellow of many 1950s liberation movements. Guinea's first president, Sékou Touré, explained the colours thus: 'red is the colour of blood, symbol of anti-colonialist martyrs; the sweat of farmers and factory workers; and the wish for progress. Yellow is for Guinean gold and African sun, the source of energy, generosity and equality. Green symbolizes the countryside and prosperity, which comes from the soil, and the difficult life of ourcountry's masses.'

GUINEA-BISSAU

Republic of Guinea-Bissau

Flag proportions: 1:2

Adopted: 24 September 1973

Capital: Bissau

Area: 36,125km² (13,948mi²)

Population: 1,3 million

Language: Portuguese, local

Religion: Traditional, Muslim, Christian

Currency: CFA franc

Exports: Cashew nuts, shrimp, peanuts, palm kernels, timber.

A slave-trading centre from 1446, Portuguese Guinea was administered with the Cape Verde islands until 1879, then as a separate colony until independence was negotiated in 1973, followed by the recognition of Guinea-Bissau as a sovereign nation in 1974 (the name was chosen to distinguish it from neighbouring Guinea). The flag adopted at independence has the full Pan-African colours of yellow, green, red and black, derived from the flag of Ghana. Red is for the blood shed in the struggle for independence, yellow represents the fruits of labour, and green is for the tropical forests and for hope. The five-pointed black star denotes African unity. (A similar flag was used by the nationalist movement in Cape Verde.)

SIERRA LEONE

Republic of Sierra Leone

Flag proportions: 2:3
Adopted: 27 April 1961
Capital: Freetown
Area: 73,326km² (27,925mi²)
Population: 4,7 million
Language: English, Krio
Religion: Muslim, Traditional,
Christian
Currency: Leone
Exports: Diamonds, coffee,
cocoa, fish, rutile, bauxite.

Sierra Leone was founded as a home for freed slaves in 1787. It became a British colony in 1808, achieved independence in the Commonwealth in 1961 and became a republic in 1971. The flag is a horizontal tricolour of equal bands of green above white and blue. Blue represents the sea (specifically, the natural harbour of Freetown, the capital), white is for unity and justice, and green for the natural resources.

Since 1991, civil war between the government and the Revolutionary United Front (RUF) has resulted in the deaths of tens of thousands and the displacement of over one-third of the population. UN-led efforts resulted in elections in 2002, but rebel fighting and ethnic rivalries require the continued presence of a UN peacekeeping force. The war has resulted in serious economic and social disruption.

LIBERIA

Republic of Liberia

Flag proportions: 10:19
Adopted: 26 July 1847
Capital: Monrovia
Area: 111,370km² (43,109mi²)
Population: 3,3 million
Language: English, local patois
Religion: Christian, Traditional,
Muslim
Currency: Liberian dollar
Exports: Iron ore, rubber, timber,
diamonds, coffee, cocoa.

Liberia was bought by the American Colonization Society as a home for freed slaves, the first of whom settled there in 1822. 'Lone star' is the familiar name for the flag, which traces its design to the US Stars and Stripes. The five-pointed white star, symbolizing African freedom, occupies a blue field in the chief canton. The field is made up of 11 horizontal stripes, six red and five white, representing the signatories to the 1847 declaration of Liberian independence. The colours have been described as blue for fidelity, red for valour, white for purity.

Years of war, plus Liberia's support for rebels in Sierra Leone, have hampered economic activity and growth. There is cautious hope for a regional peace initiative begun in 2003.

CÔTE D'IVOIRE

Republic of Côte d'Ivoire

Flag proportions: 2:3
Adopted: 3 December 1959
Capital: Yamoussoukro
Area: 322,463km² (124,504mi²)
Population: 17,6 million
Language: French
Religion: Traditional, Christian,
Muslim
Currency: CFA franc
Exports: Cocoa, petroleum
products, cotton, tinned tuna.

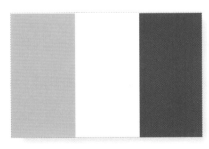

The vertical tricolour resembles the *Tricolore* of France, the former colonial power. Côte d'Ivoire (Ivory Coast) was part of French West Africa before independence in 1960 and maintained an alliance with Niger for a period afterwards. The colours have been officially described: 'Orange is for the grasslands, rich and generous, the meaning of our fight, the blood of a young people fighting for emancipation. White is for the rivers and for peace with justice. Green is for the coastal forests, for hope and the certainty of a better future.'

The resemblance to the Irish flag (see p50) is incidental.

GHANA

Republic of Ghana

Flag proportions: 2:3
Adopted: 6 March 1957
Capital: Accra
Area: 239,460km² (92,456mi²)
Population: 19,3 million
Language: English
Religion: African Traditional, Muslim, Christian
Currency: Cedi
Exports: Gold, cocoa, timber, tuna, bauxite, aluminium, manganese ore, diamonds.

Ghana, formerly Gold Coast, was the first British colony in Africa to gain independence, and its flag was copied by other former colonies. Ghana's black star, the 'lode star' of African freedom, came from the emblem of the Black Star shipping company, founded in 1919 by Marcus Garvey, a Jamaican nationalist who promoted the Back to Africa movement. Red, yellow and green (from the Ethiopian flag) plus black created the combination that became known as 'Pan-African colours'. Red represents blood shed for independence, yellow the wealth of the country, and green the natural environment. The colours are those of the Rastafarian movement, which is based on Garvey's ideas.

Ghana has a red ensign for commercial shipping and a white ensign for naval vessels.

TOGO

Republic of Togo

Flag proportions: 2:3
Adopted: 27 April 1960
Capital: Lomé
Area: 56,785km² (21,934mi²)
Population: 5 million
Language: French
Religion: Traditional, Christian
Currency: CFA franc
Exports: Cotton, coffee, cocoa beans.

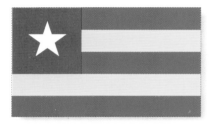

The German protectorate of Togoland was divided between Britain and France after World War I. Britain's portion was incorporated with Ghana and the French part gained independence, as Togo, in 1960. Official publications describe the flag thus: 'Red is for patriotic blood shed in the defence of integrity and sovereignty against aggressors. Green symbolizes nature, hope that represents Togo rising from colonization, and the dawn of a new era. Yellow symbolizes national unity and a common destiny. White is for peace, wisdom and dignity. The star is the symbol of liberty, life and the strength necessary for the people's development. The five horizontal bands represent strength and action in overcoming obstacles.'

BENIN

Republic of Benin

Flag proportions: 2:3
Adopted: 1 August 1990
Capital: Porto Novo
Area: 112,622km² (43,502mi²)
Population: 6,6 million
Language: French
Religion: Traditional, Christian, Muslim
Currency: CFA franc
Exports: Cotton, crude oil.

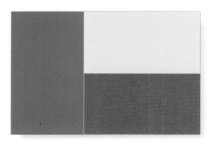

From the 17th to the 19th centuries, the kingdom of Dahomey, as Benin was then known, was active in the slave trade. A former French colony, Benin became self-governing in 1958 and independent in 1960. The flag adoped then had equal horizontal bands of yellow above red, with a vertical green band at the hoist. Green stands for the hope of renewal, red for the courage of the ancestors, and yellow for the natural riches. As Pan-African colours, they also represent unity and nationalism. Following the establishment of a Marxist-based People's Republic in 1975, a plain green flag with a red star in the canton was used. The original flag was restored in 1990 after a referendum favoured a return to multiparty politics.

MALI

Republic of Mali

Flag proportions: 2:3
Adopted: 1 March 1961
Capital: Bamako
Area: 1,248,574 km² (482,077mi²)
Population: 10,2 million
Language: French
Religion: Muslim, Animist
Currency: CFA franc
Exports: Cotton, livestock, gold, manufactured goods.

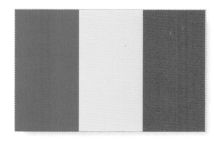

A former French colony, Mali achieved independence in 1960, forming a short-lived confederation with neighbouring Senegal. The vertical tricolour in the Pan-African colours of green, yellow and red is based on the French *Tricolore*. The original flag bore a black stylized human figure, known as a *kanaga*, which was dropped in 1961. Green is for the natural environment, yellow for purity and mineral resources, and red for courage and sacrifice in the cause of independence.

BURKINA FASO

People's Democratic Republic of Burkina Faso

Flag proportions: 2:3
Adopted: 4 August 1984
Capital: Ouagadougou
Area: 274,122km² (105,884mi²)
Population: 12 million
Language: French
Religion: Muslim, Roman Catholic, Traditional
Currency: CFA franc
Exports: Cotton, gold.

Red symbolizes the revolution against French colonizers, and the star its guiding principles, while green represents the land's abundance of natural riches. Red, yellow and green are also the Pan-African colours. When the country achieved self-government in 1958 (as Upper Volta), the flag was a horizontal tricolour of black, white and red, representing the three major tributaries of the Volta River. The present colours were chosen as being more strongly expressive of solidarity with other former colonies in Africa.

NIGER

Republic of Niger

Flag proportions: 6:7
Adopted: 23 November 1959
Capital: Niamey
Area: 1,267,000km² (489,401mi²)
Population: 11,8 million
Language: French
Religion: Muslim
Currency: CFA franc
Exports: Uranium, live animals, hides and skins, peas, cotton.

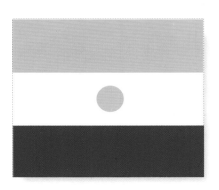

On Niger's horizontal tricolour, the orange band is said to signify the country's savanna grasslands, while the disc at the centre represents the sun. White symbolizes the great Niger River, green the country's plains and dense rainforests. Other interpretations are that orange is for the Sahara Desert, green for fraternity, and white for purity and hope. The orange disc is sometimes interpreted as signifying sacrifices made by the people in their struggle to uphold justice and human rights.

The flags of Niger and Côte d'Ivoire are similar as they were designed in 1958 when both countries had an informal alliance with Chad and Dahomey (Benin), former colonies of French West Africa. Niger achieved independence in 1960.

NIGERIA

Federal Republic of Nigeria

Flag proportions: 1:2

Adopted: 1 October 1960

Capital: Abuja

Area: 923,773km² (356,669mi²)

Population: 146,6 million

Language: English, Hausa

Religion: Muslim, Christian, Traditional

Currency: Naira

Exports: Petroleum, cocoa beans, rubber, palm products, minerals, fish.

From the 12th to 14th centuries, Nigeria was home to the Yoruba and Ife cultures. English and Portuguese slave traders were active from the 15th century. In 1881 a British trader bought the town of Lagos from a local chief. Further acquisitions resulted in Nigeria becoming Britain's largest West African colony. It became a federation in 1954 and achieved independence in 1960 as a constitutional monarchy within the Commonwealth. The green, white, green vertical tricolour adopted at independence was chosen from nearly 3000 entries in a national competition. The designer, Abadan student Michael Akinkunmi, described green as representing the land and agriculture, with white for peace and unity.

CHAD

Republic of Chad

Flag proportions: 2:3

Adopted: 6 November 1959

Capital: N'Djamena

Area: 1,284,000km² (496,000mi²)

Population: 7 million

Languages: French, Arabic

Religion: Muslim, Traditional, Christian

Currency: CFA franc

Exports: Cotton, cattle, textiles, fish.

The pattern and colours derive from the *Tricolore* of France (the former colonial power) and the Pan-African colours. An official description states that blue represents the sky, hope, and agriculture in the southern part of the land. Yellow is for the northern deserts and the sun. Red is for prosperity, unity and the readiness of citizens to make sacrifices for their country. Chad was settled by Arabs in the 7th century, before being conquered by Sudan. A province of French Equatorial Africa from 1913, Chad became an autonomous republic in 1958 and achieved independence in 1960. Since then, the flag has not altered, despite unrest and regime changes. Unintentionally, Chad's flag is identical to Romania's (see p64).

CAMEROON

Republic of Cameroon

Flag proportions: 2:3

Adopted: 20 May 1975

Capital: Yaoundé

Area: 475,442km² (183,648mi²)

Population: 16 million

Languages: French, English

Religion: Christian, Muslim, African Traditional

Currency: CFA franc

Exports: Timber products, cocoa, coffee, aluminium, cotton, bananas.

Cameroon was the next West African state after Ghana to adopt a flag comprising Pan-African colours. A former German colony, it was partitioned between Britain and France after World War I. A plain green, red and yellow flag, based on the *Tricolore*, was first used in 1957. When Southern Cameroon, a former British colony, joined French Cameroon in 1961, two yellow stars were placed in the chief canton (the upper part of the green band). With a change of government in 1972, the stars were replaced with a single, five-pointed yellow star in the red band, representing unity between the north and south. Green stands for hope, as well as the natural vegetation, and yellow for prosperity, the soil and the sun.

CENTRAL AFRICAN REPUBLIC

Central African Republic
Flag proportions: 2:3
Adopted: 1 December 1958
Capital: Bangui
Area: 622,436km² (240,324mi²)
Population: 3,7 million
Languages: French, Sangho
Religion: Traditional, Christian, Muslim
Currency: CFA franc
Exports: Diamonds, timber, cotton.

The former French colony of Ubangi-Shari became the Central African Republic (CAR) on independence in 1960. Adopted in 1958, the flag's unusual design combines French and Pan-African colours. Four horizontal bands of blue, white, green and yellow are bisected by a central vertical red band. In the chief canton, on the blue, is a five-pointed yellow star. Barthélémy Boganda, the country's first president, described the red band as symbolizing the people's willingness to shed blood for their country. Red also admonishes Europeans and Africans to respect one another. 'Placed as the sky', blue represents freedom and serenity. Green is the colour of hope and faith, white is for dignity and equality, and yellow for tolerance and charity. The star forecasts a bright future.

EQUATORIAL GUINEA

Republic of Equatorial Guinea
Flag proportions: 2:3
Adopted: 21 August 1979
Capital: Malabo
Area: 28,051km² (10,831mi²)
Population: 466,000
Language: Spanish, Fang, Bubi
Religion: Roman Catholic
Currency: CFA franc
Exports: Timber, textile fibres, cocoa, coffee.

This tiny country incorporates five offshore islands, including Bioko (previously Fernando Po), off the coast of Cameroon. The islands came under Spanish rule in the mid-19th century, and mainland territory of Río Muni (now Mbini) in 1885, the colony, known as Spanish Guinea, was a Spanish Overseas Province from 1959 until independence in 1968.

The horizontal tricolour of equal bands of green above white and red has a blue triangle at the hoist, its base occupying the full depth of the flag. Blue represents the sea that links the mainland and the islands, green is for the country's forests and natural resources, white is for peace, and red symbolizes the struggle for independence from Spain.

SÃO TOMÉ AND PRÍNCIPE

Democratic Republic of São Tomé and Príncipe
Flag proportions: 1:2
Adopted: 5 November 1975
Capital: São Tomé
Area: 1001km² (387mi²)
Population: 136,000
Language: Portuguese, Creole
Religion: Roman Catholic
Currency: Dobra
Exports: Cocoa, copra, coffee, bananas, palm products.

The country comprises two main islands, São Tomé and Príncipe, plus several smaller islands in the Gulf of Guinea. Uninhabited until the arrival of the Portuguese in 1471, the islands played a role in the slave trade. The colony was given self-government in 1973, leading to independence in 1975.

A horizontal yellow band, half the depth of the flag, is enclosed top and bottom by equal bands of green. A red isosceles triangle, its base occupying the full depth, is placed at the hoist. Two five-pointed black stars, representing the main islands, complete the Pan-African colours. Red represents blood shed for freedom, and green the forests, while yellow is for cocoa, a key agricultural product.

GABON

Gabonese Republic

Flag proportions: 3:4
Adopted: 9 August 1960
Capital: Libreville
Area: 267,667km² (103,391mi²)
Population: 1,3 million
Language: French, local patois
Religion: Roman Catholic
Currency: CFA franc
Exports: Crude oil, natural gas, timber and wood products, manganese, uranium.

First visited by Portuguese slave traders in the 15th century, Gabon became part of the French Congo, and was a province of French Equatorial Africa from 1908. Virtually the whole country is covered with tropical rainforest, and its reserves of uranium, manganese and iron make Gabon one of the richest countries in central Africa. The flag adopted at independence in 1960 has the unusual proportions of 3:4 (most flags are 2:3). The colours are described as yellow and green for the natural resources, especially timber, and blue for the sea.

CONGO (BRAZZAVILLE)

Republic of the Congo

Flag proportions: 2:3
Adopted: 10 June 1991
Capital: Brazzaville
Area: 342,000km² (132,103mi²)
Population: 3 million
Language: French, local patois
Religion: Christian, Animist
Currency: CFA franc
Exports: Petroleum, timber, plywood, sugar, cocoa, coffee, diamonds.

The area came under French administration in 1889 and was part of French Equatorial Africa from 1910. The Congo became an autonomous republic in 1958 and achieved independence in 1960. After a Marxist revolution in 1964 the country became the People's Republic of the Congo in 1970. The present flag, first used in 1959, was retained after independence. With the formation of the People's Republic a new flag was introduced, consisting of the national emblem in the chief canton, on a field of red. Marxism was abandoned in 1990 and multiparty democracy restored in 1992, along with the original flag. The colours are Pan-African, but the diagonal pattern sets this flag apart from those of most other African nations.

DEMOCRATIC REPUBLIC OF THE CONGO

DRC

Flag proportions: 2:3
Adopted: May 2003
Capital: Kinshasa
Area: 2,344,885km² (905,365mi²)
Population: 56,6 million
Language: French, Kiswahili
Religion: Christian, Traditional
Currency: Congolese franc
Exports: Diamonds, copper, coffee, cobalt, crude oil.

From 1885 to independence in 1960, the former Belgian Congo used a blue flag with a large five-pointed yellow star at the centre. Blue represents the mighty Congo River; the large star, hope for the future. At independence, a row of six yellow five-pointed stars was added at the hoist to signify the provinces that existed at the time. Changes of government resulted in three new flags between 1963 and 1996, and the name Zaire being used from 1971–97. Following a coup in 1997, the 1960 flag was re-established and in 2003 the shade of blue was changed from dark blue to United Nations blue.

In recent years, an on-going civil war in the DRC has impacted upon the entire Great Lakes region, but steps have been taken towards ending the conflict and securing peace.

RWANDA

Rwandan Republic

Flag proportions: 1:2
Adopted: 31 December 2001
Capital: Kigali
Area: 26,338km² (10,169mi²)
Population: 8 million
Language: Kinyarwanda, French
Religion: Roman Catholic, Protestant, Muslim, Traditional
Currency: Rwanda franc
Exports: Coffee, tea, tin, cut flowers.

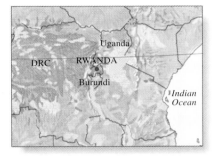

Rwanda came under Belgian administration after 1919, and gained independence in 1962. In 1959, fighting between the majority ethnic Hutus and rival Tutsis sent thousands of Tutsis into exile. In 1990, the children of these exiles formed the Rwandan Patriotic Front, beginning a civil war that culminated in the 1994 genocide of ±800,000 Tutsis and moderate Hutus, with two million refugees fleeing to neighbouring countries. Most have since returned but, despite local elections in 1999, tensions remain. A new flag, introduced in 2001, comprises a half-depth band of blue above yellow and green bands. A radiant golden sun at the upper fly symbolizes enlightenment, leading to unity. Blue is for hope and the promise of peace, green is for prosperity, yellow for the need for reconstruction.

BURUNDI

Republic of Burundi

Flag proportions: 2:3
Adopted: 27 September 1982
Capital: Bujumbura
Area: 27,834km² (10,751mi²)
Population: 7,4 million
Language: French, local patois
Religion: Roman Catholic
Currency: Burundi franc
Exports: Coffee, manufactured goods, tea.

Burundi, a former German colony, became an independent kingdom in 1962. The emblems on the flag were a symbolic drum and a stalk of sorghum but when the country became a republic in 1966, they were replaced by three red six-pointed stars in a white disc at the centre of a white saltire. The stars represent the national motto of 'Unity, work, progress', as well as the main ethnic groups: Tutsi, Hutu and Twa. The arms of the saltire create four triangles, the apexes clipped by the central disc. The triangles at the hoist and the fly are green, those at the upper and lower edges are red. White is for hope, red for sacrifices made in the struggle for independence, and green represents hope for a peaceful, prosperous future.

SUDAN

Democratic Republic of the Sudan

Flag proportions: 1:2
Adopted: 20 May 1970
Capital: Khartoum
Area: 2,505,815km² (967,500mi²)
Population: 36,8 million
Language: Arabic
Religion: Muslim, Christian
Currency: Sudanese pound
Exports: Cotton, sesame seed, gum arabic, sorghum, livestock, hides and skins.

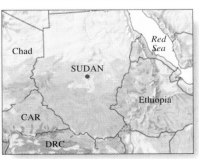

Sudan was ruled jointly by Egypt and Britain until it became independent in 1956. After the formation of the Democratic Republic of Sudan in 1968, a national competition was held to choose a new flag, and the winning entry was adopted in 1970. Equal horizontal bands of red over white and black echo the flags of Egypt and other Arab countries, but Sudan adds a green isosceles triangle with its base occupying the full depth at the hoist. Red is for socialism and the blood shed for liberty, white is for peace and optimism, black is for the 19th-century ruler, known as the Mahdi, who led a revolt against Egypt, and green symbolizes agriculture and Islamic prosperity.

ERITREA

State of Eritrea

Flag proportions: 1:2
Adopted: 24 May 1993
Capital: Asmara
Area: 93,679km² (36,171mi²)
Population: 3,9 million
Languages: Tigrinya, English, Arabic
Religion: Muslim, Christian
Currency: Nakfa
Exports: Drinks, leather, leather products, textiles, oil products.

Eritrea was part of the Ethiopian kingdom until the 7th century. It subsequently fell under Turkish, Italian and British rule before reverting to Ethiopia in 1962. The red, green and blue of the three triangles are the colours of the Eritrean People's Liberation Front (EPLF), which waged a lengthy campaign for independence from Ethiopia, finally obtaining it in 1993. Following independence, the EPLF emblem (a gold star) was replaced with a golden olive branch set within a wreath of olive leaves, to symbolize the winning of the country's autonomy.

DJIBOUTI

Republic of Djibouti

Flag proportions: 21:38
Adopted: 27 June 1977
Capital: Djibouti
Area: 23,200km² (8958mi²)
Population: 787,000
Languages: French, Arabic
Religion: Muslim, Catholic
Currency: Djibouti franc
Exports: Hides, cattle, coffee.

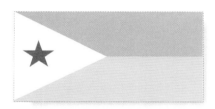

The country was formerly called French Somaliland and, later, the Territory of the Afars and Issas. Opposition to French rule grew in the 1970s, with frequent and sometimes violent clashes occuring until independence was achieved in 1977. The national flag is adapted from that of the former liberation movement, *Ligue Populaire Africaine pour l'Indépendance*. It is divided horizontally into equal bands of light blue over green, with a white equilateral triangle occupying the full depth at the hoist. Blue represents the Issa people, and green the Afars – the two main ethnic groups. Within the triangle is a five-pointed red star, a symbol of unity. White is for the peace eventually attained.

ETHIOPIA

Federal Democratic Republic of Ethopia

Flag proportions: 1:2
Adopted: 6 February 1996
Capital: Addis Ababa
Area: 1,133,880km² (437,794mi²)
Population: 68 million
Language: Amharic
Religion: Ethiopian Orthodox, Muslim
Currency: Ethiopian birr
Exports: Coffee.

Ethiopia's hereditary rulers, the last of whom was Emperor Haile Selassie (1892–1975), claimed direct descent from the biblical King David. The green-yellow-red tricolour, first used as a flag in 1897, once referred to the Holy Trinity. A more contemporary interpretation is green for hope, the land and fertility; yellow for peace and justice, and red for power, faith and sacrifice. The five-pointed Seal of Solomon, added in 1996, signifies unity in diversity. Rays emanating from it symbolize prosperity, and the blue disc is for peace.

In the 1930s, Ethiopian colours were adopted by Jamaicans who saw Africa as a spiritual homeland. With the addition of black, the colours now represent the Rastafarian movement, named after Ras Tafari, the original name of Haile Selassie.

SOMALIA

Somali Democratic Republic

Flag proportions: 2:3
Adopted: 12 October 1954
Capital: Mogadishu
Area: 637,657km^2 (246,201mi^2)
Population: 8 million
Language: Arabic, Somali
Religion: Muslim
Currency: Somali shilling
Exports: Livestock, skins and hides, bananas, fish, charcoal, scrap metal.

Somalia went through periods of British and Italian rule and UN trusteeship prior to independence in 1960 and adopted its flag when the territory was under UN administration. Set on a field of UN blue, a five-pointed star represents countries where the Somali people traditionally lived (Ethiopia, Kenya, Djibouti and the former British and Italian Somaliland). Since independence, Somalia has engaged in disputes with its neighbours over the right of Somalians to self-determination regardless of where they settle. The country has been in a state of civil war since 1991 and border disputes, factional fighting and clan rivalry have created a long-term refugee and humanitarian crisis. A transitional government, in place since 2000, expired in 2003 amid attempts to set up an interim government.

KENYA

Republic of Kenya

Flag proportions: 2:3
Adopted: 12 December 1963
Capital: Nairobi
Area: 582,646km^2 (224,961mi^2)
Population: 31,5 million
Languages: Kiswahili, English
Religion: Christian, Muslim, Traditional
Currency: Kenya shilling
Exports: Tea, coffee, horticultural products.

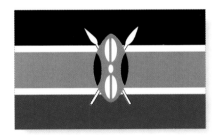

Parts of the region were inhabited by early humans over five million years ago. The coast was settled by Arab traders in the 8th century and fell under Portuguese rule in the 15th century. The country became a British protectorate in 1896 and a colony in 1921. Kenya gained independence in 1963 and joined the Commonwealth in 1964. Black, red and green are the colours of the Kenya African National Union, which came to power at independence. On the flag they are separated by white stripes, representing democracy, peace and unity. Black represents the majority of the people, red is for sacrifice, and green for natural resources. A traditional Masai shield and two crossed spears symbolize readiness to defend freedom.

UGANDA

Republic of Uganda

Flag proportions: 2:3
Adopted: 9 October 1962
Capital: Kampala
Area: 241,038km^2 (93,072mi^2)
Population: 23,5 million
Language: English
Religion: Christian, Muslim
Currency: Uganda shilling
Exports: Coffee, tea, cotton, tobacco, oil seed, fruit, textiles, hides and skins.

Uganda gained independence from Britain in 1962 as part of the Commonwealth. By 1971, following a series of coups, it was under the dictatorial regime of Major-General Idi Amin Dada, who suspended the constitution and took absolute power. He was overthrown in 1978, but Uganda remained in a state of unrest until the establishment of a broad-based coalition government in 1986. The flag adopted in 1962 was based on the tricolour of the dominant Uganda People's Congress. The colours symbolize the people (black), sunlight (yellow) and brotherhood (red). Uganda's national bird, the crested crane (*Balearica pavonia*) is depicted on a central white disc. Despite regime changes, the flag has endured.

TANZANIA

United Republic of Tanzania

Flag proportions: 2:3
Adopted: 30 June 1964
Capital: Dodoma
Area: 945,037km² (364,881mi²)
Population: 34 million
Language: Swahili, English
Religion: Christian, Muslim
Currency: Tanzanian shilling
Exports: Coffee beans, cotton, tobacco, tea, cashew nuts, cloves, minerals, petroleum products.

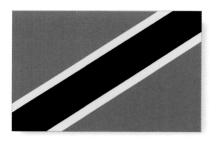

The flag represents the union of the former British Tanganyika and the island of Zanzibar, whose long-ruling Sultanate was overthrown in 1964. Zanzibar's flag was a horizontal tricolour of blue above black and green, while that of Tanganyika had a green field equally divided by a horizontal, gold-edged black band. The flag of the United Republic of Tanzania combines elements of both. Green symbolizes the land and blue the sea, while gold is for mineral wealth and black for the people.

Tanzania's attractions include Africa's highest mountain, Kilimanjaro (5895m/19,340ft), Olduvai Gorge, home to some of the oldest humanoid fossil finds, and Stone Town, the oldest part of Zanzibar, and a UN World Heritage Site.

MALAWI

Republic of Malawi

Flag proportions: 2:3
Adopted: 6 July 1964
Capital: Lilongwe
Area: 118,484km² (45,747mi²)
Population: 11 million
Languages: Chichewa, English
Religion: Christian, Muslim, Animist
Currency: Kwacha
Exports: Tobacco, tea, sugar, cotton, groundnuts.

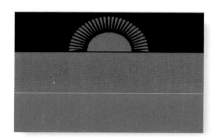

Midway along the uppermost band of the horizontal tricolour of Malawi is a representation of a radiant rising sun, or *kwacha*, in red, symbolizing a new dawn of hope and progress in Africa. The role of the sun is underscored by the fact that Malawi's currency is termed the kwacha. At independence in 1964, the colours chosen were those of the dominant Malawi Congress Party. Black represents the people and their heritage, red is the colour of sacrifice, while green represents the land and its natural resources.

ANGOLA

Republic of Angola

Flag proportions: 2:3
Adopted: 11 November 1975
Capital: Luanda
Area: 1,246,700km² (481,354 mi²)
Population: 10,7 million
Language: Portuguese, local
Religion: Christian, Animist
Currency: Kwanza
Exports: Crude oil, diamonds, refined oil, natural gas, coffee.

Angola's constitution decrees that the flag be divided into red and black horizontal bands. Black represents Africa, red is the blood shed for liberation, yellow is for the country's wealth. The cogwheel symbolizes workers and industry; the machete is for peasants, agriculture and the armed struggle; and the star stands for international solidarity. The design is based on the former Soviet flag, but Angola has abandoned Marxism, raising the possibility of a new flag. After a lengthy civil war to end Portuguese rule, the People's Liberation Movement (MPLA) took power in 1975. Unrest continued until 1994 when a peace accord integrated government and rebel (UNITA) forces. Fighting resumed in 1998, leaving thousands homeless, but UNITA leader's death in 2002 renewed hopes for peace.

ZAMBIA

Republic of Zambia

Flag proportions: 2:3
Adopted: 24 October 1964
Capital: Lusaka
Area: 752,614km² (290,586mi²)
Population: 11 million
Language: English
Religion: Christian
Currency: Kwacha
Exports: Metals (copper, cobalt, zinc), tobacco.

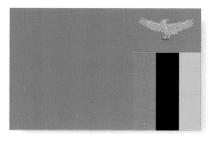

Unusually, the charges (objects) depicted on the Zambian flag are placed at the fly rather than the hoist. In the lower corner a vertical red-black-orange tricolour represents, respectively, the struggle for independence, the people, and the country's mineral wealth, chiefly copper. The colours are also those of the dominant political party at independence in 1964. In the upper fly, an eagle in flight represents liberty and freedom. The green field signifies the land's natural resources. As the former British colony of Northern Rhodesia, Zambia was part of the Federation of Rhodesia and Nyasaland (now Malawi), and it remains in the Commonwealth. The southern border is the Zambezi River, on which the mighty Victoria Falls are situated.

ZIMBABWE

Republic of Zimbabwe

Flag proportions: 1:2
Adopted: 18 April 1980
Capital: Harare
Area: 390,759km² (150,872mi²)
Population: 13,9 million
Language: English
Religion: Christian, Animist
Currency: Zimbabwe dollar
Exports: Metals, tobacco, textiles, cotton, clothing.

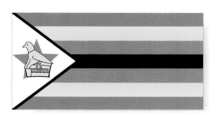

After years of UN sanctions and a protracted civil war, the former British colony of Rhodesia became Zimbabwe in 1980. Since independence, the once-prosperous country has slid into economic and political chaos under Robert Mugabe. The green, yellow, red and black of the ruling Zimbabwe African National Union (ZANU) appear as equal horizontal stripes. A white isosceles triangle, its base at the hoist, occupies the full depth. It points to a peaceful future, while the black border represents the postcolonial leadership and a five-pointed red star symbolizes Marxism. The yellow Zimbabwe bird is based on stone carvings from the centuries-old ruins near Masvingo.

MOZAMBIQUE

Republic of Mozambique

Flag proportions: 2:3
Adopted: 1 May 1983
Capital: Maputo
Area: 799,380km² (308,642mi²)
Population: 17,7 million
Language: Portuguese
Religion: Traditional, Roman Catholic, Muslim
Currency: Metical
Exports: Shellfish, cashew nuts, cotton, sugar, copra.

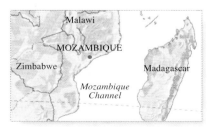

The colours come from Frelimo, the leading political party. Red symbolizes resistance to colonialism, green the richness of the land, black the African continent, yellow the mineral riches, and white peace and justice. The rifle stands for vigilance in defence (although it is fitted with a bayonet, an offensive weapon), the hoe is for agriculture, the book for education. The yellow star is for Marxism. Mozambique is one of the poorest countries in Africa, exacerbated by drought and a protracted civil war. Strenuous economic reforms, including abandoning Marxism in 1989, have resulted in improvements, but much of the population lives below the poverty line. Despite severe floods in 1999 and 2000, the country is making progress.

NAMIBIA

Republic of Namibia

Flag proportions: 2:3
Adopted: 21 March 1990
Capital: Windhoek
Area: 824,268km² (318,275mi²)
Population: 1,8 million
Language: English, several local languages
Religion: Christian
Currency: Namibian dollar
Exports: Diamonds, fish, live animals, meat, uranium.

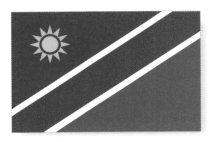

Namibia was part of Imperial Germany, Great Britain and South Africa prior to independence in 1990. The new flag was chosen from designs submitted by the public. The field is divided into two right-angled triangles by a diagonal red band, bordered with white, rising from the hoist. The lower green triangle symbolizes natural resources, while the upper blue triangle represents the sky, Atlantic Ocean, marine resources, and the importance of rain in this dry land. White is for peace and unity, yellow for the Namib Desert, and red for future hopes. The colours came from the main political parties at independence. A gold radiant sun depicts life and energy. The rays are separated from the sun's body by a narrow blue circle, a feature also found on Taiwan's flag (p88).

BOTSWANA

Republic of Botswana

Flag proportions: 2:3
Adopted: 30 September 1966
Capital: Gaborone
Area: 582,000km² (224,808mi²)
Population: 1,7 million
Languages: English, Setswana
Religion: Traditional, Christian
Currency: Pula
Exports: Diamonds, copper, nickel, beef.

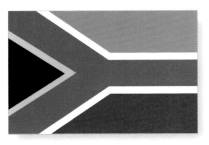

Rain, a rare and precious commodity, is depicted on the Botswana flag by two equal horizontal bands of pale blue. In the desert, water is life, and the Setswana word *pula* means not only 'water' and 'rain', but also the life that is derived from it. The country's currency is the pula and the term forms the national motto as well. Between the blue bands is a narrow horizontal band of black bordered with white, symbolizing the harmonious coexistence of the country's large black population with the relatively small number of whites.

SOUTH AFRICA

Republic of South Africa

Flag proportions: 2:3
Adopted: 27 April 1994
Capital: Pretoria
Area: 1,221,037km² (471,647mi²)
Population: 45 million
Language: English plus 10 others
Religion: Christian, Traditional, Muslim, Hindu
Currency: Rand
Exports: Gold, diamonds, metal ore, minerals, wool, chemicals, maize, fruit, sugar.

Many flags have flown over South Africa during the 350 years since European settlement, and the new flag reflects this historical legacy. Thus, red, white and blue derived from the Dutch and British flags; and black, green and yellow are from the African National Congress (ANC), which came to power in 1994. The pall (Y-pattern) symbolizes the merging of formerly disparate groups and embodies hope for progress. From its establishment as a republic in 1961 to the first democratic elections, South Africa was fragmented between an economically powerful white minority and a disenfranchised black majority. Under Nelson Mandela, the country united behind largely common goals, although issues of poverty reduction and economic growth still prevail.

SWAZILAND

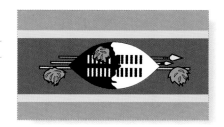

Kingdom of Swaziland

Flag proportions: 2:3
Adopted: 30 October 1967
Capital: Mbabane
Area: 17,400km² (6705mi²)
Population: 1 million
Languages: siSwati, English
Religion: Christian, Traditional
Currency: Lilangeni
Exports: Sugar, wood pulp, cotton yarn, tinned fruit.

Swaziland was a British protectorate until 1968. The flag is derived from one presented by King Sobhuza II to the Swazi contingent of the Africa Pioneer Corps in 1941. The blue bands represent peace and stability after battles of the past (red); yellow is for natural resources. On the red band is a traditional cowhide shield with two assegais (spears) and a fighting stick with *injobo* tassles, comprising feathers of the lourie and the whydah (widowbird). Another tassle is attached to the shield.

Since 1968, Swaziland has been ruled by King Mswati III, whose family founded the kingdom in the 19th century. A hereditary monarchy, political parties are banned, but there is pressure for political reform and the implementation of democratic representation.

LESOTHO

Kingdom of Lesotho

Flag proportions: 2:3
Adopted: 20 January 1987
Capital: Maseru
Area: 30,355km² (11,720mi²)
Population: 2,4 million
Language: Sesotho, English
Religion: Christian
Currency: Loti (Maluti)
Exports: Cattle, wheat, wool, mohair, vegetables, diamonds.

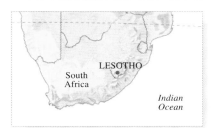

The colours of the flag embody Lesotho's motto *Khotso-Pula-Nala*, 'peace (white), rain (blue) and prosperity (green)'. A blue diagonal band rising from the hoist, and a green right-angled triangle in the lower fly, symbolize the link between water and prosperity. The white right-angled triangle in the upper half has a traditional Sotho shield with a plume, crossed spear and ball-headed club (*knobkerrie*).

Lesotho (formerly Basutoland) gained independence as a constitutional monarchy in 1966 and has been ruled by King Letsie III since 1990. A mountainous country, the highest point is Thaba Ntlenyana (3482m/11,424ft), while the lowest is a lofty 1400m (4590ft) above sea level.

MADAGASCAR

Democratic Republic of Madagascar

Flag proportions: 2:3
Adopted: 21 October 1958
Capital: Antananarivo
Area: 587,041km² (226,658mi²)
Population: 15 million
Language: Malagasy
Religion: Traditional, Christian
Currency: Malagasy franc
Exports: Coffee, shrimps, cloves, vanilla, chromium, cotton fabrics.

The flag comprises equal horizontal bands of red above green, and a broad vertical band of white occupying the full depth at the hoist. Red and white come from the pre colonial Merina Kingdom, under which most of the country was united. Green is for the Hova people who comprise the agricultural peasant class. Madagascar became a French protectorate in 1885, achieved self-government in 1958 and independence in 1960. Martial law was imposed in 1975 under a Marxist constitution, which was abandoned in 1980. Elections in 1992–93 ended 17 years of single-party rule, but the hotly contested 2001 presidential election nearly caused secession of half the country. Agriculture is the mainstay of the economy, with coffee and spices, like vanilla and cloves, dominanting.

COMOROS

Union of the Comoros

Flag proportions: 2:3
Adopted: 23 December 2001
Capital: Moroni
Area: 1862km² (719mi²)
Population: 611,100
Language: Arabic, French
Religion: Muslim
Currency: Comorian franc
Exports: Vanilla, cloves, ylang-ylang, cocoa, copra, coffee.

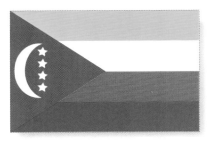

Since gaining independence from France in 1975, there have been repeated coups or attempted coups by the islands of Mohéli/Mwali, Anjouan/Nzwani, Grand Comore/Njazidja and Mayotte, to give both their French and local names. Anjouan and Mohéli declared independence in 1997. Mayotte remains a territorial collectivity of France, although it is claimed by the Comoros. A new constitution was adopted in January 2002 and it is hoped the situation can be resolved.

At the hoist, a green triangle bears a white crescent, pointing towards the fly, with a row of four five-pointed stars between the tips. Both the crescent and the colour green are emblems of Islam. The stars represent the larger islands, as do the equal horizontal stripes of yellow, white, red and blue.

SEYCHELLES

Republic of Seychelles

Flag proportions: 1:2
Adopted: 8 January 1996
Capital: Victoria, on Mahé
Area: 455km² (175mi²)
Population: 81,000
Language: Creole, English, French
Religion: Roman Catholic
Currency: Seychelles rupee
Exports: Fish, cinnamon, copra, refined oil products.

The Seychelles comprises over 100 islands scattered across the Indian Ocean. As a result of political upheavals, there have been three flags since independence from France in 1976. The present flag was designed to effect reconciliation after the Seychelles became a multiparty democracy in 1993. The five bands radiating from the lower hoist represent the colours of two major political parties. Red, being common to both, is placed between white and green, for the ruling Seychelles People's United Party, and blue and yellow, for the opposition Democratic Party.

RÉUNION

Department of Reunion

Flag proportions: 2:3
Adopted: 5 March 1848
Capital: Saint-Denis
Area: 2512km² (970mi²)
Population: 755,000
Language: French, Creole
Religion: Roman Catholic
Currency: Euro
Exports: Sugar, rum, molasses, vanilla, pefume essences.

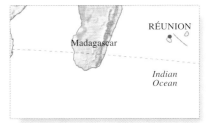

Réunion is an overseas department of France, so the official flag is the *Tricolore*. In 1642 the Mascarene Islands, which includes Réunion and Mauritius, were claimed by Louis XIII of France, but only Réunion (also known as Ile de Bourbon) is still French. During the 17th and 18th centuries, French settlers, Africans, Chinese, Malays and Malabar Indians established the rich ethnic mix that prevails today.

Rugged and mountainous, Réunion is the site of an active volcano, Piton de la Fournaise, on the southeastern coast. The region is subject to periodic cyclones from December to April, and a cyclone centre at Saint-Denis acts as the monitoring station for the entire Indian Ocean.

MAURITIUS

Republic of Mauritius

Flag proportions: 2:3
Adopted: 12 January 1968
Capital: Port Louis
Area: 2040km² (788mi²)
Population: 1,2 million
Language: English
Religion: Hindu, Muslim, Roman Catholic
Currency: Mauritius rupee
Exports: Sugar, clothing, tea, molasses, jewellery.

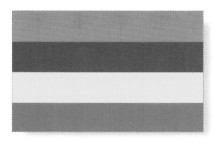

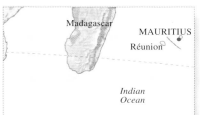

The four equal horizontal bands recall the colours of the island's coat of arms. Red stands for independence, blue for the Indian Ocean, yellow is a symbol of a bright future, and green is for the lush vegetation. A French colony from 1715, Mauritius was siezed by Britain in 1810. African slaves worked in the sugar-cane plantations, but the abolition of slavery in 1833 saw the arrival of indentured labourers from India, whose descendents now constitute about 70 per cent of the population. Internal self-government in 1957 was followed by independence within the Commonwealth in 1968. Tourism is important to the economy, as borne out by the country's motto *Stella Clavisque Maris Indici* ('The star and key of the Indian Ocean').

ST HELENA

Saint Helena

Flag proportions: 1:2
Adopted: unknown
Capital: Jamestown
Area: 410km² (158mi²)
Population: 7000
Language: English
Religion: Christian
Currency: Saint Helenian pound
Exports: Fish (frozen, canned and dried), coffee, handicrafts.

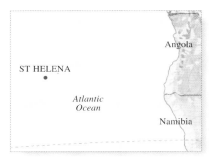

This tiny volcanic island is situated in the Atlantic Ocean, about 1900km (1200mi) west of Africa. It became a British possession in 1673 and a colony in 1834, and remains one of Britain's overseas territories. The island flag, and also that of its dependencies, Ascension Island and the Tristan da Cunha group, is the British Blue Ensign with the arms of St Helena at the fly. The arms consist of a shield on which is depicted a three-masted British warship, with furled sails, below a steep cliff. The ship is flying the Cross of St George. In the upper part of the shield, against a yellow field, is a wirebird, a species endemic to St Helena.

BRITISH ANTARCTIC TERRITORY

British Antarctic Territory

Flag proportions: 1:2
Adopted: 21 April 1998
Capital: British bases at Halley in Coats Land, Rothera on the Antarctic Peninsula and Signy in the South Orkney Islands.
Area: 660,000km² (170,874mi²)
Population: No permanent inhabitants. Research personnel fluctuate from summer to winter.

Occupying only a small portion of this vast continent, the BAT administers all British territories south of latitude 60°S (South Orkney and South Shetland islands, Antarctic Peninsula and adjacent land, and Coats Land, extending to the South Pole). The ensign used by research stations and their vessels has the Union Flag in the canton and a plain white field, for the ice and snow which covers Antarctica. The arms, at the fly, consist of a shield on which a 'pile' (wedge) is placed on a chief of three wavy blue lines symbolizing the sea. On the pile is a torch, signifying exploration (as on the arms of South Georgia, see p131). The supporters are a lion, standing on a base of grass, and a king penguin, standing on ice. The three-masted ship on the crest is the polar exploration vessel *Discovery*.

Glossary

Armorial banner Flag bearing an exact depiction of a coat of arms.

Arms (coat of arms). Heraldic symbols of honour, granted to families, states, organizations etc.

Banner Rectangular flag, originally flown with the long side at the hoist. Almost always bear a personal coat of arms.

Battle flag Flown by armed forces, or a warship on active service (*see also* Colours).

Becket Short line attached to the hoist, with a toggle at the top and an eye splice or grommet at the bottom.

Bicolour Flag with two bands of different colours, either horizontal or vertical.

Blue peter Signal flag for the letter P (blue with a white square at the centre), flown by a vessel about to leave port.

Burgee Private or club flag flown at the masthead by yachts.

Canton (also called chief canton or upper hoist). The uppermost corner of the flag, nearest the hoist or flagpole. Considered to be the position of highest honour on a flag.

Charge Any design, pattern or device on a flag or coat of arms.

Chief The upper portion (one third) of a heraldic shield.

Civil flag A national flag as displayed on land by private citizens.

Cleat Two-pronged fastener on the staff, within reach of the person securing the halyard by looping it over the cleat several times.

Cockade A coloured ribbon worn on caps to show political persuasion.

Colours A flag that indicates nationality. Also the name given to a pair of silk flags carried by a military unit, usually at battalion or regimental level, and to the ceremony of hoisting or lowering the colours.

Compartment In heraldry, a panel or base below the shield, on which supporters sometimes stand.

Counter-change To place one design or pattern on top of another so that the underneath image remains visible.

Couped A cross cut cleanly, usually before reaching a border, like the cross on the flag of Switzerland.

Courtesy flag Flag of the country in whose territorial waters a foreign ship is sailing. Usually flown when entering port.

Crest In heraldry, an object placed above a helmet on a shield.

Cross On a flag, a vertical and horizontal stripe placed at right angles, extending across the whole flag to divide it into four.

Depth The vertical dimension of a flag as measured along the hoist.

Dexter The right-hand side of a shield or coat of arms (the side opposite the left hand of the observer).

Ensign Rectangular flag flown at the stern of a vessel to denote its nationality. The ensign may differ from the national flag.

Field The whole of the flag or shield surface. When a design is applied, the field is effectively the background.

Fimbriated Having a narrow edge or border.

Flag A piece of coloured cloth attached to a pole. Usually decorated with a design and used as an emblem, symbol or means of signalling.

Flag captain Commander of a flagship.

Flag Day June 14, an annual holiday in the USA, to celebrate the adoption in 1777 of the Stars and Stripes.

Flag lieutenant Junior officer who is aide-de-camp to an admiral.

Flag of convenience Flag of a country in which a ship is registered for the sake of legal or financial advantage.

Flag officer Naval officer of the rank of Rear Admiral or above.

Flag of truce White flag raised on a battlefield indicating willingness to negotiate or surrender.

Flagpole/flagstaff A pole on which a flag is hoisted and displayed.

Flagship A naval warship on which the fleet commander is based. In a merchant fleet, usually the newest or most impressive ship.

Fleur-de-lis Heraldic flower of three leaves.

Fork-tailed Describing a flag with a shallow split at the fly.

Fly That part of the flag farthest from the staff, sometimes divided as upper fly and lower fly.

Garrison flag Large US flag flown on military posts on special days.

Gonfalon (gonfanon) A banner hanging from a crossbar; also a flag with three or more tails.

Guidon Cavalry flag, usually long and narrow with two rounded tails.

Half-mast (half-staff) A prescribed position below the full height of the flagstaff, but not necessarily halfway, at which a flag is flown as a sign of mourning.

Halyard The rope by which the flag is hoisted (raised) or lowered, with a toggle at one end and an eye splice or grommet at the other.

Heraldry Armorial bearings, insignia or symbols representing a person, family or dynasty. Also the study of the classification of these items and the allocation of the right to bear arms.

Hoist That part of the flag nearest to the staff, sometimes divided as upper hoist and lower hoist.

House flag Flag of a commercial undertaking, such as a shipping line.

International flag Flag used by an organization that is recognizable wherever in the world it is flown, such as the UN.

Jack Rectangular national flag, smaller than the ensign, flown from the jackstaff (see below).

Jackstaff Short staff at the bow of a warship, for flying the national flag. A jackstay is a wire rope to which the edge of a sail is fastened.

Lay up the colours A ceremony in which military colours are placed in safekeeping before going on active service.

Labarum Standard or banner carried in Christian religious processions; also the military standard bearing a Christian monogram, once used by Constantine the Great.

Maritime flag Flag flown by civilian ships (merchant vessels), usually from the stern or rear-mast. Also called a civil ensign, merchant ensign or merchant flag (*see also* Ensign, Naval ensign).

Mast Vertically fixed pole on a ship, for attaching the rigging. The term is also generally used, as in radio mast.

Metals In heraldry, gold (or) and silver (argent), often represented as yellow and white respectively.

Motto Word(s) or short sentence accompanying arms, often written in Latin or medieval French.

National flag Flag used by citizens of a country and also to represent the country abroad. Many countries have only national flags and use them for all purposes, including on vessels (*see also* State flag).

Naval ensign Flag flown by naval vessels and at naval bases. Often plain coloured or of a simple right-angle cross design, with the national flag in the canton (*see also* Ensign, Maritime flag).

Obverse The 'front' of a flag, usually identical to the back or reverse.

Passant In heraldry, a beast walking, with the head in profile.

Pennant Long, tapering or triangular flag flown from the masthead of a warship in commission.

Pile In heraldry, the shape of a wedge, usually point downward.

Post flag Large US flag normally flown on military posts (bases).

Proper In heraldry, displayed in natural colours.

Proportion A flag's proportion is the ratio between the vertical depth (width) and the horizontal length.

Q-flag Quarantine flag. The yellow signal flag for the letter Q, flown from a vessel to indicate there is no disease on board and request permission to enter port. Also called a yellow flag.

Quarter Quadrangular form containing one fourth of the field.

Quartered Flags or shields may be divided into quarters containing different designs. The commonest division is four equal quarters, but a shield may be divided into 16, 32 or 56 quarterings.

Queen's Colour Flags representing a military unit in the British armed forces (*see also* Colours, Regimental Colour).

Radiant Emitting rays, as a radiant sun, for example.

Ratio The relative proportions of a flag described as height against width (1:2 describes a flag twice as wide as it is high).

Red Ensign Flag (ensign) of the British Merchant Navy.

Red Flag Flag with a red field and hammer and sickle emblem in the chief canton. First used during the French Revolution, it became the flag of Russia after the 1917 Bolshevik Revolution, then of the Soviet Union. It remains the flag of extreme left-wing political organizations.

Regimental Colour Flags showing the crest and battle honours of a regiment, especially in the British armed forces (*see also* Colours).

Saltire (Also called a cross in saltire) A diagonal cross stretching from corner to corner of a flag.

Scandinavian cross On a flag, a cross with the upright set closer to the hoist than to the fly.

Shield In heraldry, the basic unit on which a coat of arms is depicted.

Show the flag To assert a territorial claim through military or naval presence. Also, to make an appearance.

Signal flags Flags representing letters and numbers, once used to communicate between ships at sea.

Sinister The left side of a shield or coat of arms and the side opposite the right hand of the observer.

Staff Vertically fixed pole from which a flag is flown.

Standard A distinctive flag, sometimes tapering to a swallow-tail, bearing a personal coat of arms of a sovereign or high-ranking noble. Formerly carried in battle to mark the army's rallying point.

State flag Flag flown by government and diplomatic missions abroad. It often consists of the national flag with the addition of the country's coat of arms or emblem. Not all countries have a separate state flag.

Storm flag Small flag flown during violent weather.

Streamer Long, narrow flag (or strip of fabric), usually single pointed. Not necessarily a flag but rather a decoration. Also called a pennant.

Strike the flag (strike the colours). To lower a flag rapidly, usually as a sign of surrender.

Sun in splendour Heraldic radiant sun, shown with a face.

Supporters In heraldry, a human or animal figure on either side of the shield, supporting it.

Swallowtail A flag deeply split at the fly, ending in two points.

Triangle A flag divided by a coloured triangle, usually at the hoist.

Triband (*see also* Tricolour) A flag with three bands of only two colours, either horizontal or vertical.

Tricolore The national flag of France.

Tricolour A flag with three bands and three different colours, either horizontal or vertical.

Truck Block at the top of the staff, through which the halyard passes.

Vexillology The study and collection of information about flags.

Vexilloid Before the origin of flags; a staff or spear topped with an emblem, used as a sign for troops to rally around.

Vexillum A square flag or banner used by Roman armies, from which the term vexillology originated.

Yellow flag (*see also* Q-flag) Another name for a quarantine flag.

Index

A Abu Dhabi 74
Afghanistan 69, 76
Africa 133
African National Congress 21
African Renaissance 133
African Union (AU) 133
airborne flags 25
Ajman 74
Akinkunmi, Michael 142
Albania 62
Algeria 34, 135
Allahu Akbar 76
American Samoa (see also Samoa) 102
Andorra 52
Anglo-Boer War 21
Anglo-Transvaal War 24
Angola 133, 148
Anguilla 119
Antarctica 125, 131
Antigua and Barbuda 120
Antilles 119
ANZUS 93
Arab League 37
Argentina 32, 125,131
Armenia 67
armorial banner 20, 102
Aruba 123
ASEAN 37
Asia 69
Australia 93, 94, 96
Austria 59
Azerbaijan 67
Aztec 113, 114

B badges 18
Bahamas 116
Bahrain 13, 75
Bangladesh 79
banners 16
Barbados 122
Bayeux Tapestry 23
Belarus 14, 66

Belgium 53
Belgrano, Manuel 131
Belize 115
Benelux 53
Benin 34,140
Bermuda 112
Bhutan 80
birds — Andean condor 127
  bald eagle 102
  condor 129
  crested crane (*Balearica pavonia*) 147
  eagle 113, 118, 149
  frigate bird 102
  King Penguin 152
  kumul (bird of paradise) 98
  quetzal bird (*Pharomacrus mocinno*) 113
  sisserou parrot (*Psittacus imperialis*) 121
  swan 96
  wirebird 152
  Zimbabwe bird 149
black 31, 72, 74, 75, 117, 119, 121, 123, 128, 135, 136, 138, 140, 145, 147, 148, 149, 150
Black Star Shipping Company 140
blue 30, 77, 79, 80, 88, 89, 90, 91, 101, 112, 113, 114, 115, 118, 122, 123, 127, 130, 138, 139, 142, 143, 144, 145, 146, 148, 150, 151, 152
Blue Ensign 29, 51, 81, 96, 100, 101, 102, 103, 116, 117, 119, 120, 131, 152
blue-white-blue 112, 114
Bolívar, Simón 127, 129
Bolivia 32, 129
Bora-Bora (see French Polynesia)
Bosnia and Herzegovina 61
Botswana 133, 150
Brazil 125, 129
British Antarctic Survey 131

British Antarctic Territory 18, 152
British army 23
British Columbia (Canada) 31
British Empire 31
British Indian Ocean Territory (BIOT) 81
British overseas territory 103, 112, 116, 117, 119, 120, 131, 152
British Virgin Islands 119
Brunei 90
Buddhism 83, 85
Buddhist prayer flags 80
Bulgaria 64
Bundesländer 58, 59
Burkina Faso 141
Burundi 145
Byron, Lord 11

C Cambodia 89
Cameroon 34, 142
Canada 105, 111
Canadian provinces 111
canton 14
cap of liberty 32, 114, 130
Cape Agulhas 133
Cape of Good Hope 133
Cape Verde 138
Caribbean 105
Cayman Islands 117
Central African Republic 143
Central America 32, 105
Chad 142
Chagos Archipelago (see BIOT)
chakra 79
charges 17, 18
Chile 125, 130
China 33, 83, 85, 86, 88
Chuuk (see Micronesia)
coats of arms 16, 17, 18, 18, 19, 20
code flags (see flags, signals)
cogwheel 148
Colombia 32, 125, 127
colours — false 27
  military 22–25

British Antarctic Territory 18, 152
Colours of Liberty 31
Columbus, Christopher 113, 115, 117, 119, 120, 122, 123, 127
common colours 30–31
Commonwealth 37, 98, 99, 100, 101, 119, 123, 128, 137, 139, 142, 147, 149, 152
Commonwealth of Independent States (CIS) 66, 69
Commonwealth Star 96
Communism 47, 56, 57, 64, 83, 85
communist emblems 66
Comoros 34, 152
Congo (Brazzaville) 144
Congo (see Democratic Republic of Congo)
Continental Colours 108
Cook Islands 103
Cook, Captain James 96, 101, 103, 131
Costa Rica 32, 112, 114
Côte d'Ivoire 139
crescent 76, 77, 80, 81, 90
crescent and star (see also star and crescent) 34, 135, 136, 137, 152
Croatia 61
cross 26 34, 101, 112, 118
  quarter cross 118, 121, 123
cross pattée (see also Maltese cross) 100
cross of Lorraine (see St Anthony's cross)
crucifix 26
Crusades 19, 34, 47
Cuba 31, 105, 116
Cyprus 63
Czech Republic 57
Czechoslovakia 65

D *Dannebrog* 54, 55
de Miranda, Francisco 32, 127
Declaration of Independence 31
Democratic Republic of Congo (DRC) 34, 133, 144

Denmark 34, 54
Diego Garcia (see BIOT) 81
displaying flags 12, 13, 14
distress signal 14
Djibouti 146
Dominica 121
Dominican Republic 118
Dubai 74
Dutch East India Company 20
Dutch flag (see Netherlands)
E Eagle of Saladin 136
East Timor 91
Easter Island 130
Eastern and Southeast Asia 83, 84
Ecuador 32, 125, 127
Egypt 13, 34, 136
El Salvador 15, 32, 112, 114
emblems 16, 17, 18, 19, 20, 21, 43
Emirates (see United Arab
    Emirates)
England 20, 50
ensign 23, 27
Equator 98, 99, 102, 129
Equatorial Guinea 143
Eritrea 146
Estonia 56
Ethiopia 34, 146
Europe 47, 49
European Union (EU) 37, 47, 36, 53
F Falkland Islands 125, 131
Far East 83
Faroe Islands 54
Federal Republic of Germany (see
    Germany)
Federated States of Micronesia
    (see Micronesia)
Fiji Islands 101
finial 14
Finland 13, 56
Flag Act 108
flag of convenience 27
flagpole (flagstaff) 13, 14, 129
flags
    as symbols of nationhood 12
    at funerals 13, 15
    at sea 26–29
    breaking 15
    common characteristics 30–35

display 12, 13, 14
draping 13
flying 13, 14, 36
history 16–21
hoisting 15
hours for flying 13
mourning (used in) 14–15
national 12, 13, 22
parts of 13, 14
qualities of 43
representatives of a people 43
saluting 15
signal 27, 28
sizes 13
France 20, 52
French Equatorial Africa 142, 144
French Guiana 128
French Overseas Territories 52,
    100, 102, 112, 120, 128, 152
French Polynesia 102
French Revolution 32, 105, 114
French West Africa 139, 141
Fujairah 74
Futuna (see Wallis and Futuna)
G Gabon 144
Galapagos Islands 127
Gambia (The) 137
Garvey, Marcus 34, 140
Georgia 67
Germany 58
Ghana 34, 140
Gibraltar 51
Gilbert and Ellice islands 100, 102
'God is Great' (see Allahu Akbar)
gold 31, 122, 128, 148
Gold Coast (see Ghana)
Gran Colombia 125, 127
Greece 62
green 30, 32, 72, 73, 74, 75, 76,
    77, 78, 79, 113, 117, 121, 122,
    128, 129, 135, 136, 137, 138,
    139, 140, 141, 142, 143, 144,
    145, 146, 147, 148, 149, 150,
    151, 152
Greenland 54
Grenada 122
Guadalcanal 99
Guadeloupe 120

Guam 97
Guatemala 32, 112, 113
Guinea 34, 138
Guinea-Bissau 138
Gulf states 69
Guyana 128
H Haiti 118
half-mast (half-staff) 15
halyard 13, 14
Hawaii 31
Hawk of Quraish 136
heraldry 18, 19
Herzogovina (see Bosnia)
Hinomaru 86
HMS Bountry 103
Holy See (see Vatican City)
Honduras 32, 112, 113
Hong Kong 83, 86
Hungary 61, 64
I Iceland 55
ICRC (see Red Cross)
Inca 125, 127, 129, 130
India 79
Indochina 83, 88, 89
Indonesia 13, 91
International Maritime Code of
    Signals 28, 41
IOC (see Olympic flag)
Iran 76
Iraq 34, 76
Ireland 50
Islam 32, 34, 69, 73, 75, 135, 136
Israel 72
Italy 59
Ivory Coast (see Côte d'Ivoire)
J Jamaica 117
Jammu and Kashmir 79
Japan 83, 86
Jolly Roger 26
Jordan 71
K Kazakhstan 77
Kenya 147
Key, Francis Scott 11
King's Colour 23
Kiribati 102
Korea (see North Korea, South
    Korea)
Kosrae (see Micronesia)

Kuwait 34, 75
Kyrgyzstan 78
L Laos 88
Latvia 56
Lebanon 71
Leeward Islands 119, 120, 123
Lesotho 151
Liberia 31, 133, 139
Libya 34, 136
Liechtenstein 58
Lithuania 57
London College of Arms 139
Louisiana Purchase 105
Low Countries 53
Luxembourg 53
M Macau 86
Macedonia 62
Madagascar 151
Magellan, Ferdinand 130
Magellan Strait 125, 130
Magen David 72
Malawi 148
Malaysia 31, 90
Maldives 81
Mali 34, 141
Malta 60
Maltese cross 60, 100
Maori 103
maple leaf 111
maritime flags 27
Marquesas islands (see French
    Polynesia)
Marshall Islands 98
Martinique 121
Mauritania 135, 137
Mauritius
Maya 113, 114
Melanesia 93, 99, 101
Mexico 105, 113
Micronesia 93, 98
Middle East 69
military colours (see colours)
modern flags, evolution of 20–21
Moldova 65
Monaco 13, 52
Mongolia 85
Montenegro (see Serbia)
Montserrat 120

moon 97

Morocco 15, 135

motor racing 39

Mount Everest 69

Mozambique 149

Muhammad 135

Myanmar 89

N Namibia 133, 150

national flags (see flags, national)

NATO 37

Nauru 99

Nazi Germany 21, 23, 34

Nazi Party 58

Nelson, Admiral 27

NEPAD 133

Nepal 80

Netherlands 20, 13, 35, 53

Netherlands Antilles 123

New Caledonia 100

New Hebrides (see Vanuatu)

New Zealand 93, 94, 101, 103

Nicaragua 32, 112, 114

Niger 141

Nigeria 133, 133, 142

Niue 103

North America 105

North American Free Trade
   Agreement (NAFTA) 105

North Korea 87

North Yemen 73

Northern Cyprus 63

Northern Ireland 50

Northern Mariana Islands 97

Norway 14, 55

O Oceania 93, 94

Olympic flag 38

Oman 73

orange (see also saffron) 79, 80,
   98, 139, 141, 149

Organization of African Unity
   (OAU) 133

ornament (see finial)

Ottoman Empire 32, 34, 61, 62, 63,
   64, 65, 72, 133, 136

P Pacific Ocean 87, 98, 100, 102

Pakistan 69, 78

Palau 97

Palestine 72

Palestine Authority 72

pall 150

Pan-African colours 31, 34, 119,
   117, 133, 137, 138, 140, 141,
   142, 143, 144

Panama 34, 115

Panama Canal Zone 115

Pan-Arab colours 32, 34, 69, 71,
   73, 74, 75, 135

Pan-Slavic colours 35, 61, 65

Papua New Guinea 98

Paraguay 32, 130

pentagram 135

People's Republic of China (see
   China)

People's Republic of Congo (see
   Congo Brazzaville)

Peru 125, 129

Peter the Great 35, 66

Philippines 83, 91

Phyrigian Cap (see Cap of Liberty)

piragua/pirogue 102

pirate flag 26, 27

Pitcairn Islands 103

Pohnpei (see Micronesia)

Poland 13, 57

Polynesia 93, 101

Portugal 35, 51

prayer flags 80

Prinsenvlag 20, 35, 53

Prophet Mohammad 72, 73

Puerto Rico 31, 105, 117

Q Q flag 41

Qatar 75

Queen's Colour 23

R rainbow 114

Ras el Khaimah 74

Rastafarian movement 34, 140, 146

red 30, 33, 72, 73, 74, 75, 78,
   81, 85, 86, 88, 89, 90, 91, 100,
   101, 111, 113, 114, 115, 118,
   119, 123, 127, 128, 129, 130,
   135, 136, 138, 139, 140, 141,
   142, 143, 145, 146, 147, 148,
   149, 150, 151, 152

Red Cross 37

Red Ensign 29, 111, 112

Red Flag 66, 67

Regimental Colour 23, 24, 24

Republic of Ireland (see Ireland)

Réunion 152

Roman army 22, 23

Romania 13, 64, 65

Romans 17

Royal Navy 26, 29

royal standard 20

Russia (Russian Federation) 35, 66

Rwanda 133, 145

S saffron 79, 80

sailing flags 41

saltire 19, 34, 50, 145

Samoa (see also American Samoa)
   101

San Marino 59

San Martín, José de 129, 130

São Tomé and Príncipe 143

Saskatchewan 18

Saudi Arabia 73

Scandinavia 34, 35

Scandinavian cross 54

Scotland 50

Seal of Solomon (see also Shield
   of David) 135, 146

Senegal 137

Serbia and Montenegro 61

Seychelles 152

Shackleton, Ernest 131

Shahada 73, 76

Sharjah 74

shield (traditional) 147, 151

Shield of David 72

Sierra Leone 139

signal flags (see flags, signal)

Singapore 90

Slovakia 35, 57, 65

Slovenia 60

Smith, Whitney 128

Society Islands (see French
   Polynesia)

Sol de Mayo (see Sun of May)

Solomon Islands 99

Somalia 147

South Africa 21, 133, 150

South America 32, 125

South Georgia and South
   Sandwich Islands 131

South Korea 87

South Pacific Forum 93

South Pole (see British Antarctic
   Territory)

Southern Asia (see Western and
   Southern Asia) 83

Southern Cross 96, 98, 101, 103

Soviet Union 66, 67, 69

Spanish conquest of Central
   America 105, 113, 114

Spain 15, 51

sports flags 38–41

Sri Lanka 81

St Andrew's cross 31, 34, 50

St Anthony's cross 35

St Chrisopher-Nevis (St Kitts and
   Nevis) 119

St George's cross 20, 29, 31, 34,
   50, 101, 103, 117, 152

St Helena 153

St Lucia 121

St Patrick's cross 50

St Pierre et Miquelon 112

St Vincent and the Grenadines 122

star/s (as an emblem) 31, 76, 77,
   78, 79, 85, 86, 87, 88, 89, 90, 91,
   96, 97, 98, 99, 100, 103, 108,
   113, 119, 121, 122, 123, 115,
   117, 128, 129, 137, 138, 139,
   140, 142, 143, 144, 145, 146,
   147, 148, 149

star, five-pointed (see pentagram)

star and crescent 78, 79

Star of David (see Shield of David)

Star of May 130

stars and stripes (flag design, not
   US flag) 31

Stars and Stripes 13, 21, 29, 90,
   91, 105, 108, 139

Star-Spangled Banner 11, 108

statement of faith, Muslim (see
   Shahada)

Sudan 34, 145

sun 77, 78, 79, 80, 86, 87, 88, 91,
   102, 145, 148, 150

sun (of liberty) 127

Sun of May 32, 130, 131

Suriname 128

swastika 21, 34

Swaziland 151

Sweden 55

Switzerland 58

symbols 17, 19, 20, 21, 25,

Syria 34, 71

T Tahiti (see French Polynesia)

Taiwan 88

Tajikistan 78

Tanzania 148

Tasman, Abel 103

Tau (see St Anthony's cross)

Tennyson, Lord Alfred 11

Thailand 89

Theseus 26

Tibet 85

Tibetan Buddhism 80

Tierra del Fuego 130, 131

Togo 31, 140

Tokelau 103

Tonga 101

Trafalgar (Battle of) 27

Tricolore 20, 52, 53, 71, 100, 102,
  118, 120, 152

Trinidad and Tobago 123

Trucial States 74

Tunisia 136

Turkey 63

Turkmenistan 77

Turks and Caicos Islands 116

Tuvalu 100

U Uganda 147

Ukraine 65

Umm al-Qaiwain 74

Union Flag 23, 31, 50, 96, 101,
  103, 108, 112, 152

Union Jack (see Union Flag)

United Arab Emirates (UAE) 34, 74

United Arab Republic (UAR) 71

United Kingdom 13, 50

United Nations 12, 36, 72

  UN blue 123, 144, 147

  UN trust territory 99

United Provinces of Central
  America 32, 112, 113, 114

USA 13, 20, 23, 31, 69, 97, 102,
  105, 108–110

  US state flags 108–110

flags based on the US flag 116,
  117, 130

US Trust Territory of the Pacific
  Islands 93, 97, 98

Uruguay 32, 130

USSR (see also Soviet Union) 67

Uzbekistan 77

V Vanuatu 99

Vatican City 60

Venezuela 32, 125, 127

vexilloid 22

vexillology 17

Vietnam 83, 88

Vikings 16, 17, 26

Virgin Islands 118

W Wales 50

Wallis and Futuna 100

Waterloo (Battle of) 23

West Bank (see Palestine
  Authority)

Western and Southern Asia 69, 70

Western Australia 18

Western Sahara 135

white 30, 74, 75, 77, 78, 79, 86,
  87, 88, 89, 90, 91, 98, 100, 101,
  111, 113, 114, 118, 119, 121,
  123, 128, 129, 130, 135, 136,
  138, 139, 140, 141, 142, 143,
  144, 145, 146, 147, 149, 150,
  151, 152

White Ensign 29

World War I 27, 30, 32, 72, 89

World War II 21, 23, 83, 88, 89,
  93, 99

Y Yap (see Micronesia)

yellow 30, 90, 117, 119, 121, 122,
  127, 129, 137, 138, 140, 141,
  142, 143, 144, 145, 146, 147,
  148, 149, 150, 151, 152

Yemen 34

yin-yang symbol 85, 86

Y-shape (see also pall) 150

Yugoslavia 13, 60, 61, 62

Z Zaire (see Democratic
  Republic of Congo)

Zambia 149

Zanzibar 148

Zimbabwe 34, 149

Information

The Flag Research Centre

PO Box 580, Winchester MA 01890-0880 USA

Tel: +1 (781) 729-9410; Fax: +1 (781) 721-4817

email: vexor@comcast.net

Lovell Johns Ltd

10 Hanborough Business Park, Long Hanborough,

Witney, Oxfordshire OX29 8RU United Kingdom

Tel: +44 (0)1993 883161; Fax: +44 (0) 1993 883096

www.lovelljohns.com – 'Leading the way in Mapping Solutions'

A member of the Maps International Group.

Fédération Internationale Des Associations Vexillologiques (FIAV)

504 Branard Street, Houston, Texas 77006-5018 USA

Tel: +1 (713) 529-2545

email: sec.gen@fiav.org

Flags of the World (FOTW)

PO Box 546, RR2, 2 Gloosecap Terrace

Wolfville NS B0P 1X0 Canada

Tel: +1 (902) 542-7767; Fax: +1 (902) 585-1816

email: rob.raeside@acadiau.ca   Web: www.flagspot.net

North American Vexillological Association (NAVA)

1977 N. Olden Ave. Ext., PMB 225

Trenton NJ 08618-2193 USA

email: pres@nava.org   Web: www.nava.org

The World Factbook: An annual publication containing up-to-date information on countries, compiled by the US Central Intelligence Agency (CIA). www.cia.gov/cia/publications/factbook/index.html

Acknowledgements

New Holland Publishing would like to thank the following for assistance with flag artwork: Lovell Johns Ltd. Oxford, UK;

Flag Research Centre, Winchester, Mass., USA; National Geographic Maps, Evergreen, Co., USA..

Statistical information from the World Pocket Atlas 2004, courtesy of MapStudio Tourist Division SA and

Lovell Johns Ltd UK, with additional input from the CIA World Factbook.

. .

Photographic credits

Front cover	ImageState
Back cover	galloimages/gettyimages.com
1	AFP
2–5	Touchline
6–9	galloimages/gettyimages.com
10–11	www.travel-ink.co.uk/Dave Saunders
12 (top)	Touchline Photo
12 (bottom)	PhotoAccess
13	Touchline Photo
14	PhotoAccess
15	galloimages/gettyimages.com
16 (top)	The Bridgeman Art Library/The Stapleton Collection
16 (bottom)	The Bridgeman Art Library/Mark Fiennes
17	The Bridgeman Art Library/Bibliotheque Nationale
19	The Bridgeman Art Library/Archives Charmet
20	The Bridgeman Art Library/Roger-Viollet, Paris
21	The Bridgeman Art Library/National Archives Trust, Pennsylvania, USA
22 (top)	The Bridgeman Art Library/The Classical Gallery
22 (bottom)	galloimages/gettyimages.com
23	The Bridgeman Art Library/Archives Charmet
24	The Bridgeman Art Library/National Army Museum, London, UK
25	galloimages/gettyimages.com
26 (top)	The Bridgeman Art Library/Christie's Images
26 (bottom)	Christelle Marais
29	INPRA/Loic Jacob
30 (top)	Touchline Photo
30 (bottom)	PhotoAccess
33	PhotoAccess
35	galloimages/gettyimages.com
36	PhotoAccess
38–40	galloimages/gettyimages.com
41	Touchline Photo
42–43	galloimages/gettyimages.com
46–132	NHIL/Danie Nel